David, King of Israel, and Caleb in Biblical Memory

Of all the Bible's personalities, David is the most profoundly human. Courageous, cunning, and complex, he lives life to the hilt. Whatever he does, he does with all his might, exuding both vitality and vulnerability. No wonder it has been said that Israel revered Moses yet loved David.

But what do we now know about the historical David? Why does his story stand at the center of the Bible? Why didn't the biblical authors present him in a more favorable light? And what is the special connection between him and Caleb – the Judahite hero remembered for his valor during the wars of conquest?

In this groundbreaking study, Jacob L. Wright addresses all these questions and presents a new way of reading the biblical accounts. His work compares the function of these accounts to the role war memorials play over time. The result is a rich study that treats themes of national identity, statehood, the exercise of power, and the human condition.

Dr. Jacob L. Wright teaches Hebrew Bible and Jewish studies at Emory University, where he is a member of the faculty of distinction. His first book, *Rebuilding Identity: The Nehemiah Memoir and Its Earliest Readers*, was awarded The John Templeton Award for one of the best first books in religion and theology. For his research on war commemoration, he received a prestigious faculty fellowship from the National Endowment for the Humanities.

Advance Praise

"This bold and original work traces the development and growth of various Davids in the Hebrew Bible, showing how different stories reflect interests centuries after David's putative reign. It argues compellingly that we cannot construct the real David, only different memories of him. This book is full of surprises, ranging from the importance of the relatively obscure Caleb for understanding David, to illustrating how modern modes of war commemoration help unlock the composition of these stories."

– Marc Brettler, Dora Golding Professor of Biblical Studies, Brandeis University

"Jacob Wright has made a significant contribution to the lively ferment that is under way in the interpretation of the David narratives. His proposal concerning the linkage between David and Caleb is somewhat of a surprise and has immense heuristic importance. This is a book to which future interpreters of David will pay attention, not least because of Wright's clear articulation of an on-going constructive tradition."

– Walter Brueggemann, William Marcellus McPheeters Professor of Old Testament, Columbia Theological Seminary

"With exquisite literary sensitivity, historiographic sophistication, and attention to questions concerning reception, political ideology, and cultural memory, Jacob Wright offers an original reading of the 'quintessential survivor,' David. Wright explores why and how biblical writers have framed and reframed not only the hero king himself but also his predecessor Saul and Caleb, another hero of biblical tradition, whose depictions are relevant to a full appreciation of the portrayals of David."

– Susan Niditch, Samuel Green Professor of Religion, Amherst College

David, King of Israel, and Caleb in Biblical Memory

JACOB L. WRIGHT
Emory University

CAMBRIDGE
UNIVERSITY PRESS

32 Avenue of the Americas, New York, NY 10013-2473, USA

Cambridge University Press is part of the University of Cambridge.

It furthers the University's mission by disseminating knowledge in the pursuit of education, learning, and research at the highest international levels of excellence.

www.cambridge.org
Information on this title: www.cambridge.org/9781107672635

First published 2014

Printed in the United States of America

A catalog record for this publication is available from the British Library.

Library of Congress Cataloging in Publication Data
Wright, Jacob L.
David, King of Israel, and Caleb in biblical memory / Jacob L. Wright, Emory University.
pages cm
Includes bibliographical references and index.
ISBN 978-1-107-06227-6 (hardback) – ISBN 978-1-107-67263-5 (pbk.)
1. David, King of Israel. 2. Caleb (Biblical figure) I. Title.
BS580.D3W75 2014
222'.4092–dc23 2013049900

ISBN 978-1-107-06227-6 Hardback
ISBN 978-1-107-67263-5 Paperback

Additional resources for this pulication at www.kingdavidsreign.com

To the memory of Frank Moore Cross (1921–2012)

Contents

Preface

This book exists in two versions. One version, with the title *King David and His Reign Revisited*, is available at the Apple iTunes store. As an iBook (for the iPad and Mac computers), it's the first of its kind in the humanities: a monograph that enhances the text in the style of medieval illuminated manuscripts, with hundreds of striking images, a fixed-page format, videos, audio clips, and an innovative new approach to footnotes. That version is focused on the figure of King David. The version you are now reading bears a different title (*David, King of Israel, and Caleb in Biblical Memory*) in keeping with the expanded nature of its contents: It includes several chapters, along with a discussion throughout, of the relationship between David and another Judahite luminary – Caleb, the warrior known for his intrepidity during Israel's wars of conquest. As I show, David and Caleb are two competing figures for the Judahite authors who were responsible for the final shape of the Hebrew Scriptures.

My work on David and Caleb began as chapters in a larger study that I conducted with the support of a Faculty Fellowship from the National Endowment for the Humanities in 2011/2012. The aim of the project was to show how the political concerns that fuel war commemoration in ancient and modern societies are very similar to the forces that gave rise to many biblical texts as well as propelled Israel's ethnogenesis as a heterogeneous people. As the book became too lengthy, we decided to break off the chapters that treat a corpus of Judahite texts. The remaining chapters, which treat war commemoration in the Hebrew Bible from a variety of perspectives related to Israel (rather than Judah), have been collected for a separate volume.

The time spent this past year preparing the present two volumes on King David has been a lot of fun thanks to the expertise and solicitude of my editors at Cambridge, Lewis Bateman and Shaun T. Vigil. I am beholden to the National Endowment for the Humanities for its generous support, and in particular for the encouragement of its officers, Claudia Kinkela and Mark Silver. My research was stimulated by many thoughtful conversations on the biblical texts with Zev Farber.

Finally, a comment about the book's dedication. The great biblical scholar Frank Moore Cross passed away as I was in the midst of this project, and his death provoked me to think about my own academic lineage. I was trained in a German tradition of biblical studies that sees the Bible's formation and Israel's history very differently from the views Cross presented in his various writings. Nevertheless I have, over the past decade, developed great respect for Cross, and especially for his extraordinarily gifted students, whose work I have come to value as indispensable conversation partners in this fantastic field of biblical studies.

Jacob L. Wright
September 24, 2013
(CH"M Sukkot 5774)
הרחמן הוא יקים לנו את סוכת דוד הנפלת

Visit the website for this book at:
www.kingdavidsreign.com

1

Slings and Arrows

Remembering King David

How many are the ways we remember David – that striking, brash lad who strides confidently upon the stage of history and, with one well-aimed shot of the sling, launches a career that has bedazzled generations for 3,000 years. We know David as majestic king and lowly shepherd boy, as valiant warrior and soothing singer, as ruthless killer and passionate lover, as enraptured dancer and pious saint.

No other figure has the mysterious magnetism that makes David such a beloved hero. His are tales of intrigue and adventure, tenderness and pain. Courageous, cunning, and complex, David lives life to the hilt. He exudes vitality and vulnerability. Whatever he does, he does with all his might. No wonder it has been said that Israel revered Moses but loved David.

"David in his faults and attainments, his losses and victories, embodies on a scale almost beyond imagining the action of *living a life*." So captures the poet Robert Pinsky the meaning of David. Paving the way for Pinsky's appreciation, the literary critic Harold Bloom observed, David "had exhausted every human possibility yet went on in fullness of being – open to more experience, more love, more grief, more guilt and suffering, more dancing in exuberance before the Ark of Yahweh." David's all-eclipsing vitality and passion prompted Bloom to assert famously that the woman who authored the oldest biblical source ("J" or the "Yahwist") created YHWH in the image of David.[1]

To later generations, the Bethlehemite both inaugurated and embodies Israel's golden age. He possessed a Midas touch that turned every obstacle into another secure step to glory, rising higher and higher on the rickety scaffolding of Saul's tumbling house.

Can any other biblical biography rival David's? In his novel *God Knows*, Joseph Heller, celebrated author of *Catch-22*, has the dying monarch reflect on his greatness:

> I don't like to boast – but I honestly think I've got the best story in the Bible. Where's the competition? . . . Moses isn't bad, I have to admit, But he's very, very long, and there's a crying need for variation after the exodus from Egypt. . . . I've got the poetry and passion, savage violence and the plain raw civilizing grief of human heartbreak. "The beauty of Israel is slain upon thy high places." That sentence is mine and so is "They were swifter than eagles, they were stronger than lions." My psalms last. I could live forever on my famous elegy alone, if I wasn't already dying of old age. I've got wars and ecstatic religious experiences, obscene dances, ghosts, murders, hair-raising escapes, and exciting chase scenes. There were children who died early. "I shall go to him, but he shall not return to me." That's for the one who died in infancy. . . . "My son, my son" was for another who was struck down in the prime of young manhood. Where in Moses can you find stuff like that?[2]

Yet David also presents problems. Undoubtedly he is a pivotal figure in the formation of the nation, forging a kingdom, capturing Jerusalem, initiating the construction of the Temple, establishing an enduring dynasty. Undoubtedly, too, he is the most fully delineated character in the Bible, the subject of the most colorful, detailed, and revealing tales. But there is more to his story than the glitz of glory. David is also calculating, ruthless, and cold – exceedingly so. Why did the biblical authors depict him in this way? In their estimation, was the precious price he paid for success worth the suffering?

Careerist and Survivor

David's portrait differs sharply from Saul's. As Israel's first king according to the biblical narrative, Saul doesn't set his sights on the throne. Instead he happens to find it while looking for lost donkeys. At the time he's anointed, they discover him hiding among the baggage. Kingship is not his ambition, and to his dying moment he harbors deep self-doubt. Insecurities, lack of faith, and angst accelerate his demise.

Not so David. He lacks not one ounce of confidence. As the youngest of eight boys, the odds are stacked against him. But the disadvantage only makes him more determined. "Whether 'tis Nobler in the mind to suffer / The Slings and Arrows of outrageous Fortune, / Or to take Arms against a Sea of troubles . . . ." The shepherd boy leaves his little flock to bring bread and cheese to his brothers on the front lines, and he returns a fêted national champion.

Whereas Israel's soldiers flee in terror before Goliath, David wants to know what prize awaits the one who fells the giant. His oldest brother discerns his motives:

"Why did you come down here, and with whom did you leave those few sheep in the wilderness? I know your impudence and your impertinence: you came down to watch the fighting!"

But David replied, "What have I done now? I was only asking!" (1 Sam 17:28–29)

But sooth to say, David does have grander designs. After learning that the champion would walk away with great riches and the king's own daughter, he resolves to go out against Goliath. With the most brazen assertiveness, he approaches King Saul:

"Let no man's courage fail him. Your servant will go and fight that Philistine!"

But Saul said to David, "You cannot go to that Philistine and fight him; you are only a boy, and he has been a warrior from his youth!"

David replied to Saul, "Your servant has been tending his father's sheep, and if a lion or a bear came and carried off an animal from the flock, I would go after it and fight it and rescue it from its mouth. And if it attacked me, I would seize it by the beard and strike it down and kill it. Your servant has killed both lion and bear; and that uncircumcised Philistine shall end up like one of them, for he has defied the ranks of the living God." (1 Sam 17:31–37)

Thanks to unwavering faith in his own future, he manages to overcome all obstacles, on the battlefield and beyond.

David's self-confidence is irresistible. He knows how to manipulate the masses. Unlike Saul, he neither fears them nor surrenders to them. Yet everyone fears David, and many love him. Saul's own children, Jonathan and Michal, willingly betray their father for this usurper. After his premature death, Saul's general Abner crosses over to David's side. An array of figures – priests, soldiers, leaders, women, and anonymous individuals – do his dirty work. To the very end, they are motivated by unflinching loyalty. He is the original "Teflon Don." Even when we know he's guilty, nothing sticks to him. On account of his friends' allegiance, his hands remain clean, and he comes out of the most compromising situations smelling like the Rose of Sharon.

Many may love David, to be sure. But whom does David love? Michal? Probably not. Jonathan? Perhaps. Himself? Most certainly.[3]

David's self-love and confidence give him an unfailing sense of timing. There is nothing rash or impulsive about his actions. He stages his success with impeccable strategy. His eyes are firmly fixed on the throne as he wields his private army against Judah's enemies and distributes shares of his war spoils with those who, predictably, will later anoint him king. At each step of the way – whether he's making his escape or returning from exile – we witness him acting at the auspicious moment. He makes his move only when he's certain that all his pawns are in formation.

The scion of Jesse is the quintessential survivor. In this regard he anticipates both the history of his dynastic line and the life of his people. He begins his career dodging Saul's spear. Hounded by the armies of Israel, he goes on the lam, hiding in the cracks and crevices of Judah's desert. Eventually he seeks refuge among the Philistines, Israel's most dangerous enemies. Then, long after he assumes Saul's throne, he is chased out again, this time by his own son Absalom. Returning to his refugee existence, he seeks asylum far away from the comforts of Jerusalem. Later, on his way back to the palace, the country erupts in another rebellion.

He must face a famine and a plague. Death consumes those round about him.

In the end, David is left shivering and hanging on for his dear life. To get some heat into his war-weary bones, he curls up next to a young body. It is there, in the bed he made over the course of his tumultuous life, that he grants Bathsheba an audience and yields the throne to her son Solomon. It is there too that, before going the way of all the earth, he admonishes Solomon to "be a man," to follow YHWH, and to settle his father's scores.

David's Women

"The story of David," Robert Alter writes, "is probably the single greatest narrative representation in antiquity of a human life evolving by slow stages through time, shaped and altered by the pressures of political life, public institutions, family, the impulses of body and spirit, the eventual sad decay of the flesh."[4]

As a way of tracing these stages of David's life, let us briefly examine his relations to women. There are four leading ladies in the narratives, and each corresponds to a phase in David's life. His interactions with them provide a litmus test of his success and failure.

In the first phase David is a wonder boy, climbing upward, sleeping his way to the top. The first woman on his path is the princess Michal. She is the boss's daughter, and she loves David, just as her brother does and father once did. But for David, she is not the goal – she's just a means: "It pleased David to be the king's son-in-law." Whereas Jacob loves Rachel, David yearns for royalty and glory.

Once he escapes through Michal's window, he returns no more. Just one scene later, he is back in town for several days, spending time with Michal's brother Jonathan, shooting arrows, and taking a tearful farewell. They kiss each other, which is perhaps more than David and Michal have ever done. Does she know that he is now within a bowshot of her window? What goes down a rope can just as easily come up. But now she will have to make do with the household idol and goat's hair that she once placed in her bed as a decoy.

Over the years David marries other women as he gradually establishes his Judahite kingdom in the south. During this time Saul had given Michal to another man. When Saul dies, David aspires to be king of Israel and sends for the princess, describing her as his possession: "my wife whom I bought with the bride-price of a hundred Philistine foreskins." His interest is motivated by his determination to mount a new throne. In contrast to David's calculations, the man to whom Saul had given Michal follows her in a trail of tears, devastated at the thought of losing his beloved spouse.

If Michal is the boss's daughter, David's wife Abigail is a "discerning and comely woman" who proves to be a fitting counterpart. We meet her when David is a wily outlaw, living by the sword and running a protection racket. He's a man on the make, doing what he does best.

Because Abigail's wealthy husband refuses to pay for the security services, David decides to make an example of him. Yet in the nick of time, Abigail intercepts the warlord with an array of costly victuals. The elegant address she delivers is longer than that of any other woman in the Bible. She speaks his language, convincing him with an appeal not to fairness or kindness, but to practicality and expediency. David listens, alters his course of action, and thanks her for preventing him from messy bloodshed. When her husband hears of the matter, he has a stroke and eventually dies, leaving his wife to marry David.

Abigail is not only a clever and eloquent partner but also an affluent widow. Not surprisingly, in this stage of his career, David prospers and becomes a powerful political player.

When David has his dalliance with Bathsheba, he's at the zenith of his career. He has successfully seized the throne of Israel and expanded the kingdom's border far beyond what Saul could have imagined. This is the perfect time for a midlife crisis.

Bathsheba is ostensibly just a sex object whom David beds at will. But the romp represents much more. The king is in Jerusalem while his men are dying on the battlefield. This is already a violation of a pact: When the people of Israel make him their king, they declare,

> "We are your own flesh and blood. Long before now, when Saul was king over us, it was you who led Israel in war; and Yhwh said to you: 'You shall shepherd my people Israel; you shall be ruler of Israel.'" (2 Sam 5:1–2)

Yet David is no longer shepherding YHWH'S people. Instead, he's sending them on an imperial mission to expand his kingdom's territory, while he stays back in the palace.

Just as he takes possession of forbidden territories, he illicitly seizes a woman, and the one he chooses is married to a man who is serving him in the field. It is the arrogance of power, and it will not go unpunished.

"All that is solid melts into air." First his infant child dies. Then his family disintegrates, with one son, Amnon, raping his own sister Tamar. David fails to mete out discipline, so that another son, Absalom, takes matters into his own hands and slays Amnon. Later Absalom, in Oedipal fashion, seduces the hearts of Israel, steals his father's throne, and sleeps publicly with David's concubines.

The pain that David undergoes is greater than that of losing his throne. He suffers from betrayal by his cherished son, and then from his death. The father's haunting cry is deafening:

> "O my son Absalom, my son, my son Absalom! Would I had died instead of you, O Absalom, my son, my son." (2 Sam 18:33)

Once David had eloquent words for grief. Now he is reduced to a broken cry, repeating a few words over and over – the price David pays for success.

The fourth woman is Abishag, David's hot-water bottle. We meet her during David's final days, when he's losing his body heat and relinquishing his power. His servants use robes to maintain his temperature, but to no avail. They then conduct a search throughout the land for a fair damsel who will warm him up, and they find Abishag, the beautiful Shunamite.

"Yet the king knew her not." The calefaction doesn't work. David is now impotent. More virile rulers will vie for the throne. In the next scene, one of his sons, the attractive Adonijah, announces that he will reign. David has one final opportunity to assert himself, and when he does, he will take his cue from a woman.

Abishag steps aside to make way for Bathsheba. No longer a passive sex object, the former wife of Uriah is now a woman of presence and authority who capably persuades the king to go ahead and allow her son Solomon to reign. All his life David was deft at manipulating others; now he is subject to manipulation. In keeping with his wife's entreaty, he lets go of the kingdom he built. Solomon is crowned, and David dies as he was born – a non-king.

How difficult it must be for a king to decide to relinquish control of his kingdom. Are we to understand that David has had a change of heart? Does a thirst for power not drive his actions still? Is David no longer David?

The decision to abdicate his throne to Solomon turns out, after all, to be extraordinarily astute. For no longer is David obliged to keep the promises he made long ago. He can charge his son, as the new king, to finish his business, rewarding friends and taking vengeance on the enemies he had once sworn to pardon. And this is exactly how David spends his final hours. As he begins his life, so he ends it: calculating his advantage.

Why David?

So why have the biblical writers devoted so much space to David's life? And why have I chosen to write another book about him?

Composing a biography of Israel's celebrated king in 1943, the British diplomat Alfred Duff Cooper, 1st Viscount Norwich, insisted that the biblical account of this figure must be factual because no people would invent a national hero so deeply flawed.

Many contemporary biblical scholars have arrived at the same conclusion about the historicity of the David accounts, albeit via an alternate route. Reading the narratives with Shakespearean suspicion ("the lady doth protest too much, me thinks," *Hamlet* III.2), they notice that the authors of the David accounts go to the greatest lengths to demonstrate David's innocence. He is *not* in the ranks of the Philistine armies when Saul and his sons die in battle on Mount Gilboa. To the contrary, he is deeply grieved at the news of their death, executing the messenger who conveys it, rending his garments in anguish, fasting, and teaching a dirge to his fellow Judahites.

The biblical writers make similar claims about the deaths of other members of Saul's and Jonathan's descendants, as well as Saul's general Abner. On the one hand, David's right-hand men wipe out Saul's house. On the other hand, he is consistently enraged by their violence and takes punitive action against them. If the biblical writers protest with such force that David was blameless – so it is typically argued – they must have completed their accounts soon after David's death. Therefore, to understand the narratives properly, one must interpret them as an *apologia pro vita sua* or *pro domo sua* (a defense of his life or household), composed in the court of Solomon or his immediate successors.

This approach seems reasonable enough, and not surprisingly many have embraced it. The problem is that it fails to explain the texts that are critical of David.[5]

In the foregoing pages, I noted how the biblical narratives portray him as a leader driven by a thirst for power. To bring Duff Cooper's observation to bear on this popular interpretation, one would expect these narratives to have presented a much more favorable image of Judah's king if their purpose were to defend the dynasty's founder and reputation.

Imagine that the Davidic court had commissioned a group of scribes to compose an account of David's life that vindicates his conduct vis-à-vis Saul's household. Would these scribes have ever thought to submit a work to their royal patron that contains a shedload of passages describing David's raw ambition, failures, and ruthlessness? Had they done so, they would have rightly feared for not only their livelihoods but also their lives.

Their biography doesn't just fail to proffer a sufficiently positive portrait of David. It even includes portions that depict David mistreating Saul's family. Take, for example, his brusque treatment of Saul's daughter Michal in 2 Samuel 6. Even more telling is the account in 2 Samuel 21, where he appeases the Gibeonites by allowing them to slaughter, in the most barbaric manner, seven of Saul's descendants. Only when Rizpah, Saul's concubine, refuses to relent from her public protest does he take it upon himself to do something favorable for Saul's house.

What we need then is a more plausible, and robust, model to explain why the biblical authors composed such colorful, detailed, and revealing tales about David. Such is precisely the *raison d'être* of the present volume.[6]

How will I interpret the David materials in the following chapters? And why I have chosen to include in this book several chapters about the figure of Caleb?

No one can deny the presence of a series of passages in the Book of Samuel that exonerate David's name by underscoring either his solicitude for Saul's house or his moral ascendancy over his royal predecessor. These texts most likely emerged, however, long after David's death, as they are easier to understand as part of the ongoing rivalry between the states of Israel and Judah. David represents the kingdom of Judah, and Saul the kingdom of Israel. By showing how the founder of their dynasty was the divinely chosen and morally superior leader, the kings of Judah invite the members of Israel to join them and submit to their rule.

The number of passages that fall into this category is relatively minimal. What remains are two different types of texts: those that articulate a penetrating critique of royal power and statehood, and those that treat issues of status and belonging in Judahite society. These two types include some of the most fascinating and popular tales of David.

In the coming chapters of this book, I will explore exemplary selections of the David narratives from the books of Samuel,

Kings, and Chronicles. My aim is to show how circles of Judahite authors, anticipating Shakespeare's work, took the greatest ruler in their collective memory and made him the most profoundly human of all biblical personalities. Their move is a radical one: According to ancient conventions, monarchs are to be represented as stoic, immutable, superhuman sovereigns.

In their efforts to unmask royal rule, the biblical writers produced a parable of power that probes new depths in the history of biography. The David they created is both larger than life and "human, all too human" – which is undoubtedly why he has long been cherished. His story reveals uncomfortable truths about the human condition. But it also displays a stupefying faith that impels an underdog to set his sights on unthinkable heights of glory. As they wrestled with the realities of passion and power, these writers affirmed the resiliency of the human spirit. Unprecedented triumphs must contend with mortality, fragility, and failure. "Oh how the mighty have fallen!"

But the David story does not only explore what it means to be human. Its larger goal pertains to collective political life. Faced with catastrophic defeat and the loss of statehood, the biblical authors set about the task of imagining a new kind of political community, one that can withstand conquest by imperial armies. (I will call this model of community "nationhood" or "peoplehood.") As part of their project, they lay out, in a highly nuanced historical narrative, the pros and cons of centralized monarchic rule. And they situate this experience of statehood in the history of a people that long antedates it and survives its demise. Not surprisingly, the authors enlisted the David account for a pivotal role in their extensive history stretching from Genesis to Kings.

Closely related to this category of texts is *the second group*: those that treat questions of belonging and status within Judahite society. I will devote more attention to this group for two reasons: First, many have not received a lot of attention in the past. Second, in interpreting them, I will introduce a new model for understanding the formation of many biblical texts, one grounded in concrete political activities that have been studied in a wide range of times and places. My contribution makes a case for what is called the "supplementary approach" to the formation of biblical literature. This approach is, I show, firmly rooted in the common social activities by which political communities negotiate belonging and status. It departs fundamentally from the strict "documentarian" approach associated with the JEDP hypothesis that once governed biblical studies and that has recently made a comeback among various circles.

In my years of teaching biblical literature, I've often heard students complain about the number of details the biblical authors include in their narratives – names of various figures, their parents' names, the places where they come from, and so on. And the students have good reason to complain: Although the David story in the books of Samuel and Kings is relatively lengthy for biblical standards, it comprises only a small fraction of the pages in a modern novel. Yet the number of characters in a massive novel such as Tolstoy's *War and Peace* is not much larger than the number of figures in the David narrative!

Why is that so? Didn't the biblical authors realize that their stories would have been much easier to read if they had focused on the plot and kept the particulars to a minimum?

The profusion of details is due, I show, to the political activity that produced these texts. The biblical authors were concerned with the privileges, honors, and authority enjoyed by groups in their society (villages, towns, regions, families, clans, professional guilds, etc.). One common way they address these matters is to report how a representative individual or group remained loyal to David, or assisted him, when the armies of Saul and Absalom sought to destroy him and his followers. These memories have direct implications for the privileges and status enjoyed by the contemporary descendants of that group.

The phenomenon can be widely witnessed in the various ways political actors use war commemoration to negotiate membership, rights, honors, and entitlements in their societies. Many of the biblical texts do the same by appeal to memories of momentous battles and war efforts, ranging from Israel's conquest of Canaan to the defeat at the hands of the Babylonians.

Such war commemoration can be conducted to define relations to neighboring peoples. In the Bible, this is particularly the case with the Edomites and their (putative) contributions to the destruction of Jerusalem by the Babylonians.

So why did the authors of the books of Samuel, Kings, and Chronicles use David for this purpose? Because they were Judahites, and David is the most beloved figure in Judahite tradition. He is the one who founded the kingdom of Judah. By claiming that a group assisted or betrayed Judah's iconic hero during this critical period in its history, the biblical authors can make a powerful case in favor of or opposition to that group in contemporary Judahite society. Seen in this light, we can understand why the David narratives are teeming with such a confusing array of figures and place names. In the next chapter, we'll begin by looking more at the nature of war commemoration.

Thus, according to the thesis of this book, we have three types of texts in books of Samuel, Kings, and Chronicles. Their agendas are, in many ways, palpably antithetical. Some affirm that David and his line are chosen by Israel's God to rule the nation. Others, however, are concerned with the nature of power and statehood *per se*. In their evaluation, they dissect the figure of David, depicting his ambitious and ruthless abuse of power. Yet even as they are at variance with one another, their combination makes David an exceptionally complex personality. It is this complexity that predestined him to a long afterlife.

Why Caleb?

This book concludes with several chapters devoted to Caleb. In the books of Numbers and Deuteronomy this biblical figure brings back a "good report" when Moses sends twelve spies on a reconnaissance mission to Canaan. In the books of Joshua and Judges he is remembered for his exceptional valor in conquering the city of Hebron. But why devote so much space to Caleb in a book about David?

Already many scholars before me have pointed to the close links between David and Caleb. The oldest references to the

Calebite clan are found in the accounts of David's activities as a warlord. David establishes the capital of his kingdom at Hebron, which was a center of the Calebites' ancestral territories. The first woman he marries, Abigail, is the wife of a prominent Calebite landowner. Several texts graft David into Caleb's illustrious line.

But who was Caleb? And why would the biblical authors have wanted to connect David to his name? In answering these questions, I will evaluate claims that the Calebites were assimilated at a late point into the tribe of Judah. The issue posed by the Calebites appears to have been less about *belonging* than about *privilege* and *honored status* in Judahite society. Rather than being outsiders, Caleb's descendants constituted a noble clan whose distinctiveness the biblical authors acknowledge and seek to explain by means of war commemoration.

As we investigate Caleb's identity and symbolic role in biblical texts, we will witness how the diachronic analysis of the Caleb legends discloses the distinctive forces and issues driving biblical war commemoration. Whereas the Judahite court created an image of the warrior David as their representative hero, Calebite circles did the same with Caleb in order to resist the encroachment of the Judahite state into their territory. After the defeat of the Judahite kingdom, Hebron and other southern Calebite territories shifted to Edomite hegemony. At this time, Caleb assumed a new representative role for the population of Judah, anticipating his iconic status in later Jewish, Christian, and Muslim texts. The investigation of this rival figure thus reveals much not only about the formation of biblical literature and the political agendas that motivated its authors but also about the political dynamics of the Judahite kingdom, both before and after its demise.[7]

2

Flesh and Stone

From War Monuments to the David Story

Across the street from the State House on Boston's Beacon Hill stands an imposing bronze relief sculpture. Although years of New England weather have dulled its glint, when the sun shines on it, the scene it depicts still comes to life. At the center rides a nineteenth-century military officer. He is surrounded by marching soldiers, young and old, with muskets resting on their shoulders. Above them hovers an angel of peace – a young woman in a flowing gown with her hand gesturing toward the horizon. The officer and his men advance under her aegis and direction. He is a white Union commander, and they are African American soldiers.

What is the purpose of this "symphony in bronze"? Why does it face the State House? Inscribed on the back of the monument, the words of Charles W. Eliot, Harvard's twenty-first president, offer an explanation:

TOGETHER
THEY GAVE TO THE NATION AND THE WORLD UNDYING PROOF
THAT AMERICANS OF AFRICAN DESCENT POSSESS THE PRIDE,
COURAGE, AND DEVOTION OF THE PATRIOT SOLDIER.
ONE HUNDRED AND EIGHTY THOUSAND SUCH AMERICANS
ENLISTED UNDER THE UNION FLAG IN MDCCCLXIII – MDCCCLXV.

According to Eliot's statement, the young soldiers stand for more than themselves. They represent an entire population: not only their many brothers who had fought in America's Civil War, but also all "Americans of African descent."

The monument portrays the Massachusetts 54th Volunteer Infantry. Formed in March 1863, this regiment consisted entirely of African American soldiers who, seizing on a clause in Lincoln's Emancipation Proclamation, flocked from far and wide to take up arms for the Union. They ended up serving for a year and a half without pay.

By contributing to a wartime effort, according to Eliot's words, these men performed a deed of historic significance. Their sacrifice proved to the country and to the world – and not least, to the occupants of the State House across the street – that African Americans have what it takes to be citizens. They have pride, courage, and devotion – the three virtues of the "patriot soldier" (i.e., the ideal citizen). The memorial graphically communicates this politically laden point. Or better said, it seeks to *remind* its audience of it.

War Commemoration and the Bible

So what does this monument have to do with the figures of King David and Caleb from the Bible? In the chapters to come, I will show how many biblical texts related to Israel's iconic king and to the honored hero of the wars of conquest, although not fashioned in bronze, are doing something very similar to what this monument does. And that something is what I call *war commemoration.*

Via memories of wars and battles, the biblical authors address issues of belonging and status within an emerging national community that they call "Israel." Like the architects of the Shaw Memorial, these authors portray how representative members of contested groups made crucial wartime contributions on the behalf of Israel, either fighting in the nation's ranks or demonstrating courage as civilians. By doing so, the biblical texts affirm the membership – or "belonging" – of this group among the people of Israel. Conversely, by claiming that an individual or group shirked their wartime duty, or failed to assist Israel at a time of crisis, the texts raise questions about the community represented by that individual or group.

Consider the case of the Kenites. This population is mentioned only in a handful of biblical texts and we know precious little about them. They appear to have been tent-dwelling nomads who herded sheep and worked with metal. In many ways they resemble the Bedouins who inhabit southern Israel in more recent times.

Although the Kenites lived within the state borders of Israel and Judah, apparently many in ancient Israel and Judah did not consider them to be MOT ("members of the tribe"). As non-Israelites, they presented the same political issues of belonging and status – something similar to what we call today "citizenship" and "rights" – that minorities and marginal groups have posed throughout history.

The biblical authors address these issues by constructing memories of the roles played by the Kenites in Israel's history. Thus we read in the books of Numbers and Judges that Hobab the Kenite, Moses's father-in-law (also known as Jethro), served as scout for Israel, bringing them safely through the wilderness. For his solidarity and service, he is awarded a portion of the Promised Land.[1]

Later in the Book of Judges (ch. 4–5), Israel goes to war with the Canaanites. But before the eruption of hostilities, a Kenite named Heber detaches his clan from the other Kenites and joins forces with the Canaanites. Although they boast formidable chariot battalions, the Canaanites cannot hold their own against Israel's army of 10,000. The enemy commander, Sisera, manages to escape with his life. He flees to the camp of his ally Heber and there enjoys gracious hospitality from Jael, Heber's wife.

What this Canaanite commander does not know is that Jael has defied her husband's political affiliations and has remained loyal to Israel. Thus Sisera gullibly drinks the warm milk Jael offers him and drifts off to sleep, confident that he is safe from all harm. At the first opportunity, Jael stealthily reaches for a hammer and drives a tent peg into his temple.

In this way the biblical writers attribute the greatest martial feat in this contest with the Canaanites to a daring Kenite woman. Flouting her husband's politics, Jael makes a memorable contribution to Israel's war effort, even if she must do so from her domestic confines. And when she fights, she wields weapons that mark her identity, not only as a woman but also as a Kenite: milk, a tent peg, and a hammer – corresponding to the Kenite activities of herding, nomadism, and metalworking.

Elsewhere I have demonstrated that the episode with Jael is likely a late addition to the battle accounts, both in their prose and verse versions.[2] But why would someone have wanted to add Jael to the story? The motivation, I suggest, is the same one that created the monument on Boston's Beacon Hill: to send a message to the larger society that a minority group deserves honor and respect. Both the authors of the Bible and the architects of the Shaw Memorial are engaging in the activity of war commemoration.

The Politics of War Commemoration

As with other forms of public ritual and performance, war commemoration is a thoroughly political enterprise. Populations on the margins of society confront "corporate amnesia" by calling attention to their own sacrifices on behalf of the larger political community. They remind others of their contribution to victory and their participation in collective suffering. In this way, these members of society – women, ethnic minorities, gays and lesbians, and other marginalized groups – lay claim to public honors and political rights. Such battles over memory make and mold the nation's identity. Conversely, where dissent and disputation diminish, a national consciousness wanes and withers.[3]

The bronze sculpture on Boston's Beacon Hill illustrates how war monuments serve as public spaces in which national identities are forged over time. The idea to create the memorial began with Joshua B. Smith. A fugitive from slavery, Smith found work in the home of the regiment's white commanding officer, Robert Gould Shaw, before going on to become a successful Boston caterer.

Despite the name the work came to bear ("Shaw Memorial"), the charter from 1865 called for a monument that would not only "mark the public gratitude to a fallen hero" (Shaw) but also "commemorate that great event . . . by which the title of colored men as citizen-soldiers was fixed beyond recall."[4]

Designed by the celebrated artist Augustus Saint-Gaudens and considered one of the finest American sculptural achievements of the nineteenth century, the memorial depicts Shaw on horseback riding stalwartly amid his regiment of Negro soldiers, each of whom is portrayed with distinctive heroic features.

Over time the monument accumulated many inscriptions. The most prominent one, on the front side, refers to Shaw, the white commanding officer:

OMNIA RELINQVIT
SEVARE REMPVBLICAM
[He left all to save the republic.]

Other lines by politicians, such as Governor Andrew, and by poets, such as Lowell and Emerson, extol the valor of Shaw and his fellow commanders. Even the cited words of Charles Eliot begin with an encomium to the white officers.

In contrast, the oration delivered at the dedication by William James calls attention to the nameless black soldiers so scrupulously sculpted: "There on foot go the dark outcasts. . . . There they march, warm-blooded champions of a better day for man."[5]

The volunteers in the 54th regiment were convinced that Frederick Douglass was correct – that they wouldn't be denied the privileges of full American citizenship if they demonstrated martial valor in defense of the nation. Yet despite their faith in American equity, the road to first-class citizenship was a long one. Their voices were not heard. It was only after the Vietnam War that new monuments emerged depicting black soldiers as emblematic American citizens. The names of (some) of the fallen members the 54th regiment were finally added to the memorial in 1981.[6]

Competing Memories and National Identity in the Bible

While an array of complex factors determines political rights, commemoration of wartime sacrifice undeniably plays a critical role. Like the Shaw Memorial, the Hebrew Bible is the bearer of a long history of competing war memories. This literary corpus is the product of collective efforts to fashion a new corporate identity in the wake of defeat and social rupture. The biblical authors use law and wisdom, song and story, to consolidate alienated populations into one united people of Israel.

Yet the biblical writings are not univocal and consistent. To the contrary, they preserve competing perspectives. This composite character is due to the Bible's long and complex history: Multiple generations inscribed on its pages memories and countermemories that negotiate membership and status for the various groups that constitute the nation. The product is a multilayered literary monument.

Consider the case of communities from the eastern side of the Jordan River. Their status in Israel was a matter of great controversy for the biblical authors and those in their societies. One series of biblical texts addresses the issue by reporting how representative members of this Transjordanian population served as a valiant vanguard for Israel during the foundational wars of conquest, fighting without personal benefit inasmuch as they would not take possession of the conquered territories. Another group of texts, however, casts aspersions on these communities by telling how they failed to contribute to subsequent war efforts.[7]

Within all these biblical passages, we repeatedly stumble upon evidence of early readers who interpolated into the text all kinds of supplements. In contrast to the inscriptions added to the Shaw

Memorial, these competing memories are difficult to date or arrange into chronological sequences. Even so, I contend that the same contested activity of war commemoration that produced monuments like the Shaw Memorial propelled the Bible's formation. The biblical writers appealed to memories of wartime contributions and sacrifice as they treated issues of belonging – both within the community of Israel and between Israel and other peoples.

If I am right, we can better explain the pervasiveness of war in the "Old Testament." The reason is not that this literature stems from a bellicose culture whose warmongering members were keen to praise martial valor and espouse theologies of "holy war." The theological dimensions are undeniable. Yet the ubiquity of war in the Bible must be appreciated in view of its authors' larger *political project*.

The aim of this project was to fashion a collective identity that could withstand the onslaught of foreign imperial powers and ultimately the loss of political sovereignty. By telling how Israel had long been a people before the establishment of centralized kingdoms, the Bible affirms that Israel can still thrive as a people even when those kingdoms are destroyed. Defeat does not mean the end of Israel. In narrating this long history, the Bible draws a sharp line of distinction between *nation* and *state*. Put simply, the nation is the people whom the state serves.

War, the most extreme form of cultural trauma, invariably shapes the life of a nation. Yet war itself is less determinative for the formation of national identities than war *commemoration*. If nations most often tell their collective histories and negotiate their identities in relation to (the memories of) the wars they fought, it makes sense that the biblical authors would do the same when constructing a new collective identity for Israel.

What's more, the conspicuous analogies to modern national war commemoration lend support to those who view the notions of peoplehood envisioned by the biblical authors as genetically akin to European definitions of "the nation." Insofar as my claims are sustainable, those interested in the dynamics of modern nationalism have much to learn by examining the formation of biblical literature, which, as we shall see, stands in a remarkable continuity with modern Jewish war commemoration.

Between Empire and Nation-State

In 1866, a year after the American Civil War had ended, Jewish women in the South created the Hebrew Ladies' Memorial Association. This organization took upon itself the task of caring for the graves of Confederate Jewish soldiers. In one of their circulars to the "Israelites of the South," they solicited funds not only to tend to the cemeteries but also to erect a large monument. Prompting the latter, more costly, project was a political concern: the fear of potential accusations that Jews, many of whom had recently migrated from the North, were not loyal to the Southern cause. As they wrote in their petition, "In time to come, when the malicious tongue of slander . . . shall be raised against us, then with feeling of mournful pride will we point to this monument and say: '*There* is our reply.'"[8]

Political rights and status in Jewish history have been closely connected to military service in foreign armies. The Roman emperor Theodosius II (d. 450 CE) issued a decree prohibiting Jews from serving in all military posts of honor (*honos militia et administrationis*). Beginning in the fifth century and continuing throughout the Middle Ages, various laws excluded Jews from carrying arms and fighting as soldiers.

Many cases are known of Jewish soldiers valiantly protecting their cities and lands during the Middle Ages and the early modern period. Yet with the rise of the nation-state in Europe and North America, Jews began to assume new roles in society, while they also faced new challenges.

In 1781–1783 Christian Wilhelm von Dohm set forth a program for "The Civil Improvement of the Jews" (*Über die bürgerliche Verbesserung der Juden*), which was directly inspired by the Jewish Enlightenment thinker Moses Mendelssohn. The proposals confronted the greatest resistance on the issue of permitting Jews to join German armies.

The most influential opponent to respond in writing to Dohm's proposal was Johann David Michaelis (d. 1791). This well-known Christian Bible scholar claimed that Jews would not make good soldiers due to their physical constitution, their strict Sabbath and dietary laws, and, not least, their reluctance to drink beer with other Germans in the taverns. For Michaelis it was clear: If Jews were permitted to serve in the military, they could lay claim to political and civil rights.

This *Kulturkampf* has a tragic history in Europe. After the First World War, monuments calling attention to the bloodshed of Jewish soldiers began to dot the landscapes of the continent. Many were sponsored by the *Reichsbund jüdischer Frontsoldaten* (RJF). Founded in 1919, this organization sought to stem the tide of anti-Jewish sentiment by commemorating Jewish service and sacrifice. In addition to sponsoring local memorials, the RJF (and others) published *Gedenkbücher* commemorating the Jewish boys and men who had fallen for the fatherland. The memorial volumes appeared in the late 1920s and early 1930s, as responses to the waves of hatred that washed over the country.

The RJF vigorously opposed proposals by Zionists to abandon Germany. Believing that the evidence of Jewish sacrifice would safeguard their communities from malevolence and ensure a bright future in their German homeland, they sorely overestimated the potential of war commemoration. As highly decorated German-Jewish officers were deported to the death camps along with those who had never served in the military, they would often proudly display their medals of honor, confident that that these marks of valor guaranteed them protection. They were mistaken.

Does this horrifying history undermine the principle I have laid out? Given the ultimate failure of the RJF, should one doubt my claim that war commemoration has been an efficacious means for Jews to affirm belonging and secure rights?

The evidence from other places and times reveals that Nazi Germany is an exceptional case that proves the rule. Thus the success story of Jews in America is closely tied to a long history of Jewish military service and patriotism. In 1895 Simon Wolf published a landmark volume entitled *The American Jew as Patriot, Soldier, and Citizen*.[9] The story of its origins and circulation attest to the way Jews have negotiated their belonging in American society by appeal to a record of loyalty and sacrifice. Today in Washington, D.C., one can visit the National Museum of American Jewish Military History. Its curators have collected evidence of the various capacities in which Jews have served in every military engagement in US history, from Colonial days to the present.

The sundry projects of Jewish war commemoration from Europe and America stand in continuity to similar efforts from antiquity. In the Persian, Hellenistic, and Roman times (from the fifth century BCE to the first century CE), many Judahites or Jews served in imperial armies. The literary sources emphasize collective allegiance to the empire. Here I will treat just one example, that of Jews in Greco-Roman Egypt.[10]

The first-century Jewish historian Josephus reports that Alexander the Great offered Jews a place in his army and received an enthusiastic response. Josephus claims that they fought valiantly in Alexander's campaign against Egypt, and in recognition of their loyal service, Alexander granted them civic privileges on par with those of Greeks and Macedonians. Although Egypt surrendered to Alexander without a fight, "the historical facts did not discourage Jewish creativity," notes Erich S. Gruen, Professor of History and Classics at Berkeley.[11]

Agatharchides (mid-second century BCE) reports that Ptolemy I Soter – Alexander's Macedonian general who founded the Ptolemaic Kingdom in Egypt – captured Jerusalem and treated its inhabitants cruelly. In contrast, Josephus cites an account from (Pseudo-) Hecataeus of Abdera according to which many Judeans, including a high priest named Hezekiah, upon hearing of the kindness and humanity (*philanthrōpia*) of Ptolemy I Soter, flocked to him after his victory at Gaza and expressed their desire to take up residence in his country.

Pseudo-Hecataeus tells of a Jewish cavalry unit that accompanied the armies on their way to the Red Sea. A Greek seer was observing the movement of a bird in order to divine the route the army should take. When the Jewish archer Mosollamos learned of this reason for the delay of the army's advance, he shot down the bird, explaining that if it could forecast the future, it would have been able to avoid his arrow. The legend draws a contrast between Jewish military skill and common sense, on the one hand, and the superstitious behavior of other nations represented in Ptolemy's army, on the other. As Prof. Gruen writes, "This is no critique of the Hellenistic ruler [Ptolemy]. Quite the contrary. It indirectly confirms his sound judgment, like that of Alexander before him, in recruiting Jewish fighters for his forces: they are loyal, accomplished, and smart."[12]

The Letter of Aristeas is more subtle. While admitting that Ptolemy I Soter, during his invasion of Coele-Syria, had captured and deported to Egypt 100,000 Jews, it emphasizes that they were skilled soldiers. In recognition of their military skills, Ptolemy stationed the Jews in garrisons throughout the land, remunerated them with handsome pay, and then bolstered the rights of the Jews already living in Egypt. Responsibility for those sold into slavery is deflected from the founder of the Ptolemaic dynasty and ascribed to the ill will of his troops.

By constructing these memories of loyal service and exceptional reward, Jewish communities in Egypt living centuries later affirmed their allegiance to Greek rule. The aim was to secure not only privileges but also protection: Native Egyptians harbored deep resentment toward the Jews who lived among them, and on more than one occasion they expressed their malice with a quality of violence that anticipates the pogroms that Jews later faced in Europe.

Aegean and Asian War Commemoration

So we can see that in both the empires of antiquity and the nation-states of modernity, war commemoration has played a key role in Jewish survival. The difference is that in the imperial context, Jews sought protection, entitlements, and (some degree of) autonomy as communities. In modernity, however, Jews have demanded membership with civic rights as individual citizens of the nation-state.

The war commemoration that we find in the Hebrew Bible is similar to both that of the modern nation-state and that of empires. The biblical authors envision a political community of "Israel" which, as already noted, bears a significant likeness to what we call today peoplehood or nationhood and has likely directly influenced these notions. Since the Bible is addressed to members of this political community, its authors use war commemoration not to assert their collective allegiance to an imperial power, but to negotiate belonging and status among themselves. The biblical texts negotiate belonging for collective groups and do so through representative individuals (e.g., Jael on the behalf of the Kenites).

Is it possible to identify similar examples of war commemoration in the ancient world? To be sure, we have a very difficult time locating parallels in ancient Western Asia, what is commonly called the "ancient Near East" (ANE). In Egypt, Anatolia, the Levant, Mesopotamia, and beyond, innumerable monuments portray rulers sallying forth against the enemy in heroic isolation. The armed forces that partake in the fighting are conceived as an extension of the king's own sovereign arm. We are thus hard pressed to find something comparable to the way the Bible uses war commemoration to negotiate belonging within a national community.

We can be confident that vassals and allies who offered their military service to the victorious king sought ways to remind others of their contributions – not only in the hope of receiving a larger share of the war spoils but also with the aim of declaring their loyalty to the king and receiving recognition and honors. Yet here again the attention is focused on the vassal kings and their successors.

For example, in a funerary monument from circa 730 BCE, an Anatolian king (Bar-Rakib) pays homage to his father Panamuwa II by describing how he served as a loyal vassal to the powerful Assyrian imperial ruler Tiglath-pileser III. In recognition of his faithful service to Assyria on military campaigns, Tiglath-pileser rewarded him by expanding the territory of his kingdom and granting him special honors. On one of the campaigns, Panamuwa died, and, according to the inscription, the Assyrian king formally mourned his death and raised up a memorial to his name.

While such monuments affirm allegiance through wartime service and sacrifice, they do so in the name of rulers and dynastic houses, *not* on the behalf of populations and political communities. In this respect, they differ substantially from the collective commemoration from the Hebrew Bible and modern nation-states.

For ancient analogies to the type of war commemoration found in biblical and modern contexts, we must look to the East Aegean. After the Persian Wars, Greek city-states erected various monuments that pay homage to the participants (either a particular city or community or an alliance) in pivotal battles.

One of the monuments at Thermopylae commemorated the bravery of the Locrians, a population who later joined the Persian side. In response to doubts about their loyalty to Greece, the inscription proclaimed, "Opus, the mother-city of the Locrians with their just laws, laments these men who died fighting the Medes on behalf of holy Hellas."[13]

An example of a monument that salutes the contributions of multiple allied communities is the famous Serpent Column. Originally erected in Delphi and currently in Constantinople, it lists the names of thirty-one (city-)states that contributed to the Persian War. The name of the Tenians was inscribed later, while five communities, including the Locrians, are conspicuously absent.

These are just a couple of examples from the Greek world. Many other monuments as well as works of historiography (e.g., Herodotus) illustrate how populations used war commemoration in a manner strikingly similar to that of the biblical authors and modern nation-states: to address questions of belonging and to jockey for status in a larger political community.

King David, Caleb, and War Commemoration

When engaging in war commemoration, the biblical texts frequently employ emblematic figures and the eponymous ancestors of ethnic groups. Thus, the Song of Deborah, one of the most impressive literary war memorials from the ancient world, ascribes singular action both to collective groups (Ephraim, Reuben, Gilead, and others) and to a representative individual – the Kenite hero Jael, discussed earlier in this chapter.

Of all the Bible's diverse figures, the one who is portrayed most graphically, and who has enjoyed the most vibrant post-biblical afterlife, is King David. In a multitude of texts, the life of this ambitious sovereign serves as a symbol around which competing literary circles struggled to come to terms with both the boon and the bane of centralized monarchic rule. Yet David is more than an illustrative example in the Bible's political-philosophical discourse. He is also an iconic figure. As I will attempt to show in the chapters to follow, the biblical writers use him as cynosure to negotiate status and belonging among the people of Israel and within Judahite society, both before and after the destruction of the state in 586 BCE.

That the biblical authors exploited the name of David for their historiographical undertaking has to do with his undisputed status: Credited with the consolidation of the kingdom of Judah and the establishment of a long-enduring royal dynasty, this Bethlehemite is the most celebrated and beloved hero in Judahite collective memory. (And those who produced the final forms of the Bible were Judahites.) David's iconic status resembles that of George Washington and other national heroes in the legends and lore cultivated in American society.

Just as the Shay Memorial places the celebrated white commander against the backdrop of numerous, yet diversely portrayed, African American soldiers, the books of Samuel and Kings present a vast, and often confusing, array of minor figures surrounding David: Doeg the Edomite, Abiathar the priest, Nabal the Calebite and his wife Abigail, Ittai the Gittite, Shobi the Ammonite, Barzillai the Gileadite, to name just a few. If the authors confine the descriptions of these characters to the essentials, it is because they are concerned with the issues posed by the polities and peoples as well as territorial regions and professional guilds that these figures represent.

By depicting how one offered succor to David in times of military conflicts, the biblical writers affirm that the particular group she or he represents deserves a privileged place in contemporary Judahite society and in the hallowed halls of Israel's history. Alternatively, by portraying an individual perpetrating perfidy and treachery, these writers can undermine the special prerogatives and honor enjoyed by those associated with that individual. Lending support to this interpretation is the fact that the biblical texts often do not use representative figures, opting instead to present whole towns or populations acting collectively when betraying David or sheltering him from his adversaries.

In the coming chapters, I develop this new approach to the study of King David by examining a series of key biblical texts and array of extra-biblical evidence. These findings will draw into question long-held assumptions about David's historical reign. We will also catch invaluable glimpses of the prodigious political vision that informs the work of the biblical authors. We will see that many biblical tales owe their existence to the same activity of war commemoration that figures so prominently in modern Jewish history.

In addition to David, this book includes several chapters on Caleb, the figure known for his exceptional valor during the conquest of Canaan. The connections between Caleb and David have long been noted by biblical scholars. My own work shows how biblical writers used war commemoration to make Caleb into the first and greatest hero in Judahite collective memory, one who as a non-king rivals David in the halls of biblical history. The biblical authors show that if Israel, during the days of Moses, had accepted Caleb's courageous counsel, they would have avoided forty years in the wilderness, marched up directly from the south into Judah, and enjoyed the fruits of the land that Caleb brought back from Hebron (the same city that David establishes centuries later as the capital of his kingdom). Judah would have then, long before David's kingship, established itself as Israel's greatest tribe.

The question is: What would have prompted biblical writers to commemorate Caleb's exceptional valor in this way? The question turns out to be a complex one, involving everything from territorial disputes (before and after the fall of the Judahite kingdom) to efforts by biblical authors to come to terms with the loss of native monarchic power.

3

King of Judah

The Earliest Account of David's Life

David is defined above all by his determination and drive. Of the countless artists who have rendered him over the millennia, Michelangelo most successfully captures this quality. In earlier representations, the revered King of Judah had appeared as a virtuous musician or as an innocent boy bearing the head of Goliath. Yet from Michelangelo's block of marble he emerged as a valiant warrior, poised for battle. He stands with unshakeable confidence. One leg bears the weight of his muscled body, while the other rests relaxed. One of his disproportionately large hands conceals stones, and the other lifts a sling that drapes insouciantly over his naked back. Yet the most dramatic feature is his eyes: his sideward gaze creates a countenance that urges caution to adversaries.

By means of the colossal, classical sculpture, Michelangelo and his patrons in Florence asserted their newfound confidence vis-à-vis their competitors and identified themselves as the heirs of the Greco-Roman legacy. The biblical David represented for the Florentines republican liberty and a willingness to defend their native sovereignty against the Medici family and Rome. For this reason, they placed the sculpture before the town hall, so that David's eyes could be fixed on Rome.

David would never have inspired republican ideals had it not been for the protracted history that his biblical biography underwent. In the present chapter I will examine this literary evolution. As we shall see, the earliest account of David's achievements that we can reconstruct from the Book of Samuel portrays the determination and drive captured in Michelangelo's sculpture. Yet in contrast to the transmitted forms of the David narratives, this account connects David solely to *Judah* and focuses on his achievements in establishing the *Judahite* kingdom. Its authors omit any reference to Saul and the kingdom of Israel.

What this means is that the earliest sources describing David's life do not recount his triumph over the giant Goliath. They have nothing to say about his relationship with Saul and his family, nothing about the scandals within his own household – the affair with Bathsheba, the rape of Tamar, the wars with Absalom, and so on.

Our findings raise a question. If the oldest narratives present David as the one who created and ruled over the kingdom of Judah, how did he come to be remembered as the one who ruled all Israel? What prompted this transformation from "king of Judah" to "king of Israel"? This question will occupy us in both the present chapter and those that follow.

Two Narrative Strands

To launch our investigation, let's examine the most curious feature of David's biography: his stint as a mercenary warlord. In several chapters from the Book of Samuel, David commands a corps of soldiers-of-fortune. Yet instead of offering his martial services to King Saul of Israel, he serves in the employ of the Philistines – Israel's archenemies!

The one who directly enlists David's services is named Achish. This Philistine ruler governs the city-state of Gath, situated on Judah's western border. David's charge is to provide protection for Achish and to yield to him a portion of the goods that he and his men collect during their raids in the Negeb (the arid region in the south of Judah extending to Eilat on the Red Sea). In return Achish grants David and his men permission to settle in the town of Ziklag.

David's mercenary activities pose a problem. In the most familiar episodes of his life, he makes his way steadily toward the throne of Israel by valiantly *combating* the Philistines.

He begins his kinetic career in idyllic solitude, tending the sheep of his father Jesse. Because of his bravery and martial skills, which he acquired in duels with predators that attacked his herds, he catches the attention of King Saul's court. He quickly makes a name for himself in Israel's ranks as an accomplished Philistine-slayer. Among his more remarkable claims to fame is the triumph over the Philistine champion Goliath. Later, as he collects foreign foreskins to win the hand of Saul's daughter, he takes down another (two) hundred Philistines.

Now if Achish, as the ruler of a Philistine city-state, had caught wind of David's penchant for killing Philistines, would he have been eager to make him his bodyguard? Most likely not. Here the Book of Samuel contains a deep disparity. What are we to make of it?

Taking the disparity seriously and following it throughout the Book of Samuel, we can discern two very different narrative strands. One strand presents David serving valiantly in Saul's forces, arousing the king's jealousy, and then going on the lam. Eventually he seeks asylum with Achish at Gath. But the Philistine ruler soon hears about David's feats as a soldier in Israel's ranks. Fearing for his life, David feigns madness and makes an escape (1 Sam 21:11–15).[1]

The other narrative strand knows nothing about David's relationship to Saul. Instead, it portrays David as a mercenary warlord. In this strand too he interacts with Achish at Gath. Yet instead of running into trouble with the Philistine king and then absconding, David gets along with him splendidly and ends up serving him for a lengthy period.

Let's consider for a moment the second strand. In an episode from it (1 Sam 31), a band of camel-mounted Amalekites make a raid on David's town of Ziklag, seizing all valuables and livestock as well as women and children. After catching up with the raiders, David and his men recover their wives and children together with the purloined property. His army declares the recovered goods to be "David's spoil." Later he sends part of the booty to the elders of Judah, saying, "here is a gift from the spoil of the enemies of YHWH!"

This tale, which I will examine later in greater detail, depicts David's exceptional political acumen as a warlord. By distributing the spoils strategically, he makes Judah's leaders beholden to him and secures widespread allegiance. The rewards of David's shrewd benefaction are reported several chapters later, where the Judahites come to make David their king:

> After this David inquired by oracle of YHWH, "Shall I go up into any of the cities of Judah?"
>
> YHWH said to him, "Go up."
>
> David said, "To which [town] shall I go up?"
>
> He said, "To Hebron."
>
> So David went up there along with his two wives, Ahinoam of Jezreel, and Abigail the widow of Nabal of Carmel.
>
> David brought with him his men, every one with his household, and they settled in the towns of Hebron.
>
> Then the people of Judah came, and there they anointed David king over the House of Judah. (2 Sam 2:1–4a)

In the versions of Samuel that have been transmitted to us, this little section is severed from the longer story of how David recovered the purloined goods from the Amalekite raiders and shared them with Judah's elders. The text that stands between the two is the chapter-long narrative of Saul's final battle with the Philistines and his death on Mount Gilboa. That account has nothing to do with David and his men.

Examining closely the seams connecting all these texts, we can witness how the editors of the Book of Samuel combined what appear to have been originally separate accounts of David and Saul. Thus they placed the Saul material right before the short paragraph that tells of David moving to Hebron and being made king of Judah. The editors' intention was to set the record straight and to defend David's name: According to the new narrative that they created, David had not mounted the throne of this secessionist state while Saul was still ruling as Israel's king. He did not become king of Judah until *after* Saul died.

What we see from this survey is how easy it is to untangle separate accounts of David and Saul. In most cases, the editors of Samuel have juxtaposed these sources without thoroughly blending them, so that the David material has nothing to do with Saul, and vice versa.

Their juxtaposition of the sources could leave false impressions. For example, one source depicts Saul dying in a battle with the Philistines on Mount Gilboa. Another source presents David fighting for Achish, a Philistine ruler. Reading them together, one might suspect that David had a hand in Saul's death. The editors went to great lengths to correct this impression. In an elaborate pre-battle scene, they report that Achish discharged David and his men right before the Philistine forces march off to fight Saul and the armies of Israel.

In the coming chapters, we will have opportunity to examine other cases in which the editors found ways to harmonize what appear to have been originally separate sources.[2]

The Earliest Accounts

Surveying the literary depictions of David throughout the Book of Samuel, we can identify three types of passages:

A) Those that relate solely to David.
B) Those that relate solely to Saul.
C) Those that relate to both David and Saul.

If divided into these three categories, the oldest versions of the David account would have to be identified with those of type A. The versions of this older account know nothing of the interactions with Saul or of David's rule over Israel. Instead they present David as warlord who consolidates the kingdom of Judah. Texts that belong to this older account include:

David's rescue of Keilah (1 Sam 23:1–5*, 13a, [14a])
His encounter with Nabal and Abigail (1 Sam 25:2–29, 31–42)

His service as a mercenary for Achish of Gath (1 Sam 27:2–3a, [5–6], 7–11)
The sharing of war spoils with "his friends" (1 Sam 30:26b–31)
The episode at Ziklag (1 Sam 30:1b–2, 8–18a, 19–20)
His move to Hebron where he's anointed king over Judah (2 Sam 2:1–4a, 11)
The lists of his wives and children at Hebron (2 Sam 3:2–5)
His capture and occupation of Jerusalem (2 Sam 5:4, 6–11*)

Possibly also:

David's military success against his former Philistine employers (2 Sam 5:17b–25)
Several episodes included in 2 Samuel 6–9 and 10–12
The names and legends of his warriors in 2 Samuel 23

Not all of these passages were composed at the same time. For example, various statements that refer to David's wives may belong to a secondary stratum of the account.[3] But conspicuous traces of editorial work, as well as common phraseology, suggest that these texts were drafted, and later expanded, as part of an independent history that recounts David's consolidation of a Judahite kingdom.

In keeping with conventional parlance, I refer to this early source as the HDR, which stands for the *History of David's Reign/Rise*. On analogy to the HDR, I assign texts of type B to an independent history of Saul's reign, which I dub the HSR (*History of Saul's Reign/Rise*).

HDR = The History of David's Reign/Rise
HSR = The History of Saul's Reign/Rise

According to the thesis argued throughout this chapter and the following ones, the authors of the Book of Samuel synthesized the HDR and the HSR and composed a great deal of material to connect them. They wove together these separate filaments in such a way that the episodes of David as a warlord become his adventures during his flight from Saul. This redactional shift has left unmistakable traces in the language. For example, David's original "roving" (*hithallek̦*) as a desperado becomes his "fleeing" (*baraḥ*) as a fugitive from Saul's court.

Introducing David

What can we say about the beginning of the HDR? This is an exceptionally thorny problem.[4] It's possible that those who combined the David and Saul histories deleted the introduction. I worked under this assumption for many years. But reading through these biblical texts one evening in a Tel Aviv cafe, I stumbled upon a promising possibility. It's a line that one can easily miss, because it is imbedded within the Goliath story and appears long after the reader has already been introduced to David.

> Now David was the offspring of an Ephrathite from Bethlehem in Judah named Jesse, who had eight sons.... David was the youngest. (1 Sam 17:12a, 14a)

Remarkably, when we eliminate all the material that has to do with Saul in the immediately following chapters, we come across another line that is closely linked to this piece of biographical data:

> And everyone who was desperate, in debt, or discontent gathered to him and he became captain (śār) over them. Those who were with him numbered about 400. (1 Sam 22:2)

By reporting that David is the youngest of no fewer than eight sons, the narrator signals to the reader that he stood very little chance of inheriting much property. One would therefore expect David to seek another way of making a name for himself. Throughout history – and still common today among some aristocracy – younger sons have sought careers in the military (and the clergy). With little chance of inhering much property in family of eight boys, it is not surprising that David becomes a warlord, forming a private army from renegades, discontents, and social outcasts.

Readers have often observed the analogies between David's story and that of another warlord in the Bible – Jephthah. This figure from the Book of Judges is the son of a prostitute. In dispute with his father's sons, he is forced to relinquish his rights to an inheritance and flees for his life. Far away from his home, on the margins of civilization, a band of desperadoes (literally "empty" or "desperate men") gather around him, and he leads them on raids of martial adventure:

> Now Jephthah the Gileadite, the son of a prostitute, was a mighty warrior. Gilead was Jephthah's father. Gilead's wife bore him other sons, and when his wife's sons grew up, they drove Jephthah away, saying to him, "You shall not inherit anything in our father's house, for you are another woman's son." Then Jephthah fled from his brothers and lived in the land of Tob. Desperadoes gathered around him and went raiding with him. (Judg 11:1–3)

Years later the Ammonites attack his country. As they prepare for war, the elders seek out Jephthah and persuade him to be their commander. The former outcast agrees on the condition that he would be the leader of Gilead.

This legend reminds us of the statement that "everyone who was in dire straits, in debt, or discontent" gathered around David, and he became their "captain." The outcasts are the same troops with whom he makes a name for himself on his way to becoming king of Judah. Just as Jephthah becomes a powerful warlord and later the head of Gilead because of a conflict with his brothers over their father's inheritance, David becomes the lord of a large corps of troops because he stood little chance of inheriting a patrimony. And just as Jephthah uses his private army to advance to the head of his society, David carves a kingdom for himself with his band of soldiers.

This opening to the oldest David account, in its length and literary style, bears striking resemblances not only to the Jephthah legend but also to the biography of Idrimi, a figure who ruled the city-state of Alalakh (on Turkey's southern coast) in the fifteenth century BCE. That biography describes how Idrimi, after a dispute, flees to the land of his mother. Later he goes to Canaan.

There many gather around him and make him their captain. In the end he returns to assume the throne of his ancestral home in Alalakh.

The many analogies to the careers of Jephthah and David are obvious. In 1976 two biblical scholars working at the Jewish Theological Seminary, Ed Greenstein and David Marcus, published a careful study that synoptically juxtaposes the accounts of David, Jephthah, and Idrimi, illustrating their many points of overlap.[5] One of the commonalities includes the passage just cited that describes how the destitute gathered around David as their captain. Yet Marcus and Greenstein did not find an introduction in the David narrative corresponding to Idrimi's and Jephthah's beginnings: Idrimi is forced to flee after some dispute, just as Jephthah is chased away after a falling-out with his brothers. In the column for David, there is a blank space.

The line that I isolated – reporting that David is the youngest of eight brothers and thus, by implication, stood to inherit little if anything from his father's estate – is a perfect candidate for that parallel introduction. As such, a biblical and an extrabiblical parallel confirms the plausibility of my reconstruction.

Creating Judah

One could perhaps argue that the authors conceived the HDR as a prelude to the account of David's succession to Saul's throne. But the complete absence of references to Saul, his family, and the people of Israel – even in later portions that have been added to it – suggests that the authors were not cognizant of any connections between David and the kingdom of Israel.

The HDR orients David's horizon in territories south of Hebron, northward toward Jerusalem on the border of Benjamin, and westward into the Shephelah. In other words, this older narrative does not present David as a ruler over core territories of the northern kingdom of Israel.

One can still feel the polemical force of the HDR. It affirms that the important Philistine city-state of Gath did not create Judah as a marionette state and that David did not owe his

Judahite throne to Achish, Gath's king. Although David begins in the employ of Achish, he exploits his patronage to assault the enemies of the Judahites along with the Jerahmeelites, or Kenites (or Kenizzites) – populations of what would become the kingdom of Judah (1 Sam 27:8–12).

Rather than rising to power as a Philistine puppet, David forges a kingdom on his own initiative and according to his own political vision. He consolidates a state out of various regions, cities, and clans, all of which unite under the banner of "the House of Judah."

The account implies that the kingdom's population includes Calebites, Jerahmeelites, Kenites (or Kenizzites), and formerly independent cities, while excluding the Geshurites, Girzites, and Amalekites. All these clans are frustratingly obscure, but several appear repeatedly within our texts, and I will discuss them later.

The HDR's authors take pride in showing how David consolidated the kingdom of Judah. If this is the greatest feat they could ascribe to him, it follows that they didn't know about his more impressive achievements, such as his rule over the much larger state of Israel.

Their silence in this regard warrants what will be for many a surprising conclusion: The traditions claiming that David ruled over a "united kingdom" of Israel and Judah emerged much later. If I am right on this point, the most popular legends about David are the creation of generations who lived long after him. David's slaying of Goliath, his exploits in the court of Saul, his relationship to Jonathan and Michal, his fate as a fugitive, his military triumphs abroad, his affair with Bathsheba, his civil war with Absalom, his succession by Solomon – all these colorfully depicted episodes were created by later generations of writers.

The HDR would have presented numerous problems for later Judahite readers who saw themselves as members of the people of Israel, especially for those living after the Assyrian conquest of Israel (722 BCE). Many of the biblical texts that we examine here likely originated as responses to this political catastrophe. Their authors portray David making his debut in the service of Israel's king, provoking his animosity and fleeing from him, and then eventually mounting his throne. We may safely regard these texts as editorial attempts to fuse what were originally two independent accounts (the HDR and HSR). As synthetic texts, they harmonize the histories in ingenious ways.

But the authors of Samuel could only achieve so much by *adding* material to the older sources. This is where the Book of Chronicles comes into play. Its authors, working in the late Persian or Hellenistic period, resorted to the radical option of text *eradication*. They erased most remnants of the oldest David and Saul accounts, creating in the process a "revisionist history" that portrays the representatives of Israel (not solely Judah, as in Samuel), after Saul's death, coming to David at his home in Hebron. There the people anoint David king over the people of Israel. Chronicles describes at length how the nation's leaders take part in this momentous event. Lest there be any doubt that these leaders represented the entire nation, we are told, "All the rest of Israel were of one mind to make David king."

Thus, in the older sources, a warlord manages – through both political calculation and brute force – to become king over "the House of Judah." In the later history of Chronicles, we have an innocent darling who is spontaneously anointed king by the entire nation of Israel.

Chronicles thus completely erases the memory of this hero's origins as a warlord serving in the employ of a Philistine ruler. It has nothing to say about how he greased the palms of the Judahite elders so that they would confer to him the scepter of royal rule. And it wipes out all traces of the older memories in which David first reigned as king of Judah before assuming the throne of Israel. According to this alternative view, there was no kingdom of Judah until much later, when Rehoboam and Jeroboam cleaved Israel into two separate states.

Confederations of Israel and Judah

Let's now take a closer look at the earliest accounts of David's reign. In the preceding pages I've claimed that the authors who composed the Book of Samuel drew selectively from the independent histories of David (HDR) and Saul (HSR), while also significantly expanding and recontextualizing them. Much later the authors of Chronicles radically reworked this history. Although based on the narrative from Samuel, their new account eliminates most of the remnants of the HDR and HSR. What remained were just a few fragments, and even they have been thoroughly reworked.

Much of twentieth-century biblical research occupied itself with the problem of Israel's origins. Today an increasing number of historians agree that the Bible's authors took many centuries to flesh out their understanding of Israel as an expansive, heterogeneous, yet unified people. Even so, many still tend to historicize the biblical account. In doing so, they follow a long-established pattern in scholarship.

Thus both the progressive German historian Julius Wellhausen (d. 1918) and the conservative Israeli historian Abraham Malamat (d. 2010), who worked a century after Wellhausen, claimed that King David managed to revive Israel's unity after it had dwindled away during the "Period of the Judges." The way in which both Wellhausen and Malamat situate David in Israel's history is little more than a selective retelling of the biblical story. Many, if not most, scholars now consider the "Period of the Judges" to be an unalloyed historiographical construction.

More troublesome is the manner in which Wellhausen and Malamat force the biblical accounts to fit their reconstruction. These accounts attribute the reconsolidation of Israel to Samuel and to Saul – yet not to David. In fact, the Book of Samuel depicts David tearing asunder Israel's unity in the process of creating the kingdom of Judah. Only Chronicles, a very late biblical work, presents David as the catalyst of Israel's unity. In claiming otherwise, one adopts its revisionist perspective.

A more elaborate model for the origins of Israel and Judah was advanced by two of the most influential biblical scholars of the twentieth century: Albrecht Alt (d. 1956) and Martin Noth (d. 1968). They claimed that the various tribes that settled in Canaan united into a large alliance or confederacy of tribes called Israel. Noth compared the confederacy to "amphictyonies" from the

East Aegean. Both Alt and Noth, and their many students, saw the "Israelite amphictyony" as more religious (or cultic) than political in character. Even so, they identified the confederacy as the direct precursor to the later kingdom of Israel.

Furthermore, according to Alt and Noth, Judah was much more centralized than Israel. Although it is said to have begun as a confederacy, called "Greater Judah," it differed from Israel in that it was more statist in character. It was also smaller, including only six tribes, all from the southern hill country: Judahites, Calebites, Othnielites, Kenites, Jerahmeelites, and Simeonites. Only two of these tribes – the Judahites and Simeonites – are included in the Bible's canonical catalogue of Israel's twelve tribes.

For the many scholars who have embraced Alt's and Noth's reconstruction, the question has been whether the confederacy of "Greater Judah" constitutes the work of the historical David or antedates his achievements. Sigmund Mowinckel and Roland de Vaux argued that David created "Greater Judah," while Alt and Noth claimed that this confederacy existed before David.[6]

This debate, which has persisted over the course of the twentieth century, rests to a considerable extent on an uncritical reading of selected passages from the Book of Samuel. Chief among them is the register of cities that received a share of David's war booty:

> When David came to Ziklag, he sent part of the spoil to the elders of Judah, his friends, saying, "Here is a gift for you – part of the spoil of YHWH's enemies." It was for those in:
>
> Bethel,
>
> Ramoth of the Negeb,
>
> Jattir,
>
> Aroer,
>
> Siphmoth,
>
> Eshtemoa,
>
> Racal,
>
> the towns of the Jerahmeelites,
>
> the towns of the Kenites/Kenizzites,

Hormah, Bor-Ashan,
Athach,
Hebron
– all the places where David and his men had roamed.
(1 Sam 30:26–31)

Alexander Fischer from the University of Jena argues that this register must have originated long after the reign of David. Fischer points to the evidence that the sites listed in the register were not occupied until the late eighth century BCE. If he is correct – as I think he is – the thesis of "Greater Judah" forfeits one of its most important intrabiblical proofs.[7]

Although the register doesn't date to the time of David, it may have belonged to early editions of the HDR. Notice how it forms a continuation (or what cuneiform scholars call a "join") to the account of David's time in the service of Achish (1 Sam 27:2–3a, 7–12a, and 1 Sam 30:26–31).

Read together, these passages report the various places where David sent a share of the booty that he had captured on his raids. The mention of "the towns of the Jerahmeelites and the towns of the Kenites (or Kenizzites)," even if it might be an editorial gloss, links back nicely to the locations David mentions in his response to Achish. Also, the concluding summary ("and to all the place where David and his men roamed") dovetails superbly with the account of David's service in the employ of Achish. Yet it makes much less sense when read in its present context – at the end of the lengthy episode describing the Amalekites' raid on Ziklag.

That episode at Ziklag provides a new context in which to understand David's distribution of war spoils to the elders of Judah. Instead of seizing wealth during his depredations of southern territories, he recaptures goods that the Amalekite marauders had taken when they assailed Ziklag. If we remove the lines that integrate the account with the larger narrative of the book, it would begin by reporting how a band of Amalekites made a razzia on Ziklag and then are pursued by David and his men (1 Sam 30:1b–2, 8:18a, 19–20).

What follows this account is the register of cities just discussed. A primary objective of the episode is to explain the origins of the goods that David distributed among Judah's elites who later place him on the throne. Its authors make it clear that David had not purloined these goods during his unsavory expeditions as a mercenary in the service of a Philistine. Rather, he had heroically recovered them from "the enemies of YHWH," who in turn had seized them as war spoils on their raids in "the Negeb of the Cherethites, and in the [territories] that belong to Judah, and in the Negeb of Caleb."[8] In keeping with its heroic portrayal of Judah's first king, the account may have originally presented Ziklag as a town that David rescues, similar to his liberation of Keilah (discussed in the following chapter). The possibility that Ziklag may have been located in the Negeb, rather than in proximity to Gath, lends weight to this suggestion.

So we can see that the register of cities that received a share of David's war spoils is not a late supplement. Although the passage likely does not derive from David's time, we have good reason to believe that it belongs to the older portions of the HDR. An excerpt from the independent Saul history (the HSR) now severs those older portions that were once tightly linked. Yet prior to the insertion of the Saul material, the earliest narrative of David's life transitioned directly from this account of him sharing his war spoils to the passage in which he is anointed king over the "House of Judah."

What all this means is that the oldest source related to David is very much concerned with *Judah*'s political constitution.

Dating Our Sources

Yet how old is this oldest source? To answer the question, we need to consider several factors. To begin with, the authors do not adopt the "canonical" view according to which Judah is one of Israel's tribes. Rather, they tell how originally autonomous regions and unrelated clans consolidated under the banner of "the House of Judah." What catalyzes their consolidation is not an ancient kinship (that is, their identity as "children of Israel"), but rather shared political and economic interests. Perennial raids by common enemies imperil these interests. It is David who rids the region of the menace. He gives the elders of the resident clans a generous share of the spoils. Predictably, the same group later crowns him king.

In presenting Judah as patchwork kingdom with regions, cities, and clans, each with their own identity and agendas, the authors of the HDR probably were not drawing on memories from the time of David or even reconstructing the period as they imagined it. More likely they were mirroring the political character of Judah during the ninth and eighth centuries BCE, when a Judahite collective consciousness was beginning to emerge.

Judah assumed a major role in the southern Levant after the defeat of Israel in the late eighth century BCE. During this period, Jerusalem underwent massive growth. If the city does not figure prominently in this early history of David's reign, it is likely because the authors knew that it had only recently become Judah's capital. For ideological reasons, later tradition claimed it was the capital already in the days of David, the founder of the Judahite state.

The HDR is, as we have seen, preoccupied with Judah. Even passages that can be identified as supplements do not have the northern kingdom of Israel in their field of vision. Instead they are entirely consumed with Judahite concerns, seeking to show how originally unrelated clans and regions came together to form a political unity, with Hebron at its center. Long after the destruction of Israel in 722 BCE, many would not have been interested in affirming commonalities with Israel. Even so, the HDR's inattention to Israel says much about its origins.

The silence suggests that this source was completed before the Assyrian conquest in 722 BCE. After Israel's defeat, and probably already in anticipation of it, many Judahite authors eagerly put forward the Davidic monarchy and Jerusalem as the rallying point for the inhabitants of the erstwhile kingdom of Israel.

One product of their activity is the synthesis of the independent Saul and David histories that we find in the Book of Samuel.

That synthesis created the many episodes in which Saul seeks David's life – the episodes most relevant to the study of war commemoration that we are about to undertake. What drives the composition of a good portion of these texts is a concern not only to show that David and Judah are part of Israel, but also to assert David's solicitude for Saul or his ascendancy – morally and politically – over him.

As I noted in Chapter 1 of this book, Saul may have originally only represented the territory of Benjamin, but in time he came to stand for Israel, just as David represents Judah. David treats Saul with respect and deference, spares his life more than once, mourns his death, and performs acts of benefaction for his household. These narratives summon Israel to join Judah by showing that Judah's royal dynasty is the one chosen by Israel's God to rule – an election that David himself manifested repeatedly vis-à-vis the reigning king.

All these texts bespeak Judah's self-consciousness as the successor state to Israel. As the youngest of eight sons, David is an underdog. Yet he is divinely chosen to replace Saul at an early point. Even so, he does not manage to mount the throne until much later – after years of wars with Israel, culminating in the death of Saul and his sons. Only then does Israel embrace him as king. The correspondences to Israel's and Judah's political histories are undeniable.

These texts, which combine and synthesize the HDR and HSR, must have been written before 586 BCE. They reflect attempts by the Davidic dynasty to address communities in the north. Asserting their authority over "all Israel," they affirm that Israel's kings had broken away from Jerusalem and the divinely chosen royal line. But those who still lived in the land could now return to it, especially now that Assyria had deported these illegitimate rulers.

While it is possible that this literary activity predates Israel's demise in 722 BCE, it is not likely: Until this time, Judah's kings were much weaker than those in Israel, and they were not in the position to expect Israel's population to recognize themselves as their legitimate rulers.

Archaeological Finds

But what about the recent archaeological finds that have attracted so much media attention? How do they affect our understanding of the biblical texts?

If I did not begin this chapter by discussing (the often sensationalistic) claims by archaeologists, it is because they run the risk of prejudicing our interpretation of the biblical writings. Archaeology, at least as it is conducted in the southern Levant, helps us to track changes over long time spans (the so-called *longue durée*). It has trouble, however, when it comes to linking finds to historical personalities. This is especially the case in cultures that failed to leave much of an epigraphic record. For the region of Judah in the southern Levant, very few finds bear any inscriptions.

Why, then, are so many archaeologists eager to date their finds to David's reign? There are two basic explanations. The first is that anything related to David is sure to create buzz, and buzz is a good thing when you are struggling to fund your excavations in the highly competitive world of Israeli archaeology. The danger of these media stunts, which often conceal the problems with the claims, is that they jeopardize the public's confidence in scholars and foster an image of archaeology as a gold-digging adventure of the Indiana Jones variety.

The second reason is that many archaeologists are working with historical paradigms and understandings of the Bible that have long been abandoned by those of us who work primarily with the textual record. The attempt to link all kinds of finds to David or Saul betrays an impoverishment of the historical imagination. The biblical account represents a thoroughly simplified historical construction, with a pronounced political message and theological-didactic function.

Careful research on both the biblical materials and the archaeological record reveals a much greater diversity of polities, which gradually coalesced into the kingdoms of Israel and Judah.

To take the important case of Khirbet Qeiyafa. This site which has been in the news for the past few years, is a fascinating one, to be sure. But it is likely part of a smaller local polity, situated strategically in the Elah Valley, with no appreciable connections to Jerusalem, Hebron, or a Judahite kingdom. Were it strategically important to an emerging territorial state, it would be difficult to explain why it was not rebuilt after being destroyed after just several decades.

If the HDR contains historical information about Jerusalem, we should not expect to find remains of monumental architecture dating to David's reign. My analysis has pointed to the likelihood that Hebron served as David's capital. Jerusalem appears to have been primarily a fortress on the northern periphery of the Judahite state; it probably would not have become the administrative center until much later. This is not to say that we will not find, or have not already found, traces of David's presence in the Jebusite town that he captured.

One find related to the historical David merits mention in conclusion. In 1993, fragments of an Aramaic inscription were found at Tel Dan in northern Israel. It refers to two states. The one designated "Israel" is mentioned first, likely in keeping with its greater political significance. The second state, called "the House of David," must refer to Judah. Its ruler appears to have fought with Israel as a vassal, or alternatively as an alliance partner. For our purposes, the inscription is important for two reasons. First, it confirms what the Bible portrays: the special relationship between Israel and Judah. Second, it confirms what critical scholarship has long maintained: the fundamental separation of Israel and Judah. That the House of David once ruled over Israel, and that its members thought of themselves as "Israelites," are ideological claims that biblical writers make for various reasons, as we shall see. But the inscription fails to lend *historical* credence to their claims.[9]

Conclusions

In this chapter I discussed the contours of an early account of David's life (HDR), one that presents an unfamiliar face of David. It differs from the way David has traditionally been viewed yet has much in common with the ambition Michelangelo imputed to him in his exquisite sculpture. Rather than a courageous shepherd or a beloved musician, David is a cunning warlord who wields his private army to chisel a kingdom from the rocky terrain of the Judahite highlands and the Negeb.

The authors of the HDR recount few if any of the feats for which this larger-than-life personality has been celebrated through the centuries. They have nothing to say about Saul and Jonathan, or Absalom and Solomon. What is more important, they do not identify him as the great ruler of a Israel. Their perspective is confined to Judah, with its capital at Hebron.

The narrative of David's life as we know it is the work of later generations who combined this history with an independent narrative of Saul's reign (HSR). The fusing of these two histories changes how they are interpreted: David's experiences as a warlord in the service of a Philistine monarch are now to be understood as necessary way stations during his flight as a fugitive from Saul.

In the coming chapters we'll see that the account of David's flight from Saul bears many features in common with the equally dramatic account of his flight from Absalom. Both served as frameworks for generations of readers to address questions of belonging. These readers amplified the narratives with an array of episodes that pursue two basic polemical agendas: Either they pay homage to those who assisted Judah's first king during his wars with Saul and Absalom, or they malign the memory of those who betrayed him during his struggles with his nemeses. To begin our exploration of this biblical "war commemoration," let us consider now the cases of two obscure populations.

4

Tales of Loyalty and Betrayal

The Cases of Keilah and Ziph

During his flight from King Saul, David valiantly rescues the town of Keilah from the Philistines. As he is residing there, he learns that Saul had discovered his whereabouts and would soon lay siege to the fortified place with the aim of capturing him. Unsure whether he should take flight or remain within the shelter of the town's walls, David inquires of the deity with the help of a priestly oracle: "Will the citizens of Keilah deliver [*hayasgirû* – "shut me up"] me and my men into Saul's hands?" The deity responds with an unequivocal affirmative: *yasgîrû*.

For the inhabitants of Keilah, which was still occupied in Persian and Hellenistic times, this account of David's early days would have undoubtedly provoked vexation. As an analogy to American history, it would be similar to someone accusing a New England village of having planned to betray George Washington to the British during the Revolutionary War. The mere allegation of such treachery would plague the place for centuries thereafter.

The case of Keilah is what I call "negative war commemoration." Instead of showing how the inhabitants of a town risked their skin for Judah's beloved king and thus deserve an honored place in Judahite memory and society, the authors assert that they were prepared to deliver David to his enemy.

A closely related example of negative war commemoration is the depiction of the Ziphites. The authors traduce the memory of this southern clan by claiming that its members had conspired against David with his enemy. In what follows, I examine these two accounts in tandem.

From Deliverance to Betrayal

Feats of military salvation were considered *de rigueur* for (would-be) kings. Thus a popular epithet for Hellenistic rulers was *sōtēr* or "savior." This Greek title corresponds to the Hebrew term *môšîaʿ*, a common designation for rulers in the Bible that also means "savior."

According to the independent HSR ("History of Saul's Reign" – see discussion in the preceding chapter), Saul became Israel's first monarch by performing the role of "savior" when he rescued the Transjordanian town of Jabesh-gilead from the Ammonites. Beholden to Saul for their liberation, the city remained his most faithful supporters. After he fell in the Battle on Mount Gilboa, the warriors of Jabesh-gilead marched all night to recover his body. As we shall see in the following chapter, these two episodes may have once framed the HSR.

In the independent David account (the History of David's Reign or HDR), David's rise to power is also closely connected to his activities of liberating, and providing protection for, various regions, populations, and towns, such as Keilah. Yet whereas the citizens of Jabesh-gilead display grateful loyalty to Saul, the citizens of Keilah, according to several lines from our account, were prepared to hand over their liberator to his opponent.

In carefully examining our story, we can discern the contours of an older version that reports how David rescued Keilah and then moved on to roam elsewhere. Notably, it does not depict Saul pursuing David:

David was told: "The Philistines are raiding Keilah and plundering the threshing floors."

David consulted YHWH, "Shall I go and attack those Philistines?"

YHWH's said to David, "Go and attack the Philistines and you will rescue Keilah."

[But David's men said to him, "Look, we're afraid here in Judah, how much more if we go to Keilah against the armies of the Philistines!"

David consulted YHWH again, and YHWH answered him, "March down at once to Keilah, for I am going to deliver the Philistines into your hands."]

So David and his men went to Keilah and fought against the Philistines; he drove off their cattle and inflicted a severe defeat on them.

[Saul material added here]

Thereafter David and his men, about 600 in number, got up and left Keilah, and continued to roam about. (1 Sam 23:1–5, 13a[1])

As proposed in the preceding chapter, the transmitted Saul–David history derives from a synthesis of the independent Saul (HSR) and David (HDR) histories. The HSR originally knew nothing of David, and the HDR knew nothing of Saul. The authors of the Book of Samuel, in splicing together these two histories, transformed the tales of David's exploits as a warlord into episodes of his flight from Saul. The tale of David's liberation of Keilah belongs, I propose, to the older, independent HDR. By inserting new material into it, later readers transformed it in line with the theme of David's flight from Saul. In this expanded narrative, Saul views David as his rival. By aggressively pursuing him, the king compels David to abandon Keilah and go back on the run. So instead of deciding on his own to leave Keilah, David absconds after learning that the town was conspiring with Saul. What follows is a section from the middle of the passage just cited:

When Abiathar son of Ahimelech fled to David at Keilah, he came down with an ephod in his hand.

Now it was told Saul that David had come to Keilah.

And Saul said, "God has given him into my hand; for he has shut himself in by entering a town

that has gates and bars." Saul summoned all the people to war, to go down to Keilah, to besiege David and his men.

When David learned that Saul was plotting evil against him, he said to the priest Abiathar, "Bring the ephod here."

And David said, "O YHWH, God of Israel, your servant has heard that Saul intends to come to Keilah and destroy the town because of me. *Will the burghers / patricians of Keilah deliver me into his hand?* Will Saul come down, as your servant has heard? YHWH, God of Israel, please tell your servant!"

And YHWH said, "He will."

Then David said, "Will the men of Keilah surrender me and my men into the hand of Saul?"

YHWH *said, "They will surrender you."* (1 Sam 23:6–12)

I suggest that this passage was inserted into the account right before the final, and original, statement that David and his men left Keilah. The older edition says nothing about Saul. It presents David as a warlord roaming about and rescuing towns that were in dire straits. The supplement transforms the story so that David is here fleeing from Saul.[2]

Now within this larger supplement, we can identify two smaller additions. I have marked them in italics. Both statements suggest that Keilah was prepared to break faith with David.

From the basic plot, these lines are superfluous. To provide a general reason why David again took flight, the narrator would have needed to report simply that the oracle had confirmed that Saul was indeed planning to storm Keilah. A separate query about Keilah's loyalty was not necessary.[3]

What, then, might have motivated the insertion of the two lines that refer to Keilah? The most likely reason is that later readers intended to cast aspersions on the memory of this town. If so, these readers would have been using war commemoration in a negative way – that is, to tell the readers how Keilah betrayed Judah's first and greatest king and thus does not deserve honor in Judah's history. To test this theory, we need to find out more about Keilah.

Keilah through Time

Keilah has a long history. Although the location of the town is not known with certainty, it is often identified with Khirbet

Qîlā, which stands at the easternmost edge of the Shephelah (approximately seven miles northwest of Hebron). Situated on a hill between two valleys that converge at a wadi, this site is connected by a north–south route to a string of other towns in the eastern Shephelah. It is also close to the Eshcol Valley, the place where Caleb and the spies reconnoiter the land of Canaan in the days of Moses, bringing back clusters of grapes from the wine-rich region.

A register from the late monarchic period (Josh 15:42) assigns Keilah to a group of "nine towns with their villages" in the Shephelah. If this group formed a territorial unit, Mareshah may have been the administrative center.

Throughout the history of the Judahite kingdom, Keilah remained an important site. Numerous LMLK ("Belonging to the King") impressions on the handles of large storage jars have surfaced at that site, and early specimens of these administrative stamps (dating to the late eighth century BCE) have been discovered at Khirbet Qîlā itself.[4]

Keilah is likely the same place as the town known as "Qiltu" in the Amarna letters, an Egyptian archive dating to the fourteenth century BCE. One dossier from this archive relates to a ruler or "mayor" of Jerusalem named Abdi-Heba. He claims that Milkilu, who governed the neighboring town of Gezer, had encouraged his alliance partners to "yield all of their demands to the men of Qiltu." Their objective was to entice Qiltu/Keilah to their side and leave Jerusalem politically isolated.

The policy appears to have been a successful one: Abdi-Heba reports elsewhere that Milkilu, together with Shuwardata of Gath (the same city David served as a mercenary), had hired men from Qiltu/Keilah, so that a small town belonging to the city-state of Jerusalem "went over to the side of the men of Qiltu."

In another group of letters, Shuwardata of Gath reports that he, in keeping with the wishes of the court, had made war against Qiltu/Keilah. Although he had recaptured it, Abdi-Heba was continuing to vie for control of it: "Now my town has been restored to me. But Abdi-Heba still writes to the men of Qiltu, saying: 'Take my silver and follow me!'"[5]

These second-millennium letters reveal how Keilah was pulled to and fro by forces from, on the one side, the hill country in the east (Jerusalem), and, on the other side, the Shephelah in the west (Gezer and Gath). The biblical texts reveal how the town continued, in the first millennium BCE, to be an object of contention between these two regions.

The tale of David's rescue of Keilah reflects a very similar territorial contest. Just as Gezer, Gath, and Jerusalem go to great lengths to exert influence over Qiltu/Keilah, David undertakes a dangerous expedition to liberate this town from Philistine control before serving as a mercenary at Gath. The biblical authors depict the Philistines attacking Keilah with the intention of plundering its grain stores, which would have been abundant given the town's location. And while they portray David's military assistance as altruistic, we have good reasons to read their account as a witness to later Philistine-Judahite border skirmishes. Given its strategic location, Keilah would have been especially attractive for any ruler from the hill country.

For Persian-Hellenistic times, we hear about Keilah in a roster of those who supported the construction of Jerusalem's wall (Neh 3:17–18). The town has two heads, each identified as a "chief of the half-district (*ḥaṣî-pelek*) of Keilah." The list identifies four other Judahite districts (Beth-Zur, Beth-Hakkerem, Jerusalem, Mizpah), most of which are also divided into two subdistricts. Keilah marks the southwestern border of Judah, which is now no longer a kingdom but rather an imperial province.

While Jerusalemite circles appear to have exploited a tale from the days of David to reproach the name of this town, this list from the Nehemiah Memoir documents the material support that both subdistricts of Keilah provided for the construction of Jerusalem's fortifications during more recent times. In the post-exilic period, contributions to public building projects began to assume the place of wartime service, and commemoration of those who supported these building projects played a very similar political role to the commemoration of wartime contributions and sacrifice (see discussion in Chapter 10).

Border Towns

From Tijuana to post-war Berlin, border towns are, not surprisingly, popular settings in modern film and literature.[6] They are also often the subject of biblical writings. Indeed, if the biblical authors pay special attention to places, it is usually because they presented historical or political issues.

The depiction of Keilah shares features with other biblical representations of border towns. I already mentioned the case of Jabesh-gilead, and in the next section I will examine the polemics against the Ziphites, a clan from a region that became Judah's southern border. Here I will examine an additional example, this time from the northern border of Israel.

When a guy named Sheba ben Bichri mounts an insurrection against David – long after he had become the king of Israel – he becomes "Public Enemy No. 1" and seeks refuge in Abel Beth-Maacah, a town on Israel's northernmost frontier. For the greater part of Israel's history, this town was not in the possession of Israel. Although we have no way of knowing how its inhabitants would have identified themselves – the city belonged to Israel less than a hundred years, all totaled – the Bible presents the city as Israelite.

As David's troops are engaged in battering the fortifications, a "wise woman" calls out from atop the wall:

> "I am one of the peaceful and devoted in Israel. But you seek to bring death upon a mother city [or: a mother and city] in Israel! Why should you destroy the YHWH's possession?" (2 Sam 20:19)

She then convinces the people of the city to cut off the head of Sheba and toss it over the wall to Joab, David's general.

By constructing this memory of Abel and its representative figure of the "wise woman," the authors identify the place not only as a true Israelite city, but also as one that brought a quick end to an insurrection against David's rule. In contrast, the account of Keilah raises doubts about the loyalties of another border town by asserting – allegedly with the support of a divine oracle – that the patricians of Keilah were willing to hand over David, or at least his head, to Saul.

The example of Abel Beth-Maacah shows again how border towns pose the same kinds of political issues in the Bible as they do elsewhere. For both Abel and Keilah, the biblical authors address these issues in the context of David's reign, and more specifically, in a setting of military conflict between two political factions.

So while we cannot say exactly why our account vilifies Keilah, the peripheral location of this town predestined it to a history (from the Late Bronze Age into the Persian period) of shifting allegiances. Keilah's political vicissitudes as a border town are reflected in the account's history: At first it tells how the greatest figure in Judahite memory once risked his skin to rescue this town from the Philistines. A later supplement, however, uses the authority of a divine oracle to assert that the town was prepared to surrender Judah's cherished hero instead of shielding him from his opponent.

Ziphite Perfidy

We now turn to a couple of episodes in David's life that are closely related to his experience at Keilah. They both involve the Ziphites, an obscure clan that possessed territories in the south of Judah. Seeking to win Saul's favor, its members offer to help find the fugitive David and hand him over to Israel's king. The formulation in Hebrew, *hasgîrô*, is the same as in the account of Keilah's betrayal. As we shall see, the authors who introduced these episodes into the Book of Samuel were intent on besmirching the reputation of the Ziphites. And this evidence in turn lends support to my suggestions for the Keilah episode.

The first of the two episodes follows directly upon the Keilah account and continues with a depiction of David sparing the life of Saul in the wilderness of En-gedi. The second is found a couple of chapters later. They both evince many of the same narrative features, actors, and even phraseology:

Then some Ziphites went up to Saul at Gibeah and said: "David is hiding among us in the strongholds of Horesh, on the hill of Hachilah, which is south of Jeshimon. Now, O king, whenever you wish to come down, do so. We will do our part to hand him over to the king."

Saul said, "May you be blessed by YHWH for showing me compassion! Go and make sure once more. Find out exactly where he is, and who has seen him there. I am told that he's very cunning. Look around and learn all the hiding places where he lurks, and come back to me with sure information. Then I'll go with you; and if he is in the land, I'll search him out among all the thousands of Judah."

So they set out and went to Ziph ahead of Saul. (1 Sam 23:19–24a)

Then the Ziphites came to Saul at Gibeah, saying:

"David is in hiding on the hill of Hachilah, which is opposite Jeshimon."

Saul rose and went down to the Wilderness of Ziph, with three thousand chosen men of Israel, to search out David in the Wilderness of Ziph. Saul encamped on the hill of Hachilah, which is opposite Jeshimon beside the road. But David remained in the wilderness. When he learned that Saul came after him into the wilderness . . . (1 Sam 26:1–3[7])

These paragraphs are tightly juxtaposed with tale of Keilah, so that it would be surprising if the editorial expansion of that tale were not closely linked to the composition of these two texts.

Because of their many points of overlap, the Ziphite texts have often served as a testing ground for models of literary composition. The parallels (what biblical scholars often call "doublets") here and elsewhere in the Book of Samuel may reflect the transmission of two or more recensions of the David–Saul account, which the editors of the book selectively synthesized.[8]

Yet it seems unlikely that the accounts, along with the widely diverging Greek and Hebrew textual versions, originated independently of each other, as some scholars assume. If the composition histories of these two parallel passages were not directly connected, one would have to explain why the correspondences are found in what are most likely very late stages of the tradition.

Instead of assuming independent origins, we may view these and other parallel texts in Samuel as early examples of

"Rewritten Bible/Scripture" – the phenomenon of reproducing a text in a reworked, expanded, rearranged, or otherwise edited form. Instead of choosing one text over the other, the authors of the book sought to preserve the competing textual recensions, even if the way in which they preserved them significantly altered their form and meaning.

When we take a closer look at the larger accounts in which our two paragraphs are embedded, we can see how an editor assimilated various details in the first account (such as the Wilderness of Ziph and the strongholds of Horesh) to the second one. Moreover, in the second account, the Ziphites are mentioned only in the first verse (marked in italics). This fact is important, as elsewhere we can be confident that editors heavily reworked the introductions to texts. If the narrative of this second account began with Saul arising to go search for David in the wilderness of Ziph, it would flow much more smoothly. What I have identified as a secondary introduction creates an incongruity in the narrative: The Ziphites had already informed Saul as to David's exact whereabouts. So it is strange that Saul takes 3,000 men to *search* for his nemesis.

These observations suggest that later readers introduced the Ziphites secondarily into the narratives. What this means is that all of the first account and the first lines (italicized) of the second account represent late supplements to their contexts. But what would have motivated these readers to assign a role to the Ziphites?

Polemics against the Ziphites

This literary activity is, I suggest, another case of "negative war commemoration" – an attempt to defame the name of a group by reporting that they failed to contribute fully to a war effort or, as in this case, behaved treacherously. Similar to the charges leveled against Keilah, these supplements claim that the Ziphites betrayed Judah's first and most cherished king to Saul and his soldiers.

A polemical motivation accounts for various aspects of the supplement. Saul promises to search out David "among all the clans of Judah," which causes the reader to wonder whether the Ziphites and other clans will either protect or betray David.

In the immediately preceding chapter, Saul scolds the Benjaminites – his own tribesmen – for their failure to inform him about the pact between David and Jonathan. Breaking the Benjaminites' silence, an Edomite named Doeg eagerly speaks up and informs the king about David's movements (1 Sam 22:6–19).

As discussed later in this book, the Edomites were a population that gradually infiltrated Judah's southern territories (including those that once belonged to the Ziphites) and took possession of them. Many texts reflect Judah's attitude toward this people; the sentiments tended to be extraordinarily hostile, as we would expect.

By juxtaposing these accounts, the authors of Samuel prompt their readers to associate the Ziphites' behavior with that of the Edomite Doeg. Whereas Saul has to wrangle with the Benjaminites at Gibeah and implores them to divulge their knowledge, the Ziphites need no incentive to go up to Gibeah and volunteer their assistance to Saul. As such, their eagerness to betray David is even more reprehensible than the actions of an Edomite.

Saul expresses gratitude for the Ziphites' devotion: "May you be blessed by YHWH for showing me compassion." His detailed directions to search diligently for David elicit a prompt response from this clan: "So they arose and went to Ziph ahead of Saul." Both of these details embellish the censure of the Ziphites. Their actions are commendable, but only from the perspective of David's enemy.

The scene of the (renewed) covenant between David and Jonathan (1 Sam 23), which has been neatly inserted into the account, serves as a backdrop to the betrayal by Ziphites. In stark contrast to Jonathan's covenant, the Ziphites, who as Judahites should have been more loyal to David than Saul's own son, are prepared to take custody of David and convey him to Saul.

Now if the Ziphites are subjected to censure in these biblical texts, they likely held some importance in Judahite politics. We need, then, to briefly consider what we know about this clan.

For the late eighth and early seventh centuries BCE, Ziph is amply attested in the royal (LMLK) Judahite jar handles. Only four names are attested on these stamps: Ziph, Hebron, Socoh, and a place called MMŠT. The handles bearing the names Ziph and Hebron are much more widely attested than the other two sites for the early seventh century.

A register from the Book of Joshua presents the town of Ziph next to others on the border to Edom in the south (15:24 and 15:55). The town of Ziph may be identified with a tell (and Palestinian village) by the same name located 4.3 miles to the southeast of Hebron, in a district that also included Maon, Carmel, and Juttah. As noted earlier, this Calebite region was – and is still – known for its excellent wines, and the LMLK jars were likely connected to wine production. While Ziph is known more for its desert area, from it one can easily view Maon and Carmel, where the Calebite Nabal owned rich estates.

According to the Book of Chronicles, which would likely have been written during the later Persian or early Hellenistic period, Caleb's firstborn was named Ziph. Although this is a clan genealogy, it reflects (or asserts) a political hierarchy, so that Ziph would have belonged to Calebite territory.

As I show in the final chapters of this book, the Calebites were a prominent clan that clashed first with the Judahite state as it encroached on its ancestral territories, and then later with the Edomites after they took possession of their territories. Some of the best-known biblical war memories portray Caleb, the eponymous ancestor of the clan, as Judah's first and greatest hero. This rivalry between Caleb and David – or more precisely, between the competing groups who identified themselves with these figures – may well be related to the polemics against the Ziphites in the texts we've examined in this chapter. While we have little evidence for the Ziphites, the case of the Calebites will fill in many of the gaps in our knowledge.

To return once more to Chronicles, this book reports that Rehoboam (the son of Solomon) fortified Ziph along with fourteen other prominent Judahite towns (1 Chr 4:15–16, 2 Chr 11:5–12). A recent study by the archeologist Israel Finkelstein rips the rug out from under those who claim that the list of fortifications in this account cannot date to the time of Rehoboam (i.e., the tenth century) or even to the monarchic period.[9] By presenting Ziph as the southernmost site, the register reflects political conditions at Judah after it had forfeited its southern territories on the border to Edom.

The fact that Ziph became a border town to territories of Edom/Idumea offers us another scenario for understanding why these texts make the town's inhabitants an object of obloquy.[10] In the chapters on Caleb that conclude this book, I show that altercations with Edomites figured prominently in constructions of Judah's identity, especially during the Second Temple period.

So, by editing these two accounts, the authors of Samuel accused the Ziphites of ignominious actions against the founder of Judah's royal dynasty. The war commemoration conducted against this clan may have been part of a larger attempt by the Judahite court to dissolve the power of clans that resisted state centralization measures.

This suggestion is admittedly conjectural, since the Bible has otherwise little to say about the Ziphites. But perhaps this silence testifies to the success of the state sanctions.

The Ziphites and Beyond

The headings, or "superscriptions," of the biblical Psalms, which are attested in the Dead Sea Scrolls from the Greco-Roman period, demonstrate how readers in the Second Temple times took the commemorative function of these narratives to a new level. Thus, the first lines of Psalm 54 read,

> For the leader; with instrumental music. A maskil of David, when the Ziphites came and told Saul, "Know, David is in hiding among us."

The psalm continues,

O God, deliver me by Your name; by Your power vindicate me. O God, hear my prayer; give ear to the words of my mouth. For strangers have risen against me, and ruthless men seek my life; they are unmindful of God. Selah.

See, God is my helper; the LORD is my support. He will repay the evil of my watchful foes; by Your faithfulness, destroy them!

Originally the psalm pronounces a curse on nameless foes. Yet the addition of the superscription identifies these foes as none other than the Ziphites. Other examples treat David's flight not only from Saul but also from Absalom. By assigning certain psalms to David, the superscriptions encourage their readers to reflect on his inner life during the time when he was pursued by enemies and betrayed by adversaries. Those who use the Psalter in private prayer and collective worship relive this hero's life and internalize it at a deeper level than what otherwise could normally be achieved through prose narrative.

What begins with these superscriptions continues in post-biblical interpretation. Thus the superscription to Psalm 57 has in mind the time when David fled from Saul and hid in a cave. One lines praises God who "completes/does good for me" (*gōmēr ʿālāy*). But what exactly does the psalmist, here identified as David, mean by this enigmatic line?

To explain the word choice, the Targum (an Aramaic translation) supplements the verse by presenting the deity causing a spider to "complete" a web for David: "I will pray before God Most High, the mighty one, who appointed the spider that completed a web for me." The translator alludes here to the legend of a spider saving David's life when he is running from Saul. The spider spins an elaborate web across the mouth of the cave where David hides so that Saul assumes that the cave was unoccupied. Subsequently David kisses and blesses this spider, whose purpose of existence he had earlier questioned.

The legend is still very popular in Jewish culture, especially among children. (It is putatively what inspired Stan Lee to help Steve Ditko create Spider-Man.) It also bears many similarities to a tale about Mohammed in his struggles with the Koraishites during his flight from Mecca. A similar legend has a wasp fighting for David, using his stinger in an assault on Abner, Saul's general.

Thus, these two insects, "most hated by men," have an indispensable role to play in not only nature but also history. Such is affirmed in these memories of the protection their members provided Israel's cherished king (see Genesis Rabbah 10:7). In these creative adaptations, of which there are countless examples in Medieval Jewish literature, we witness how the war commemoration that began in the David narratives continues to weave its web far beyond the social world of ancient Judah.[11]

Conclusions

In this chapter, I examined tales of fidelity and treachery that have grown out of the activity of war commemoration around two populations on Judah's borders: the city of Keilah and the clan of the Ziphites. My examination has revealed a close connection between war commemoration and literary expansion.

The texts we studied here represent advanced stages in the development of the David narratives. The independent David history (HDR) focuses on the person of David and tells how he wielded his private army to carve out for himself the kingdom of Judah. Prompted by the rivalries between Israel and Judah, later authors who produced the Book of Samuel combined this history with the Saul account (HSR). When synthesizing the histories of these two figures, the authors composed new material that calls to mind towns and groups within Judah who either were loyal to their first king or betrayed him to Saul. These authors thereby negotiated belonging and defined status in Judahite history and society.

In the following chapter, we will witness how other circles in Judah not only engaged in war commemoration but also radically transformed war memories of competing Israelite authors.

5

The Bones of Saul

And the Loyalty of the Gileadites

One way to impugn a population's reputation is to claim that that they had betrayed the nation's revered leader. In the preceding chapter we looked at two cases in which biblical authors did just that. Yet one can also achieve the same vilifying effect by drawing attention to the group's history of loyalty, if the object of their loyalty is *the enemy*. The present chapter treats an example of this clever use of war commemoration.

Jabesh-Gilead and Saul's Death

After vanquishing the forces of Israel on Mount Gilboa, the Philistines return the day after battle to plunder the slain. In doing so, they discover the corpses of Saul and his three sons. They send Saul's head and armor throughout their lands, announcing the victory "to the houses of their gods and to the people." Later they deposit his armor in one of their temples. (This is a widely attested postwar ritual in the ancient world.) His body they pin to the wall that surrounds the city of Beth-shan.

The continuation of the story, which was likely composed by early editors, portrays the reaction of the Transjordanian town of Jabesh-gilead to the news of the defeat. In a demonstration of daring and fearlessness, all the armed men of the town immediately rise up and march the entire night to Beth-shan. There they recover the corpses of Saul and his sons that were hanging on the city's fortifications.[1] After bringing the bodies to Jabesh-gilead, they burn them and bury the bones "under the tamarisk tree" of the city. Finally we're told that they mourn for Saul and his sons by fasting for seven days:

> But when the inhabitants of Jabesh-gilead heard what the Philistines had done to Saul, all their valiant warriors set out, traveled all night long, and took the body of Saul and the bodies of his sons from the wall of Beth-shan. They came to Jabesh and burned them there. Then they took their bones and buried them under the tamarisk tree in Jabesh. They fasted seven days. (1 Sam 31:11–13)

According to the thesis presented in Chapter 3, the Book of Samuel combines two earlier sources: the History of Saul's Reign (the HSR) and the History of David's Reign (HDR). It stands to reason that the authors of the HSR composed the episode at Jabesh-gilead as the final episode in the life of Saul. If this is the case, the HSR would begin and end at the same location: Saul becomes king by saving the city (1 Sam 11), and when he dies, the city repays their debt to him by salvaging his bones and burying them under the tamarisk tree that stood prominently in the city (1 Sam 31).[2]

The account of Saul's liberation of Jabesh-gilead in 1 Samuel 11 presents Saul moving from the plow to the throne. Butchering his oxen in a symbolic threat, he mobilizes an army from the people of Israel and rescues the beleaguered town across the Jordan.

Early audiences of this legend likely would not have viewed the citizens of that town as Israelites. One line of the passage suggests that they belong to Israel. Yet evidence from Qumran (see following section) confirms that later readers reworked the passage. When we remove this line, we can see how the account traces Israel's claims in the Transjordan to the very beginning of Saul's kingdom.

The depiction of Saul's burial likewise identifies Jabesh-gilead as a non-Israelite town. What early readers would have assumed is made explicit by the statement that the citizens of the town burned the bones. Cremation is a non-Israelite practice, and by ascribing it to Jabesh-gilead, the authors likely intended to mark it as "other."[3]

The authors draw a distinction between Israel and Jabesh-gilead in yet another way. We are told that, after Israel's defeat and Saul's death, members of Israel who had migrated to the Transjordan took flight and abandoned their settlements. The statement suggests that some had moved from the Ephraimite hill country (Israel's core territory) and had established settlements across the Jordan to the east and across "the valley" to the west. After the catastrophe at Gilboa, they flee from their settlements in the valley and on the eastern side of the Jordan back into the central highlands of the Cisjordan. By reporting how the citizens of Jabesh-gilead risked their lives to retrieve the corpses of Saul and his sons, the account draws a contrast between the bravery of the Transjordanians and the craven Israelites.[4]

The view of the Transjordan in these texts differs starkly from that of later biblical narratives. The Book of Numbers tells how Israel came to possess extensive landholdings in the Transjordan. Two (and a half) of Israel's tribes settle there right before the other tribes cross the Jordan to conquer and occupy Canaan. In the Book of Judges, Jephthah the Gileadite and the king of the Ammonites wrangle over this history in a lengthy prebattle exchange. Later, the residents of Jabesh-gilead fail to take part in a collective Israelite military action against Benjamin. In this final text, the biblical authors use war commemoration to disparage the name of the city, yet they do not deny that it belongs to Israel. Indeed, because they are full members of the nation, the rest of Israel punishes them for their dereliction of duty with extremely harsh measures – by exterminating all its inhabitants except for 400 virgin girls (see Num 21 and 32, Judg 11 and 21).

Evidence from Qumran

A biblical manuscript found at Qumran, as well as the retelling by the Jewish historian Josephus (d. circa 100 CE), significantly alters the story of Saul rescuing Jabesh-gilead. The differences are most pronounced in the introduction:

> Now Nahash, king of the Ammonites, had been grievously oppressing the Gadites and the Reubenites. He would gouge out the right eye of each of them and would not grant Israel a deliverer. No one was left of the Israelites across the Jordan whose right eye Nahash, king of the Ammonites, had not gouged out. But there were seven thousand men who had escaped from the Ammonites. They entered Jabesh-gilead . . . (See NRSV at 1 Sam 10:27)

Although widely thought to represent an earlier edition of the account, this preface is very likely a later expansion – what some would call an "aggadic expansion" – that harmonizes the older edition with the preceding biblical narratives. It corrects the story so that it no longer conflicts with the Book of Numbers, which depicts two Israelite tribes (Gad and Reuben) settling in the Transjordan. Precisely these tribes are the ones named in the Qumran version: The newly crowned Saul comes to save all "the Israelites beyond the Jordan" who had fled from the Ammonite king and sought refuge in this unoccupied city. The 7,000 refugees, we are told, belonged to the tribes of Gad and Reuben.[5]

The Qumran text not only presupposes that Jabesh-gilead is an Israelite town. It also explains specifically how the place could have been occupied if, as we are told in the Book of Judges, Israel's armies had just recently annihilated its delinquent male inhabitants except for 400 virgin girls.

The preface resembles many editorial passages from Judges that reinterpret older material from a pan-Israelite perspective. Yet it also reaffirms that Israel's presence in the Transjordan is not the work of Israel's first king (as claimed by the monarchic HSR) but rather the result of a collective-national military campaign from the time long before Israel's kings (in keeping with the Pentateuch).

If Jabesh-gilead did not belong to Israel, why would its citizens have risked their skin for Saul and his sons? Curiously, the passage itself does not provide a reason. Is the reader to assume that the citizens of the town remembered the great deeds that Saul had once performed for them? As already noted, the account of Saul's coronation tells how this yeoman from Benjamin mobilized his fellow farmers into a fighting force that rescued the beleaguered Gileadites. It and the story of his burial in Jabesh-gilead are the two "bookends" that frame the HSR narrative, which begins with Saul rescuing Jabesh-gilead and concludes with Jabesh-gilead rescuing Saul.

So how does this account relate to the History of David's Reign (HDR)? In Chapter 3, we saw how easy it is to extricate the accounts of the Philistine battle on Mount Gilboa from the passages that relate to David. When later authors decided to synthesize the HDR and HSR (presumably after the conquest of Israel in 722 BCE), they faced a problem: While the Saul account presents its protagonist dying in a battle with the Philistines, the David account presents its protagonist and his band of warriors fighting in the ranks of the Philistines.

To exculpate David from any responsibility in Saul's death, later readers (likely the same ones who combined the HDR and HSR) composed a passage in which the Philistine commanders muster out David and his men and send them home just before the battle. At the same time that Saul is dying on Mount Gilboa in the north, David is killing Amalekites deep in the south. The passage draws attention to Saul's failure to exterminate the Amalekites, which initiated his demise (see 1 Sam 28:1b–2 + 29:2–11).

These late readers are responsible for other texts. Thus they inserted a lengthy passage that portrays David's deep sorrow at the news of Saul's death. An Amalekite brings Saul's crown and informs of the king's death. Grief stricken and angered, David has the messenger killed. What follows is the lengthy dirge that David intones for Saul and his son Jonathan:

> Your glory, O Israel, lies slain on the heights.
> How the mighty have fallen! (2 Sam 1:19)

The authors placed this supplementary passage directly before an older one that describes how the elders of Judah came to crown David king of Judah (2:1–4a). Directly after it, they append a short paragraph in which David, as his first royal act, pronounces a solemn and ceremonious blessing upon the inhabitants of Jabesh-gilead in acknowledgement of their deeds:

> When they told David that it was the people of Jabesh-gilead who had buried Saul, David sent messengers to the people of Jabesh-gilead and said to them:
>
> "Blessed be you by YHWH, for you have performed this act of faithfulness to your lord Saul and have buried him. May YHWH perform true faithfulness for you in return. As for me, I will do a good thing for you because you have done this. Now take courage and be valorous men, for your lord Saul is dead, and the house of Judah has anointed me king over them." (2 Sam 2:4b–7)

In contrast to earlier texts, David's words here presuppose that Jabesh-gilead, along with the region of the Gilead that this town represents, belongs to the kingdom of Israel (although not necessarily to the people of Israel in an ethnic-national sense). If this town's warriors recovered the bodies of the royal family, it was not because Saul had been their friend or ally, and had rescued them from the Ammonites (as seems to be the case in the original account). It is rather because he, as Israel's king, was their "lord." By offering them a reward for their valorous deeds, and by promising them special covenantal relations, David strives to persuade Jabesh-gilead (representing the rich region of the Gilead) to swear allegiance to him, as he makes his bid for Israel's throne. By embracing his authority, Jabesh-gilead, as Saul's most loyal subjects, would set a precedent for other regions, towns, clans, and guilds in Israel.

The authors of the HSR assign Jabesh-gilead such a prominent place in their story because the Gilead had come to play a significant political role in the expanding state of Israel during the ninth century BCE and thereafter. By commemorating how "all the warriors" of this important town undertook a heroic mission on the behalf of one of Israel's royal families, and by claiming that the bones of this family were buried under "the tamarisk tree in Jabesh," the older source underscores the Gilead's special affiliation with Israel. In the introduction to the HSR, the authors make the same point by claiming that Saul became Israel's first king by undertaking a brave mission to rescue Jabesh-gilead from Israel's enemies.

The Transjordan in Israel's History

Over time, the Gilead was identified as an integral part of the kingdom – and later of the people – of Israel. These developments are reflected in the strata of biblical literature.

The Transjordanian territories that belonged to Israel posed problems for Judah, and some texts project this troubled relationship back to the beginning of David's reign. They present Saul's general Abner bringing a son of the dead king to the eastern city of Mahanaim from where they organize military resistance to David. As we shall see in my treatment of the Absalom account, other Judahite writings responded to such negative images of the Transjordan by reporting that David enjoyed asylum in Mahanaim and was received warmly by various representative figures from the region.

Eventually Mahanaim became more than just a place of refuge. A constituent component of the Jacob cycle in Genesis lays a claim to this Transjordanian town, along with other centers of the regions (e.g., Penuel and Succoth), by identifying them as places where the Israelite patriarch roamed, built houses for himself and his cattle, and encountered YHWH, who would become Israel's national deity.

Yet in contrast to the Samarian and Judean hill country, the Gilead and related Transjordanian territories never achieved an undisputed status as Israel's core territory. A dominant – yet certainly not uncontested – attitude in biblical and later rabbinic literature regards the Jordan as marking the border of the Promised Land.

In the Book of Deuteronomy, Moses delivers all his speeches, including the law code, in anticipation of crossing this river. YHWH's marching orders, with which the book begins, do not include the Jordan's eastern bank when defining the borders of the land that was promised to the ancestors and that Israel was to conquer. The threat that Israel will perish from the land is notably confined to the western territories.

In the Book of Joshua, the ceremonious crossing of the Jordan is told at great length. As soon as Israel encamps at Gilgal, they build a monument that connects the parting of the Jordan with the parting of the Red Sea. Later they circumcise all the males, "rolling away" the reproach of Egypt that they had carried with them until this point. At that point, the manna ceases, and they celebrate Passover. These and many other things happen in Canaan, not in the territories of the Transjordanian tribes.

One could cite evidence from other texts. Thus Ezekiel's "Temple Vision" includes expansive portions of the southern Levant in Israel's borders. But when it comes to the eastern limit, it draws a line "between the Gilead and the land of Israel, with the Jordan as a boundary" (47:18).

The issues posed by the Transjordan are often addressed through biblical war commemoration. The Song of Deborah from the Book of Judges indicts Transjordanian tribes for failing to participate in a major war effort:

> Among the clans of Reuben
>   there were great searchings of heart.
> Why did you stay among the sheepfolds,
>   to hear the piping for the flocks?
> Among the clans of Reuben
>   there were great searchings of heart.
> Gilead dwelt beyond the Jordan . . .
>
> (Judg 5:15–17)

Responding to this indictment, a chapter in the Book of Numbers paints a scene in which the earliest representatives of Israel's Transjordanian communities approach Moses and petition him to exempt them from the obligation to cross the Jordan and participate in the conquest of Canaan. The appeal outrages Moses: "Will your brothers go to war while you stay here?" (Num 32:6).

The narrative gives the Transjordanian tribes an occasion to respond to larger questions about their belonging and status among the people of Israel. The tribes take a pledge not merely to participate in the conquest, but also to fight in the vanguard – the most dangerous position in military formations. Only after Israel had taken possession of Canaan would they return to their homes on the eastern side of the Jordan. These tribes thus fight for other members of the nation, conquering territories that are not their own.

Other texts take a much more negative attitude toward the Transjordanian communities. As a case in point, consider Gideon's wars. After attacking the Midianite armies with lanterns and torches, he pursues them to the left bank of the Jordan. There he implores the towns of Succoth and Penuel to provide bread for his 300 men. These are the same towns famous for their history with Jacob. Yet both towns refuse to make any contribution to Gideon's war effort. Consequently they are later subjected to harsh sanctions: After returning triumphantly from his campaign, Gideon tramples the town elders with briars, kills the men of both places, and tears down the tower of Penuel (Judg 8:4–17).

Thus, while the Jacob traditions confer on these towns a place of honor in the history of Israel, the Gideon account uses war commemoration to raise questions about their loyalty to Israel and commitment to its welfare.

Counterhistory in Chronicles

By reshaping earlier war memories, Judahite circles from the late Persian or early Hellenistic period continued to address issues presented by the Transjordan. The Book of Chronicles bears witness to their activities.

In retelling the story of Saul's death, this work emphasizes this ruler's culpability in his own demise and eliminates any trace of Gileadites' heroism. The Philistines, in this rendition, deposit Saul's armor and head in their temples, yet leave the decapitated body on the battlefield. It is there that Gileadites find the corpses of Saul and his sons. No risk is involved on their part. They leave the head of the king hanging in the temple of Dagon. We are told nothing about these warriors marching all night to execute their mission. In fact, one cannot speak of military mission here at all. They bring the bodies back, bury them, and fast seven days.

By omitting the reference to the cremation of the corpses, the authors eliminate the identity marker with which they flagged Jabesh-gilead as non-Israelite. They also deleted words "from across the Jordan" from the description of the Israelites who flee in fear. In this way, they eradicated the contrast between the Israelites and the courageous Gileadites who come to rescue the bodies of the royal family.[6]

Yet why didn't Chronicles just pass over the Gileadites in silence? Its authors clearly felt no compunctions about deleting extensive passages from the materials they inherited, especially when it came to the reign of Saul: They begin their history with his death, reporting none of the many episodes from his life that we read about in Samuel.

The fact that they preserve the memory of the Gileadites' deeds – even if they have thoroughly expunged any aspect of valor from them – fits the wider tendency in biblical writings to malign the memory of Transjordanian communities. If Chronicles portrays Saul as a foil to David, then any affiliation with this enemy would be objectionable.

This point is highlighted in the next chapters, which commemorate the names of individual warriors and tribal groups by claiming that they had joined David and abandoned Saul already during his lifetime (see discussion in Chapter 10). By reporting that Jabesh-gilead remained on Saul's side and mourned his death, Chronicles traduces the name of this town and the region it represents.

In Chronicles we witness a complete reversal in the commemorative function of the older account. By adding this passage to the independent Saul narrative, the authors of the HSR paid tribute to the exceptional sacrifice and solidarity displayed by an outside group for Israel. However, the circle that produced Chronicles transmitted this memory with the aim of casting aspersions on Jabesh-gilead. By telling how the town buried Saul and his sons and mourned their deaths, they remind their readers that this community stood on the side of the contemptible arch-nemesis of the book's illustrious protagonist. Rather than simply denying what was written or attempting to erase it, the authors of Chronicles use the memory, counter to its original intention, to traduce the record of this representative Transjordanian town.

Chronicles is not a unified work. Like all biblical literature, it reflects a range of competing opinions, even while maintaining emphases that are distinct from those of other works. Thus the book contains several passages that commend the exceptional bravery and martial prowess of the eastern Israelite tribes. According to one passage, the Gadites are as fierce as lions and as agile as gazelles. They are able to cross the Jordan in the first month when it is at its crest and can easily put to flight all lowlanders east and west. Fearlessness and soldierly skill are the characteristic traits ascribed to the Transjordanian tribes by other texts. It is indeed the quality that should render them indispensable as members of Israel.[7]

Although the author of the Jabesh-gilead passage in Chronicles likely meant to cast aspersions on the entire of region of the Gilead, the reader who expects the book to have a consistent stance will read this passage as referring solely to the city of Jabesh-gilead. Harmonizing the conflicting texts, she or he will view the citizens of the city as an anomaly among the valorous population in the region that the city represents. Such harmonization may be in keeping with the intention of the book's final authors.

Cowardly Thieves at Jabesh-Gilead

The transitional stages between the older Saul narrative (the HSR), on the one hand, and the late retelling in Chronicles, on the other, are found in late passages from the Book of Samuel that bring together the figures of David and Saul. On the one hand, they portray how David mourns Saul's death and performs acts of piety for Saul's household; on the other, they show how David outshines Saul in various ways. We've already looked at a couple of these late texts. Let us now examine one more that relates to Jabesh-gilead.

The final episode in the HSR reports the end of Saul's line: "Thus Saul, his three sons, and his arms-bearer, as well as all his men, died together on that day" (1 Sam 31:6). In other words, the house of Saul witnessed its complete and total demise on Mount Gilboa. When later authors wanted to construct a narrative about David's relations with the house of Saul, they had to give birth repeatedly to new sons of Saul. This narratival necessity explains not only the sudden appearance of Ishbosheth/Ishbaal but also David's persistent efforts, on two occasions, to find other sons of Saul. One of these sons (called Mephibosheth or Mephibaal) the authors secondarily identify as Jonathan's descendant.

Like Jabesh-gilead, David mourns the death of Saul and his sons. Yet he also expects Saul's former friends and allies to shift their allegiances to his house. This is the address (2 Sam 2:4b–7) that was quoted in the section "Evidence from Qumran."

In the passage that immediately follows this one, Abner brings Saul's son Ishbosheth across the Jordan to the town of Mahanaim, where he makes him king over the Gilead and then over "all Israel." In other words, Jabesh-gilead and the Transjordanian region it represents spurn David's goodwill and become the launching grounds for the opposition to his reign. Thereafter David no longer approaches Jabesh-gilead with open arms.

During a three-year famine, he inquires of the deity about the reasons for the country's plight. An oracle then reveals the causes for the famine: "because of Saul, and because of his bloody house that put to death the Gibeonites" (see 2 Sam 21). The cause for the famine is twofold. In his "zeal for the people of Judah and Israel," Saul had attempted to exterminate the Gibeonite people who lived in the territory of Benjamin. When asked what David could do to make reparations for the atrocities Saul committed, the Gibeonites ask that they be given seven of his male descendants whom they could "impale before YHWH" in Saul's hometown of Gibeah. David complies with their brutal wishes, and the Gibeonites put to death the men at the beginning of the barley harvest.

The bloody massacre is followed by a courageous act of protest by Rizpah, Saul's concubine. For a lengthy period, she stays next to the impaled bodies (two of whom are her own sons), fending off "birds of the sky by day and wild beasts by night." Her protests effect change. To rectify the mistreatment of Saul, David exhumes the bones from Jabesh-gilead and reinters them at Benjamin, on Saul's patrimonial burial site. Because David finally understands that the oracle does not refer solely to Saul's wrongdoing, he performs these pious obsequies toward Saul's house and thereby brings an end to the famine:

> David went and took the bones of Saul and the bones of his son Jonathan whom the people of Jabesh-gilead had stolen them from the public square of Beth-shan, where the Philistines had hung them up, on the day the Philistines killed Saul on Gilboa. He brought up from there the bones of Saul and the bones of his son Jonathan. [And he gathered the bones of those who had been impaled.] They buried the bones of Saul and of his son Jonathan in the land of Benjamin in Zela, in the tomb of his father Kish. They did all that the king commanded. After that, God heeded supplications for the land. (2 Sam 21:12–14)

According to the medieval Jewish commentator Rashi (d. 1105), the actions of Jabesh-gilead were partly responsible for the famine: Saul's body "had been buried quickly and surreptitiously when the people of Jabesh-gilead stole and buried it, so that he was not mourned in keeping with his (royal) honor."[8]

Rashi's interpretation draws not on earlier rabbinic literature but also on the wording of the biblical account itself. The authors of the latter do not refer to the "valiant warriors" of Jabesh-gilead, as they are designated in the older account of Saul's death. The men are called instead merely the "citizens/patricians" of the city. Likewise, the authors of the passage do not remind their readers that this people subjected themselves to great peril when they recovered the bodies of the royal family. Instead we are told that they *purloined* Saul's and Jonathan's bones by bringing them back to their city. (The Hebrew word is *ganav*: "robbed, stole, made away with.") We are not even told that these thieves buried the bones or mourned the death of the king.

This countermemory, which discredits the actions of Jabesh-gilead, likely originated in the same milieu as Chronicles. Yet in keeping with its more radical censure of Saul, Chronicles does not report that David brought up Saul's bones to Benjamin. By suggesting that they remained in Jabesh-gilead, Chronicles agrees with the earlier version of the memory in the Book of Samuel. Within the new framework of Chronicles, however, this fact takes on a much different meaning: Instead providing testimony to Jabesh-gilead's solidarity with Israel, the bones of Saul serve as material evidence of this town's solidarity with the one who sought to do harm to a beloved hero. In this way, the authors took a memory and turned it on its head with the aim of reproaching a prominent city in Israel's history.

Conclusions

The independent History of Saul's Reign (HSR) must have originated in the northern kingdom and likely represents the interests of Benjaminite circles. This work affirms, as we have seen, the special relationship between the Gilead and Israel. It begins with Saul becoming king after he rescues the town of Jabesh-gilead and ends with the inhabitants of Jabesh-gilead bravely rescuing the bodies of Saul and his sons after their death in the Battle of Gilboa.

Writing from a Judahite perspective, the authors of other texts in Samuel and Chronicles perpetuated this Benjaminite-Israelite memory. Yet the reason they transmitted it was not to praise Jabesh-gilead. Instead, these writers exploited it for an originally unintended purpose, namely to cast aspersions on Jabesh-gilead – and, by extension, on the communities throughout the Gilead and Transjordan.

Instead of erasing the memory, the biblical authors turned it against itself. The significance of our findings for comparative historiography is apparent: Inasmuch as the authors here "brush history against the grain" (*die Geschichte gegen den Strich bürsten*), in the words of Walter Benjamin's maxim, they partake in the kind of "counter-history" that is widely regarded as unique to modernity.[9]

6

Uriah the Hittite

A Tale of Royal Immodesty

A major turning point in the Book of Samuel is a tale that contrasts two men and their allegiances. On the one side is David. He has now traded the vagaries of the wandering warlord for the comforts of kingship. Rather than marching off to war with the rest of the nation, he tarries behind in Jerusalem – in what he presumes to be his bed of roses.

Over against this enthroned, and recumbent, figure stands Uriah the Hittite. A soldier of foreign descent, he demonstrates his belonging among the people of Israel first through his refusal to forsake his comrades in the field, and then later through his death in battle.

"It Is Good to Be the King"

This is not a story of military triumph, as we are used to reading in the accounts of David's life. We don't have here any *veni, vidi, vici*. This is instead a tale of lust and adultery: *vidit, cupivit, tulit* – "he saw, he desired, he took."

It all begins with David's siesta in the palace, after he had sent Israel off on a campaign of conquest. He arises from his couch, takes a stroll on his roof, looks down on the homes of other Israelites, and notices a "very beautiful" woman bathing. He knows she's married to one of his soldiers on the front lines. Even so he has her brought to him, and he sleeps with her.

As fate would have it, the woman conceives after the afternoon dalliance. David summons her husband from the battlefield. His intention is not to reveal the infidelity with his wife. Instead, he bids the soldier to "bathe his feet" at home, sending along a gift in the hope that he would have intercourse with her and then later assume that the child was his own. Not such a bad idea, perhaps. The scheme however precipitates a series of decisions that brings the king to the brink of ruin.

Although told succinctly, the narrative contains the elements from which a modern author could spin many pages. Yet, as elsewhere, the biblical authors require their readers to do the work: We must reflect upon the few lines provided to us, filling in ourselves the gaps in the plot's details and the characters' reasoning.

Failing to comply with David's wishes, the soldier spends the night at the entrance of the palace "along with all the other servants of his lord." He explains his actions to the king:

> The Ark, Israel, and Judah are all dwelling in tents. My lord Joab [the general] and the servants of my lord are camping in the field. Should I then go to my home, to eat and drink and to sleep with my wife? By your very life, I cannot do such a thing! (2 Sam 11:11)

It is at this point that David reluctantly resolves to eliminate the unyielding soldier. "Stay here today, and I will send you back tomorrow." When he returns to the battlefront, it will be to meet his orchestrated demise.

David initially has qualms about such a pernicious plan. In the hope that the soldier might in a moment of weakness break down and go visit his wife, he invites him a second time to his own table, where he attempts to inebriate him with wine. Yet again the irreproachable soldier takes his place among "the servants of his lord," rather than going down to his home.

David thus takes the next step. The reader can sense the tragic agony of this chain of events. (One is reminded of Woody Allen's *Crimes and Misdemeanors*.) The king sends the soldier back to the front lines with his own death warrant in hand. Following the confidential orders from the palace, the general assigns the soldier a place over against the most experienced enemy combatants, where he predictably falls in the line of duty.

Because David is not willing to admit his wrongdoing, he ends up designing his servant's murder in cold blood. Later the prophet Nathan appears before the king and indicts him as the one who is directly responsible for the murder: "You killed him with the sword of the Ammonites."

A Hittite Soldier of Civic Virtue

Before continuing, we need to consider the character of this soldier. His name is Uriah the Hittite. The authors omitted a patronym ("son of so-and-so") and used in its place an ethnonym ("the Hittite"), identifying him thereby as an outsider. Neighboring texts use these identity markers for a wide range of non-Israelites (such as Doeg the Edomite, Barzillai the Gileadite, or Ittai the Gittite).[1]

We can distinguish two different groups of "Hittites" in biblical literature. First, there are "the sons of Heth," who predate the arrival of Abraham in the land. This Canaanite population dwells near Hebron and belongs to "the seven nations" whom Israel is commanded to annihilate.[2] Another group, often designated "Neo-Hittites," are located in the north and near the Euphrates. Instead of Canaanites, they are associated with the populations that established states in southern Anatolia and northern Syria after the fall of the Hittite Empire (from 1180 to ca. 700 BCE).

It is possible that Uriah belongs to the second group, especially as they were known for their skills in warfare. Many would have sought refuge in neighboring lands and served as mercenaries. Yet both groups are often indistinguishable in biblical texts, so that "Hittite" is often used in a more generic sense, similar to "Canaanite" or "Amorite."[3]

It is ultimately unclear what the biblical authors mean when they call Uriah "the Hittite." Because Hittites in the Bible lack a distinctive identity and do not figure as significant enemies, Uriah likely functions in our account, at least after it took on its present proportions, as a generic nonnative Israelite – or as a paradigmatic Other, in the same way Rahab represents a population of "Canaanites" in Joshua.

David employs an exotic range of foreign soldiers as mercenaries in his elite brigades. Yet Uriah is no typical soldier-of-fortune. His name (meaning "Yah is my light/flame") already signals his unusual character.[4] Whereas Ahimelech the Hittite noticeably fails to put his life at risk for David (1 Sam 26:6), Uriah fights valiantly. At a time of war, he denies himself pleasure and thinks only of the nation's welfare. He cannot enjoy the comforts of home and hearth as long as "the Ark, Israel, and Judah" are domiciled in the war camp. Instead of returning to his "place" among his native population, as David urges Ittai the Gittite to do (see the following chapter), he leaves no doubt that he belongs to the people of Israel.

The Citizen-Soldier as Paragon

When justifying their claims to authority, those at the highest echelons of hierarchical societies tend to view courage and martial valor as hereditary virtues, as the distinctive preserve of the nobility. In contrast, more horizontally structured societies exalt self-sacrifice as a duty incumbent upon all members of society. This democratic civic virtue is most often celebrated in the figure of the *citizen-soldier* – those who, like Saul and the armies he rallies, leave their plows to take up arms for a temporary war effort.

Later we will see that the oldest reference to Uriah identifies him as a professional mercenary in the ranks of David's private army. Yet the authors who shaped this dramatic tale ascribe to him a much deeper motivation for his actions, one that is emblematic of the citizen-soldier ideals that we find elsewhere in biblical literature.

What drives Uriah is his deep allegiance to the nation and to its deity, not to the king. He is the incarnation of Israelite civic virtue and stands over against Ittai the Gittite – a foreign soldier who swears undying allegiance to the person of David. As an outsider, Uriah must go to greater lengths to demonstrate that he belongs. The phenomenon is widely observable in human behavior: Through meritorious conduct, one compensates for perceived deficiencies in genealogy. This is the tension in Jewish identity between *yichus* and *zechus*, between descent and deed (see discussion of Caleb in Chapter 11).

After 586 BCE, when the political borders of the Judahite kingdom had been erased, one needed to *do something* to be a Judahite. In a multiethnic empire, identity was severed from location. We witness at this time a more deliberate combination of descent and deed – a combination that marks the birth of Jews (in contrast to Judahites as those who reside or originated in the land of Judah). The archetype of this new Jewish identity is Ezra. He boasts an envious priestly ancestry. But more decisive is what he *does*: He dedicates himself to Torah, both studying and teaching it to Israel. Thereby he earns the title "skilled scribe" (*sōfēr māhîr*).

If one with such an illustrious pedigree as Ezra needs to demonstrate his worth through meritorious performance and contributions to the collective good, how much more must an outsider like Uriah?

One of the themes of this study is the way individuals and groups negotiate belonging and achieve status via wartime contributions. Yet the principle is the same, and those who were reading and redacting biblical literature in the post-exilic period would have undoubtedly discerned essential continuities between participation on the battlefield, on the one hand, and contributions to education, public building programs, and the Temple cult, on the other. (I discuss this subject at greater length in Chapter 10.)

Literary Precursors

This section may seem a bit more technical than the rest of the chapter. But it is worth the effort to see how later generations repurposed older material. I have done my best to keep the discussion simple and straightforward.

The depiction of Uriah as a devoted and pious warrior in David's army appears to have grown from an otherwise inconspicuous reference to this figure in the roster of David's elite forces. Uriah's name appears at the end of the list, preceded by a number of fighters with diverse origins, such as Bani the Gadite, Zelek the Ammonite, Naharai the Beerothite, and Ira the Ithrite. Although Uriah's name could have been added to this list based on the tale of his death, it is more plausible that the authors of the tale took their cue from this roster, since it contains many names not found elsewhere in the book.

This historical scenario – that the authors of our account drew upon the reference to Uriah in the register – appears all the more likely if the tale originally consisted of a brief report. From the first expansions to the account that I have reconstructed, one can easily see that the authors do not present David in a favorable light. David tarries back in Jerusalem and lets his general do all the work, yet he takes the credit for the conquest, mustering the large national army ("the people") so that they can witness him vanquishing the city and taking the crown:

The First Expansions of the Account

In the spring of the year, the time when kings go out to battle, David sent Joab with his servants/warriors and with all Israel (i.e., the militia). They destroyed the Ammonites and besieged Rabbah. But David stayed in Jerusalem. The inhabitants of the city made a sortie against Joab, so that some of David's servants/warriors fell in battle along with some the militia troops. Then Joab sent and told David all the news about the fighting.... David responded to the messenger: "Say to Joab, 'Do not let this matter trouble you. For the sword devours now one and now another. Press your attack on the city, and overthrow it.' And encourage him." ... So Joab fought against Rabbah of the Ammonites and took the royal city. And Joab sent messengers to David, and said, "I have fought against Rabbah; moreover, I have taken the water city. Now, then, gather the rest of the people, and encamp against the city, and take it; or I myself will take the city, and it will be called by my name."

[Possibly the oldest portion of the account:] Then David mustered all the people and went to Rabbah, and fought against it and took it. He took the crown of Milcom from his head; the weight of it was a talent of gold, and in it was a precious stone; and it was placed on David's head. He also brought forth the spoil of the city, a very great amount. He brought out the people who were in it, and set them to work with saws and iron picks and iron axes, or sent them to the brickworks. Thus he did to all the cities of the Ammonites. Then David and all the people returned to Jerusalem.[5]

The additional expansions, inserted between the two paragraphs presented here, appear to have been prompted by the notice of casualties during the siege:

The inhabitants of the city made a sortie against Joab, so that some of David's servants/warriors, along with the militia troops, fell in battle. *Among them Uriah the Hittite was killed.* Then Joab sent and told David all the news about the fighting. David responded to the messenger: "Say to Joab, 'Do not let this matter trouble you. *For the sword devours now one and now another.* Press your attack on the city, and overthrow it.' Encourage him." *When Uriah's wife heard that her husband was dead, she made lamentation for him. After the mourning was over, David sent and brought her to his house. She became his wife and bore him a son.* (2 Sam 11:17–18, 25–27)

The older lines of this passage tell how the death of the conscript army along with members of the royal standing army ("David's warriors/servants") prompts Joab to inquire whether the commander-in-chief wished to terminate the campaign. David responds by exhorting his general not to be deterred by the casualties and by ordering him to step up the offensive. In the supplementary lines, marked in italics, later readers underscored David's determination to prolong the battle even after the death of Uriah, one of David's most elite warriors.

To honor the name of his fallen soldier, David takes his wife into his palace and grants her the privileged place of royal wife. This act of paying tribute to a fallen soldier is not unusual. We know that ancient monarchs recognized their fallen soldiers in various ways, similar to honorary funerals and special privileges conferred on the families of the war dead in contemporary societies.[6]

The same theme of honoring Uriah continues with the addition of various lines that bestow prominent names on Uriah's wife and the son she bears to David: She is none other than Bathsheba, David's beloved wife, and the child is Solomon, who will be David's successor on the throne. These supplementary lines are composed with the legend of Solomon and Bathsheba (in 1 Kings 1–2) in view. The legend has a very different provenance than the earliest formulation of the Uriah account: David and Solomon were likely separate figures who later became father and son (see Chapter 7).

Various clues support my suggestion that the account has been reworked. The earliest editions of the account do not refer to Bathsheba by her name. They call her simply "Uriah's wife." Many interpreters insist that this designation, instead of "Bathsheba," is dictated by the emphasis that David took another man's wife. That rule may obtain elsewhere, but it does not work well here. Moreover, the description of David giving Uriah's wife a place within the palace does not presuppose that she is already pregnant. The syntax and word choice ("she became his wife and bore him a son") mean that she conceives only after becoming part of the royal household. There is also a discrepancy in the battle report. The redactors seem to have had trouble transforming the older statement about Uriah's death into a depiction of an orchestrated execution: David commands Uriah to be placed on the front line where he would face the most dangerous enemy fighters. But the older statement depicts him falling in the fray when the Ammonites undertake a surprise sortie.

The final episode describes how Joab almost captures the Ammonite royal city of Rabbah. Just as he elsewhere plays an indispensable role in David's name-making feats, so now he sends messengers to David urging him to come and claim the victory for himself. Inasmuch as David is presented here as a fame-thirsty monarch residing back in Jerusalem while others do his dirty work in foreign lands, the passage is incongruous with the directly preceding depiction of David's contrition. If he had just admitted to his guilt, pled for mercy, and was punished with the death of his child, why in the very next scene would he persist along the same route that led to his affliction? It makes much better sense if this scene belongs to an early stage of the narrative, before someone introduced the mass of material telling how David executes Uriah and later faces the prophet Nathan and divine retribution.

We could consider additional clues, yet these should suffice for our purposes. Such evidence supports the conclusion that the remaining portions of the pericope, which portray an act of adultery and divine punishment, were composed at a later point. The question is now: Why?

The Politics of Dying

Already the first editions of the Uriah account express ambivalence toward David's ambition. His determination to capture the Ammonite capital results in the death of Israel's troops: "and some of David's servants/warriors fell along with members of the militia." This loss of life casts dark shadows on his triumph.

A peculiar characteristic of biblical battle narratives is that they do not report any casualties when Israel is victorious. As I have argued elsewhere, this fact reflects the Bible's character as *national*, rather than *statist*, literature.[7]

Strong states require military triumph, and military triumph requires the willingness of many to sacrifice themselves on the battlefield. To cultivate this willingness among its subjects, states have developed elaborate memorials and monuments through which they demonstrate their reverence and esteem for all those who lay down their lives for the country.

The Bible conspicuously avoids the move to glorify noble death. We would expect the Book of Joshua, for example, to contain a prominent scene in which the nation pauses to bury the war dead and pay tribute to their self-sacrifice that made the conquest of the Promised Land possible. Yet such is not the case. The only casualties in Joshua are those who, like Achan, die as punishment for their misconduct. The one who comes closest to the noble death ideal is Samson, who brings the house down on a Philistine party, killing himself along with the enemy. Yet even here the biblical writers hesitate to extol his actions.

There's a good reason why the Hebrew Bible doesn't exalt heroic death on the battlefield: Its authors were writing in the aftermath of defeat, during the reign of imperial powers. The devastation of their society and the loss of territorial sovereignty was due in large part to what we might call the Patrick Henry mentality: "Give me liberty, or give me death!" From the Book of Jeremiah and other texts we learn about those who refused to "bend their necks to the yoke and live," rejecting compromise as an option and instead stubbornly contending with the Babylonian armies. Their political intransigence brought only destruction and suffering.

Yet the Patrick Henry mentality persisted among many circles of the post-exilic period. In their striving to create a strong *national* consciousness that could survive defeat, the biblical authors had to address this political stance and offer an alternative to it. One of the things they did was eliminate depictions of noble death, producing a strange corpus of battle stories in which Israel achieves victory without any loss of life whatsoever. Uriah's death in our story is therefore highly atypical for biblical battle stories.

Name-Making Megalomania

As the account assumed its present contours, the authors shifted their censorious sights from the problems posed by monarchic territorial ambitions to the deeper tensions between nation and state. A line from the introduction elicited this shift. At the beginning of his illustrious career, David personally leads Israel into battle (see especially 1 Sam 18:12–16 and 2 Sam 5:1–3). Now he resides back in the comforts of Jerusalem and sends out "all Israel" to fight his wars.

Before the composition of the immediately preceding chapters, the early edition of the account would have been directly connected to the lengthy description of David *making a name for himself* through his impressive triumphs abroad (see 2 Sam 8, especially v. 13). The theme of "name-making" is central in our account too. After Joab captures the royal city of Rabbah, he urges David to come and take credit for the victory. Otherwise, Joab says, "I myself will take the city, and it will be *called by my name*."

After David had already made a name for himself in conquering a long list of peoples, his desire that Rabbah be called by his name is nothing other than vainglorious. The type of name-making described here involves legal claims of land possession established by the act of conquest. Various biblical texts forbid Israel from laying claim to Ammonite territory.

The composition of the preceding chapter seeks to absolve David from any imperialistic wrongdoing by presenting the war as a defensive measure.[8] Yet without it, David is possessed by a megalomaniacal determination to conquer this famous capital.

The city of Rabbah is remembered as a home to fabled monuments. According to one legend, it is there that King Og's massive iron bed once stood (see Deut 3:11). The immense size of this object resembles the dimensions of the crown of Milcom (an Ammonite royal deity). We are told that it weighed an entire talent (75–95 pounds). Despite its unusual weight, David has it lifted over his head in the climatic moment of triumph. This is the first and only time that we hear of David donning a crown. (Even when an Amalekite brings him Saul's diadem, he does not wear it – 2 Sam 1:10.)

As a tale of royal immodesty, our account constitutes the turning point in the David narrative – at least in the shape that it has assumed in the transmitted versions of Samuel–Kings.[9] From this point on, disintegration will threaten every one of David's great achievements. He will face two consecutive popular insurrections, and he will choose to quell them by brute force with the help of his royal troops. The two crises will culminate in the national census that he commissions the military to undertake. In this final act we see how David regards the tribes of Israel as if they were nothing more than his own professional warriors, there to do his bidding. Instead of working for the welfare of the nation, David expects the nation to bend to his will and subordinate their collective concerns to his personal aspirations. These developments in David's life presage Israel's subsequent history, in which the *state* gradually eclipses the *nation*.

Tukulti-Ninurta and Zimri-Lim

To better appreciate the message of our account, let us compare it to scenarios from several other ancient texts.[10]

In the correspondence between a Hittite king (probably Tudhaliya IV) and an influential adviser to Tukulti-Ninurta I, heir to the Assyrian throne (1243–1207 BCE), the Hittite ruler writes about the plans of the young Assyrian ruler to undertake a campaign against Mitanni as soon as he assumes power, a move that was contrary to Hittite interests. Noteworthy here is the motivation the Hittite king places on the lips of Tukulti-Ninurta: "In this way I will establish a good name for myself."

Apparently the mature Hittite ruler recognized the importance of a monarch manifesting his strength immediately upon accession to the throne. The campaign against Mitanni would not only demonstrate preparedness to protect and expand Assyrian influence but, if successful, also secure for Tukulti-Ninurta a prominent position among the international players of his day.

We can set this account side-by-side with two letters sent to the Mari ruler Zimri-Lim (eighteenth century BCE). In the first, his general petitions him to come quickly and rescue the besieged city of Razama; otherwise the enemy may prematurely lift the siege, and Zimri-Lim would forfeit a good opportunity to be "called by the name of savior." In the second letter, one of his servants writes,

> With respect to the king [of Yamhad], I have, in keeping with all that you wrote me, established a great name for my Lord. Hence his servants and the entire land are saying now: "Zimri-Lim is the one! He conquered the city of Azara and gave it Yarim-Lim." This news should make my Lord happy!

These two letters reflect the role played by Zimri-Lim's general and servant in public relations, political spin, and propaganda. For our present purposes it is important to bear in mind the genre of these texts. Rather than official inscriptions meant for public display, these are top-secret letters between a king and his right-hand men (his general and one of his representatives). It was, to be sure, in the interest of Zimri-Lim that no one outside his most trusted circle ever become privy to the correspondence.

The public image that Zimri-Lim, as many other rulers, wished to present was that of an accomplished sovereign who stands head and shoulders above his subjects. To accumulate "symbolic capital," he needed to be the one who conquered these cities and therefore who earned the name of victor. The messy details of how he actually made his name should, of course, remain concealed.

The correspondence between Zimri-Lim and his general is strikingly similar to that between David and Joab. Joab's rationale of name-making strikes a chord with David, and in the end, the magnificent crown of Milcom is placed on David's head. The act of making a name by conquering a city is of course not unique to this passage.[11] However, in contrast to the actual achievements earlier in his career, the name David makes for himself in the conquest of Rabbah was primarily the work of his competent right-hand man.

Opening Letters, Leaking State Secrets

There is nothing inherently wrong about David's actions at Rabbah. They are indeed no different from those of other kings. The name he makes, like that of Zimri-Lim, is the result of collaborative action with his trusted general. He behaves like many other savvy leaders in history who arrive in the final moment of a momentous victory to take a lion's share of the credit and make a name for themselves. Just as David first achieved renown with the help of Israel's women who hailed him as the one who "has slain his myriads," so too in the later stages of his rise to power, he, like Zimri-Lim, counts on devoted servants to protect and strengthen his name.

Even so, this narrative is a truly remarkable achievement: Whereas we know about the correspondence between Zimri-Lim and his general through modern research and discovery, we know about the correspondence between David and Joab because biblical authors disclosed it to their readers.

Yet this is not a political exposé written by journalists. It is a literary construction, a fiction. By unveiling the very human and fallible nature of the progenitor of the great Davidic dynasty, its authors effectively shatter the superhuman masculine self-image that ancient rulers (including those in Israel and Judah) were wont to present in their official inscriptions, iconography, state rituals, and monumental architecture.

The most striking parallels to this narrative are works of drama from early modernity, especially those composed by Shakespeare, which scrutinize political affairs and institutions at a time before newspapers began to publish exposés. What makes Shakespeare great – and what has sustained the long afterlife of his work – is his ability to take the greatest rulers in the English imagination and reveal their all-too-human qualities.[12] In a similar fashion, the authors of Samuel create an epic account in which the most beloved king in Judahite memory is the most human and fallible character in the narrative. Rulers in the ancient Near East are never portrayed with emotion. They are immutable. Not so the biblical David. He is "human, all too human."

The episode of David making a name for himself as "conqueror" of Rabbah frames the Bathsheba affair. As a whole, the narrative provides one of the most penetrating critiques of royal power in the Western tradition. Instead of joining his royal peers in making a name for himself on the battlefield, David stays back in the capital reclining on his couch, and then with Uriah's wife. Later he attempts to pass their child off as Uriah's namesake. Then he kills Uriah and takes his wife under his own name. The authors formulate this critique notably by divulging to their readers the disturbing contents of *letters* the king conveys to his general via his trustworthy soldier. In this narrative, what was once closed is opened; what was formerly clandestine is now unveiled.

The authors' aim is not to deny the legitimacy of the monarchy. Rather they seek to humanize it, to cut it down to size, and to subject it to the scrutiny of a common code of conduct, just as the authors of Deuteronomy bring it under the authority of a specific legal code of conduct (see Deut 17:14–20). Such a move in many ways preserves royal rule. For example, it paved the way for the model of constitutional monarchies that has a long history in Europe. Yet since the king often embodies the hegemonic masculinity, the denial of his absolute authority necessarily challenges the identification of self-sufficiency as an essential element of manhood.

As part of their work to challenge the self-sufficiency of the king, the biblical authors often superimposed a "theological" layer on the king's success in making a name for himself. The interpolation of the covenantal promise to David (2 Sam 7) shifts the king's success from his own virility and power to the deity. Instead of David making a name for himself, the deity proclaims, "I will make for you a great name, like the name of the great ones of the earth." The principal way in which this international renown will be achieved is martial – by granting the king "rest" from all his enemies and making a place for Israel to dwell in peace.

By including this text in 2 Samuel 7, the authors provide their readers with a new lens through which to read the long list of David's conquests. The text also provides a corrective to the explicit statement in the next chapter that "David made a name for himself." The redactional activity extends to the account of David's very first success, where a later hand has made David declare to Goliath: "You come with sword and shield, but I come in the name of 'Yhwh of the military hosts.'"

These new layers do not wipe out the older traditions of military power and territorial sovereignty. Rather, they amplify them with a component that was, according to the biblical authors, critical to Israel's survival in times when military power and territorial sovereignty were not available options.

The Ethics of Reading

Uriah's unwavering service in the ranks of the nation incarnates what is known today as "republican civic virtue." It contrasts sharply with the situation in which the state has become an end in itself, represented in David's willingness to sacrifice this faithful soldier in a scheme to preserve his royal power. Biblical and republican ideals converge on an essential point – that the state's primary duty is to safeguard the welfare of the nation. Electing to exploit his most loyal subjects for the sake of his own renown, the imperious David personifies the state's propensity to abdicate its most basic responsibility and to become an end in itself.

David resembles the ambitious and power-thirsty Jephthah, who sacrifices his sole child on the altar of triumph (Judg 11). The theme is common to classical Greek literature, with the most popular expression being Agamemnon's sacrifice of Iphigenia.

Within modern Jewish culture, the issues related to the sacrifice of soldiers by the state have been treated more often in relation to the Akedah ("Binding of Isaac" from Gen 22). A beautiful example is Amichai's poem "The Real Hero," which has often been interpreted in reference to Israel's war fallen, especially with those from the First Lebanon War in 1982. The poem begins by affirming that the real hero of the Akedah is the ram, who doesn't know about a "conspiracy between the others." It is as if he had volunteered himself to die in the place of Isaac. The poet announces his desire to "sing a song in his memory." He begins by describing the curly hair and human eyes, and then turns to the horns "that were silent on his living head." When the ram is slaughtered, the horns are made into shofars (trumpets) "to sound their battle cries or to blare out their obscene joy."

Using techniques of defamiliarization, Amichai beckons us to think anew about one of the most foundational stories in the Jewish tradition. He directs our attention, as readers and as social actors, to the plight of the ram in the bush – that is, to those on the margins consigned to oblivion in the war memories that become hegemonic.

Singing a memorial song for those who are sacrificed and then forgotten, Amichai engages in the same activity of commemoration that produced much biblical literature. Thus, the authors of Genesis direct their readers' attention to the suffering of Hagar and confer on this Egyptian servant her own story of redemption, one that resembles in many respects Israel's collective history.

Similarly, our account sensitizes the reader to take notice of an otherwise negligible figure, Uriah the Hittite. Within this story the prophet Nathan uses a parable to awaken David's moral faculties: Instead of consuming one of the members of his own flock, a wealthy man seizes and slaughters a beloved little lamb from his humble neighbor. This lamb is reminiscent of the ram in Amichai's poem "who was volunteered to die" in the place of another.

The biblical authors could have easily censured David by painting him in dictatorial garb, comfortably issuing death orders for faceless masses. But their account renders a much more subtle critique, and it does so by giving the peripheral figure a face and identity. Only one individual is executed, and he is a Hittite. Even so, the circumstances that result in this soldier's death are all the more scandalous. He must die because his commitment to the collective cause of Israel jeopardizes the name and fame of Israel's megalomaniac monarch.

Conclusions

In contradistinction to the callously self-indulgent ruler who willingly sacrifices the lives of his people for the sake of triumph and territorial expansion, Uriah takes an oath (on the life of the king!) that he would not abandon his lord, the general Abner, and his comrades-in-arms. The decisive criterion for belonging, according to this account's authors, is embodied by a Hittite soldier and his unfaltering commitment to Israel's wellbeing. In his speech, Uriah could have appealed to a yet unachieved victory by declaring, "I will not go to my home as long as Rabbah has not been conquered." Yet he eschews the statist concern with name-making and triumph. Instead he thinks only of the Ark of YHWH, the people of Israel and Judah, and his commander Joab. Self-sacrifice and battlefield death are the defining gesture.

Lacking Uriah's steadfast solidarity, David sends off the troops to fight his wars while he, in an act of statist hubris, stays behind to enjoy the comforts and security of Jerusalem. This spatial division between palace and people precipitates a spiral of transgressions that results in the gratuitous loss of Israelite lives and the imperilment of the throne itself. By selecting a Hittite soldier to display the civic virtue that defines a sustainable form of nationhood, the biblical authors have thrown into sharp relief the degeneracies of a state (personified in the figure of King David) that detaches itself from the plight of the people.

We may compare such literary tributes to physical victory monuments in modern nation-states. One of the most poignant instances is the colossal Arc de Triomphe in Paris. Lying beneath it is the "Tomb to the Unknown Soldier." The edifice echoes a message: State triumph requires the sacrifice of its citizens and rests on the graves its soldiers. Its statist message is much different from the one communicated in our account.

7

Ittai the Gittite

Mercenary Allegiance versus National Solidarity

After the account of Uriah, the remainder of the Book of Samuel, as well as the first chapters of Kings, depicts the problems that beset David throughout the remainder of his reign. The authors recount these problems as a way of proving the veracity of Nathan's declaration – that "the sword shall henceforth never depart from your house."

Of all the blocks of material portraying the crises within David's household, the largest is the account of David's flight from Absalom. It illustrates the scourge that plagued David after his murder of Uriah. But it also frames the story of his life. It depicts him ending his career in the same way he began it – seeking refuge from his adversaries.

Although the identity of his adversary has changed, many other features remain the same. As in the account of David's flight from Saul, the authors used this narrative as a framework in which they embed little episodes that commemorate the loyalty and wartime contributions of some groups and document the duplicity and betrayal of others.

My task in this and the following chapter will be to examine the texture of the Absalom account. I will focus on the various political issues that its authors address through the means of war commemoration.

The Succession Narrative

The account of Absalom's rebellion and David's flight is conventionally thought to constitute the centerpiece of what is called the "Succession Narrative" (or "Court History"). The work also tells of the rape of Tamar as well as of a second insurrection, this time mounted by a figure named Sheba ben Bichri.

Many scholars consider the Succession Narrative to be one of the oldest biblical narratives. This consensus, as so many others in the research on King David, needs to be questioned. The entire complex appears to have grown gradually from a modest core. That core may have been secondarily appended to a heavily augmented version of the History of David's Rise (HDR) in which David is no longer king solely of Judah but of all Israel.

A growing number of scholars agree that the earliest versions of the account did not present David absconding from Jerusalem.[1] Several considerations support this conclusion:

1) David dispatches against Absalom a much vaster army ("hundreds and thousands") than the entourage that escorts him to the Transjordan.
2) The description of the battle locates the fighting in the forest of Ephraim, located in the West Bank. From the transmitted version of the account, however, we would expect the battle to take place in the Transjordan ("the land of the Gilead").
3) David seeks refuge in the town of Mahanaim. This location is incongruous with the battle account: David sits "between the two gates," the troops return to a city, and finally David mounts his throne at the gate, where all the people come before him. These details make little sense if they refer to the more modest town of Mahanaim. The story would be much more coherent if David never leaves the gates of Jerusalem, the capital, where it all begins.

In light of these and other observations, I would suggest that the unusually complex narrative originally consisted primarily of two passages: an introduction and a report of the battle and events thereafter (2 Sam 15:2–13 + 18:2–19:9). The lengthy report of David leaving the city and crossing over to the Transjordan (15:14–17:29), and then returning to his throne (19:9–44, 20:3), represents the work of early readers who successively embellished a much simpler putsch account. This reconstructed form depicts David hearing news of a coup d'état and then ordering troops to be mobilized at Jerusalem just as he does in the episode of Sheba ben Bichri's insurrection that follows on the heels of this account (2 Sam 20).[2]

The prequel and sequel to this account are, according to my thesis, a secondary framework to the older account. (We can identify many other cases in the Bible and ancient Near Eastern texts in which later readers add new introductions and conclusions.) The prequel depicts violence among David's children: Amnon rapes Tamar, Absalom slays Amnon, David banishes Absalom. The sequel, which recounts Sheba ben Bichri's putsch, is tightly connected to the insurrection that Absalom mounts. Yet the perceptive reader can discern how redactors have sewn this originally independent account to Absalom's story as well as supplemented it with new material.

Within the secondary prequel, one paragraph sticks out: a short description of Absalom (2 Sam 14:25–27). Its authors introduce this character as if we had not already read about him in the preceding passages. The paragraph, along with an introductory line ("there was a man from PN named Absalom"), would make an excellent beginning to the earliest versions of the Absalom account. The description of his hair, even if it is supplementary, anticipates his demise: He dies when his thick mane traps him on the branch of tree, making him an easy target for David's troops.

The paragraph is in tension with various parts of the account. For example, its information about Absalom's sons contradicts the transmitted narrative. Elsewhere we are told he died in dishonor without a male descendant to carry on his name. Likewise, the statement about Tamar, Absalom's *beautiful daughter*, is confusing right after the episode of the rape of Tamar, his *beautiful sister*. Such incongruities witness to the activities of later readers who reworked this material.

Absalom Becomes David's Son

If this suggestion is merited, the oldest versions of the account would not identify Absalom as David's son. This is a remarkable finding, one to which additional observations lend credence. For example, Nathan's prophecy declares that YHWH would take David's wives and give them to his neighbor, who will "lie with them in the sight of this very sun." Absalom is the one who later sleeps with David's concubines "in the eyes of all Israel" (2 Sam 12:11–12 and 16:20–22). Thus, Nathan's prophecy, written with Absalom's deed in view, does not seem to presuppose that David's challenger was his own son.

Originally Absalom might have been no more David's descendant than Sheba ben Bichri, who stages a putsch in the immediately following account. By means of the lengthy prehistory and various additions to the account of Absalom's death, later readers reidentified David's political opponent as his own progeny. Angered by his father's response to his sister's rape, the scion Absalom plots, in oedipal fashion, to take his throne. In this way, the chapters give a new twist to the judgment prophesied by Nathan – that the sword would never depart from David's house.[3]

This editorial move to relate originally independent characters is not confined to the present case in biblical historiography. The biblical writers went to great pains to collect independent (and sometimes competing) traditions and create from them a single narrative. In this way, they took diverse pasts and synthesized them to create one history of the people of Israel.

This is easiest to observe in the Book of Judges: The authors of this book arranged competing local traditions into a chronological succession and thereby constructed an unbroken narrative.

Another way the biblical authors did this was by descent: They genealogically connected Abraham to Isaac, Isaac to Jacob, Jacob to the twelve tribes, Moses to the descendants of one of these tribes, and so on. Each of these figures, however, originally represented independent traditions. (Scholars generally agree that the patriarchs have been secondarily aligned into a succession and that the patriarchal texts as whole were originally unrelated to the much different Moses–Exodus account.)

In the case of David's family, it is quite possible that not only Absalom but also Solomon was not originally portrayed as David's son. The oldest literature depicting his reign, with its focus on Jerusalem and his major construction projects there, differs substantially from the David narratives.

These redactional moves to construct continuities across Israel's diverse pasts tell us a lot about the concerns that propelled biblical historiography. The biblical writers sought to pull together the disparate traditions of competing factions and divided communities in order to appeal to a wider array of actors who could join forces as the members of Israel. Seen from this perspective, the Bible's history of composition and canonization is more about collecting and combining than editing and excluding.

An Exemplary Mercenary and Vassal

So why did later readers expand the Absalom account into a complex narrative of David's departure and return?

The literary dilation did more than make Absalom into a son of David. It also generated the kind of spatial denouement, at the end of a transformative voyage, that makes the travel-account such a popular genre – even in antiquity (examples include the Tale of Sinuhe, the Gilgamesh Epic, the Lugal-banda myths, the Odyssey, and the Anabasis). The crossing of the Jordan is also loaded with symbolic valences, such as the reversal of Israel's national history from the time of the conquest. The authors also evidently attached some significance to the Transjordan, and the city of Mahanaim in particular, where David seeks asylum. Moreover, the editorial expansions undermine David's achievements. Now, at the end of his life, he must return to the same fugitive existence that he faced during his days before taking the throne, when King Saul was hounding him. As the casualty of Absalom's ambition, the exiled David is forced to come to terms with the thirst for power and renown that catapulted his own political career.

Yet there is more to the amplification than narrative denouement. As in the Saul–David episodes, which we have studied in the preceding chapters, the story of David's flight from Absalom offered an ideal literary space in which later readers could address issues of Judah's identity. These readers did so by constructing memories of those who either broke faith with the kingdom's founder during a pivotal moment in its history or contributed valorously to his cause. Again, what propels the expansion of these texts is the political activity of *war commemoration.*

The first episode in this expanded narrative relates to a figure named Ittai the Gittite. It is embedded in the account of David's departure from Jerusalem after he relinquishes his throne to Absalom. As David leaves, his followers march in procession past him. The cavalcade includes the foreign troops who serve as his royal guard: the Cherethites, the Pelethites, and the Gittites. The latter are described as "600 men who came to [David's] side from Gath." David urges Ittai to take his men and their families back to Absalom:

> Then the king said to Ittai the Gittite: "Why should you too go with us? Return and stay with the king. For you are a foreigner, an exile from your place. You came only yesterday; should I make you go with us today? I must roam about. But you, go back, and bring your comrades with you. May mercy and truth be shown to you." (2 Sam 15:19–20)

The phrase "you too (go) with us" in the first line (*gam-ʿattâ ʾittānû*) is likely a play on the name of Ittai (*ʾittay*), which in unvocalized Hebrew appears the same as "with me."[4] Ittai should return, instead of accompanying David, because he is a "foreigner" (*nokrî*). He is not a member of the people in whose land he and his troops dwell. Like Uriah, Ittai lacks longstanding ties to his new abode. As such, he is not expected to show the same degree of devotion as David's Israelite kin.

Not only is Ittai a nonnative; he is also "an exile (*gôleh*) from [his] place." The combination of "exile" with "place" – rather than with "land/country" – is unusual. It underscores the similarity between Ittai's identity and David's plight. The latter is now also "an exile from his place" (i.e., his palace). Pushed out by Absalom, he must return to a life of wandering, the course of survival he had adopted before ascending the throne.

One might presume that issues of belonging posed by a particular population prompted the composition of this passage. In the preceding chapter we saw that the Uriah account addresses larger issues than those presented by a Hittite population within the societies of Israel or Judah. Yet since Ittai is said to lead a band of 600 Gittite men and their families, the authors may have been concerned with the issues posed by Gittites in their society.

To be sure, the prodigious city of Gath, easily the largest city in the region, has a long political history in the central hill country. It was apparently known among the Philistine cities for producing great warriors, such as the redoubtable Goliath, who, in a late tradition, is brought down by David's sling. Gittites may have served in the armies of Judah or Israel. Several LMLK jar handles from the eighth century were found there, and Judah may have controlled the city after the Arameans besieged it (c. 830 BCE) and before the Assyrian king Sargon II subjugated it (711 BCE).

Despite the important role that Gath had long played on the borders of Israel and Judah, what prompted the composition of the passage likely was not the presence of a foreign population (Gath or the Gittites) in Judahite society. Instead, its authors, as I will show, were interested in the issue that the Uriah account addresses: the purpose and function of states and royal rule.[5]

However, this passage differs from the Uriah account on one basic point. Whereas Uriah portrays what happens when the state becomes an end in itself, Ittai represents the special type of allegiance indispensable to the exercise of state power. Uriah expresses his solidarity with the nation in wartime and thereby sets himself in opposition to the king: "The Ark, Israel, and Judah are dwelling in booths, just as my lord Joab and the servants of my lord are in the field." Ittai, by contrast, is concerned solely with the king's welfare. Both Uriah and Ittai are foreign mercenaries. Yet where Uriah is part of the people of Israel, Ittai pledges his life to the person of King David.

The fact that Ittai is not an Israelite makes his allegiance all the more meaningful. As a soldier of fortune, he is expected to go where the fortune is to be made. Hence David enjoins him to return to Absalom, now identified as "the king." But Ittai represents more than just a self-serving condottiere. He is the paragon of a faithful vassal who, like a noble knight, pledges to protect his liege with his life: "Ittai replied to the king, 'As YHWH lives and as my lord the king lives, the place where my lord the king is, there your servant will be, whether for death or for life!'"[6]

Ittai expresses here the essence of statehood. His use of "place," the same word that David speaks, drives home his point. As an exile from his own *place*, he swears to accompany the king to whatever *place* the king's fate brings him, even if it means that he, his men, and their families must abandon the assured alimentation of the royal table for the destitute life of asylum seekers – and eventually their death.

Ittai's Likeness to David

David and Ittai have several other features in common. During his early days as a wandering fugitive, David leads a band of 600 warriors (and their families) – the same number of Gittites whom Ittai commands (1 Sam 27:2 and 30:9). David also entered the employ of a Gittite ruler (Achish). Just as this passage portrays Ittai's allegiance to David, the account of David's time in the service of Achish addresses concerns of mercenary loyalty.

After witnessing David's devotion, Achish decides to make him his bodyguard in perpetuity. Later, in keeping with his trust and confidence in David, Achish expects his mercenary commander to take the field against Israel with his forces along with the other Philistine alliance partners and their respective armies. When asked if he'd be prepared to fight against Israel, David declares his allegiance.

In those days the Philistines gathered their forces for war, to fight against Israel. Achish said to David, "You know, of course, that you and your men are to go out with me in the army." David said to Achish, "Then you shall know what your servant will do." Achish said to David, "And then I will make you my bodyguard for life." (1 Sam 28:1–2)

Sure enough, David follows through with his promise. The other Philistine leaders are suspicious of David's loyalties. What concerns them is not that David secretly harbors love for his people, but rather that he might decide to return to and seek the favor of his former master, King Saul of Israel. Hence they demand that he be sent home:

Now the Philistines gathered all their forces at Aphek, while the Israelites were encamped by the fountain that is in Jezreel.

As the Philistine lords were passing on by hundreds and by thousands, and David and his men were passing on in the rear with Achish, the Philistine commanders said, "What are these Hebrews doing here?"

Achish said to the Philistine commanders, "Is this not David, the servant of King Saul of Israel, who has been with me now for days and years? Since he deserted to me I have found no fault in him to this day."

But the Philistine commanders were angry with him and said to him, "Send the man back, so that he may return to the place that you have assigned to him; he shall not go down with us to battle, or else he may become an adversary to us in the battle. For how could this fellow reconcile himself to his lord? Would it not be with the heads of the men here? Is this not David, of whom they sing to one another in dances:

'Saul has killed his thousands,
  and David his ten thousands'?"

Even though Achish can attest to David's irreproachable record for the years during which he faithfully served him at Gath, the other Philistine lords do not want to run the risk that he would reconcile himself with Saul, his former liege. (Once again, they do not fear that David will turn against the Philistines in a show of loyalty to *the people of Israel.*) In the end Achish has no other choice than to muster out David and his men:

> Then Achish called David and said to him,
>
> "As YHWH lives, you have been honest, and to me it seems right that you should march out and in with me in the campaign; for I have found nothing wrong in you from the day of your coming to me until today. Nevertheless the lords do not approve of you. So go back now; and go peaceably; do nothing to displease the Philistine lords."
>
> David said to Achish, "But what have I done? What have you found in your servant from the day I entered your service until now, that I should not go and fight against the enemies of my lord the king?"
>
> Achish replied to David: "I know that you are as blameless in my sight as an angel of God; nevertheless, the Philistine commanders have said, 'He shall not go up with us to the battle.' Now then rise early in the morning, you and the servants of your lord who came with you, and go to the place that I appointed for you. As for the evil report, do not take it to heart, for you have done well before me. Start early in the morning, and leave as soon as you have light."
>
> So David set out with his men early in the morning, to return to the Philistines' land. But the Philistines went up to Jezreel. (1 Sam 29:1–11)

Thus whereas Achish claims that he found no fault in David since the time he defected and entered his employ, his Philistine confederates remind him that David has a reputation for being a great warrior in Saul's army.

When the Philistine leaders refer to the widely known ditty ("Saul has killed his thousand, and David his ten thousands"), which first appears in the Goliath account, it is not because the lyrics allude to David's history of killing Philistines or because it presents him fighting bravely for his Israelite kin. The reason is rather that the lyrics link David to Saul. They wonder whether David might look for an opportunity to demonstrate his abiding allegiance to this king by offering him a pile of Philistine heads.[7]

In sum, the Philistines correctly perceive that what motivates David is not national loyalty but rather mercenary allegiance.

In the end Achish urges David to return to his "place," which, however, is not understood as David's homeland ("the place I appointed for you").

Peoplehood versus Statehood

Both David and Ittai represent the virtues of an exemplary mercenary or vassal, willing to "fight against the enemies of my lord the king." The mentality he represents pays no heed to national allegiance. Belonging is instead a personal bond between liege and lord. That bond is often expressed in the vassal's oath to make the suzerain's enemy his own foe.

Thus Niqmaddu, the fourteenth-century ruler of Ugarit (Ras Shamra in northern Syria), swears to Šuppiluliuma, his Hittite overlord in Anatolia: "With the enemies of my lord, I am enemy; with his ally, I am ally" (RS 17.340.13). Likewise, Assyrian kings obliged their vassals to love those whom they love, and hate whom they hate – sentiments that were to be displayed through sacrifice on the battlefield.

The fact that both Ittai and David serve their lords as foreigners is not coincidental. In antiquity, as in more recent times, one recognized the benefits of an elite guard of nonnative soldiers. Standing outside local familial and political networks, its members could be trusted to protect the king from the reach of nemeses and to execute their assignments more professionally.[8] This fact explains why so many monarchs throughout history have employed foreign mercenaries in their royal guards. For example, rulers in early modern Europe hired Swiss mercenaries (*Reiseläufer*) and so-called Swiss Guards, while Turkish Ottoman courts used Christian boys (Janissaries) as their household troops and bodyguards.

Within the Bible, the accounts of Solomon's accession and of the Joash putsch highlight the role played by foreign warriors (1 Kings 1 and 2 Kings 11). Elsewhere, the Book of Samuel describes the devotion of elite multiethnic corps (2 Sam 23:8–39) that fought in David's employ as "his men" or "servants."

Thus we read how David once expressed his thirst for water from Bethlehem, which was at the time occupied by Philistine forces. Three of his best warriors then imperil their lives by stealing into the town and bringing him a flask of water from its municipal well (2 Sam 23:13–17). The devotion of these men to David (see also 2 Sam 21:15–17) corresponds in turn to David's allegiance to Achish. In the same way, the 600 Gittites fight faithfully in the ranks of their lord Ittai, and Ittai in turn swears to accompany his lord David.

Two concerns propelled the authors who synthesized the originally independent histories of David and Saul (the HDR and HSR). First, they sought to come to terms with Judah's relationship to the older and more powerful kingdom of Israel. They treat this issue by constructing stories of David's irreproachability vis-à-vis Saul and his ultimate ascendancy over this earlier king. This Israel–Judah duality drives the earliest syntheses of the independent Saul and David histories.

Second, in addition to addressing Judah's relationship to Israel, the book's authors, at a later stage, addressed the problem of political consolidation and national kinship. In keeping with the history of political philosophy – from Plato and Aristotle to Machiavelli and Hobbes – the biblical authors treat this problem in terms of military organization. They draw a line between nonprofessional "citizen-soldiers" who fight for their own collective interests, on the one side, and a standing army of professional troops and mercenary warriors who fight for the king, on the other.

The image of David portrayed here is not one of a devoted champion of Israelite "peoplehood." Instead we have a ruler determined to expand his rule. Formulating thereby a sophisticated critique of state power, the authors of Samuel affirm that David consolidated Judah into a state before taking the throne of Israel. Yet they present him as a political opportunist who had long aspired to be great. His unsavory personal ambition may promote Israel's security, yet it also imperils the nation's collective life.

This duality of David pervades the narrative, from the earliest texts to the final form. As we shall see in Chapter 10, it stands in stark contrast to the narrative in Chronicles, which resists any criticism of Judah's iconic monarch.

Ruth versus Ittai

To grasp the significance of the Ittai episode, let us compare it with the legend of Ruth. The biblical tale begins with a woman from Bethlehem named Naomi moving to the land of Moab during a famine in Judah. In time, her husband and two sons died, leaving Naomi with her two Moabite daughters-in-law, Ruth and Orpah. Once the famine ceases, she makes her way from her "place" in Moab back to the land of Judah.

The scene culminates with Naomi urging the wives of her deceased sons to turn back to their homeland of Moab. The two women are reluctant to take leave of her. Eventually one of them, Orpah, kisses Naomi goodbye and departs. Ruth, however, "clings" to her Judahite mother-in-law and refuses to return. Just as David urges Ittai to go back to Absalom in his "place," Naomi pleads with Ruth to follow Orpah back to her people and her gods. Yet Ruth does not give in:

> Do not urge me to leave you, to turn back and not follow you. For wherever you go, I will go. Wherever you dwell, I will dwell. Your people shall be my people. Your God, my God. Where you die, I will die. And there I will be buried. Thus and more may YHWH do to me if anything but death parts me from you. (Ruth 1:16–17)

In her award-winning commentary, Tamara Cohn Eskenazi identifies the similarities to the scene with Ittai: "In both these instances, a foreigner leaves the comfort of home and joins a wandering Judean. The comparison suggests an altruistic motive for both. Each places the welfare of the other person ahead of self-interest."[9]

The overlap between the two scenes also underscores the significant differences between the statements of the protagonists. By means of her profoundly personal pledge, Ruth expresses her pertinacious resolve to join Naomi's people. This transformation involves the worship of a new god and a new place of interment. Ittai resembles Ruth when he insists on accompanying David wherever he goes. Yet he says nothing about adopting David's people as his own or making David's God his own. Instead, he pledges – as befitting his role of vassal and royal guard – to protect the king "whether for death or for life."

Tikva Frymer-Kensky, a scholar of Bible and ancient Near Eastern Studies at the University of Chicago before her untimely death in 2006, juxtaposed Ruth's vow with expressions of fraternity between partners of international treaties and military coalitions.[10] The Moabite woman's personal pledge to her Judahite mother-in-law does in fact share many features with the formal declarations of kings forming war alliances. Consider two examples from the Bible:

> He [the king of Israel] said to Jehoshaphat, "Will you go with me to battle at Ramoth-gilead?" Jehoshaphat replied to the king of Israel, "I am as you are. My people are your people. My horses are your horses." (1 Kings 22:4)

> As [the king of Israel] went, he sent word to King Jehoshaphat of Judah, "The king of Moab has rebelled against me. Will you go with me to battle against Moab?" He answered, "I will. I am with you. My people are your people. My horses are your horses." (2 Kings 3:7)

These two asseverations made by one king to another are more reminiscent of Ittai's oath to David than of Ruth's pledge to Naomi. In the cases of these monarchs and Ittai, we witness coalition partners or vassals representing armies and pledging military assistance. Jehoshaphat's affirmation of unity – "my people will be as your people" – refers to his armed forces (like Ittai's company of soldiers), not to the peoples of Israel and Judah in the national sense. Just as the king possesses stables of horses, he controls these people/troops. They answer to his beck and call – a far cry from the Torah's ideal of the nation determining its own destiny in direct covenant with their God.

The differences in formulation between Ruth's and Ittai's vows correspond to the ubiquitous tension in the Bible between peoplehood and statehood. Ruth expresses the willingness to become a member of Naomi's people. Ittai swears allegiance to the person of the king, embodying the state.[11] David embodies the statist tradition that characterizes Judahite politics. It is therefore fitting that Ittai's oath is depicted precisely at the point in his biography where he loses his hold on the throne.

David's Place within Biblical History

Within the history extending from Genesis to Kings (the so-called Enneateuch), the Book of Samuel depicts a political transition. It begins with a people in their homeland yet without a centralized state. Then Saul assumes the throne. As Israel's first king, he unifies the people but fails to vanquish the nation's enemies. The task of achieving national security falls on David. As a strong-armed ruler, he brings real respite from external threats, but also often inflicts death upon his own people.

As to be expected, the authors of the Enneateuch view this political evolution ambivalently. The palace's monopoly of power challenges and ultimately undercuts the demotic strategies of peoplehood that the biblical authors deem indispensable to the survival of the nation after the destruction of the state. In the Enneateuch's remarkably complex and nuanced narrative, we can study the dangerous threat posed by a strong centralized state that guarantees security from enemies abroad while simultaneously suffocating collective-national political life. This extensive history concludes by portraying a horrific vacuum created by the eradication of the last remnant of the people who figure so prominently in the centuries of history prior to the establishment of the centralized state.

The transition to a centralized state is a gradual one. The authors present Saul's kingdom as unified but weak. Beginning with his first campaign to rescue the town of Jabesh-gilead in the Transjordan, Saul mobilizes the entire nation, *kol-yiśrā'ēl*, for the nation's war efforts. Thereafter he consistently makes use of conscripted irregular troops – yet with only moderate success.

Within this narrative, the oldest sources present Saul as the commander of 600 soldiers, who likely constitute his private army. However, the Book of Samuel thoroughly transforms this force: We're told that these 600 men are the remainder of the large host of nonprofessional fighters who voluntarily rally to his call.[12] In the same way, the authors of Judges transformed Gideon's 300 elite warriors into those who remained from the 32,000 who originally volunteered for service.

Tellingly, the biblical writers did not undertake such editorial work with respect to David's 600. Throughout the Book of Samuel, David represents the powerful state that employs strong-arm methods and elite corps of professional warriors – many of whom are nonnatives – to vanquish Israel's enemies, to establish strong borders, and, most alarmingly, to enforce its will upon the people within these borders.

Although many have claimed that David established a grand "united kingdom" of Israel, the authors of Samuel depict him tearing asunder the unified state Saul established. David greases the palms of the Judahites with the spoils of his raids, and then Judah's elders predictably come and appoint him their king (see the discussion in Chapter 3 of this book). David therefore becomes king only at the cost of Judah's secession from Israel. The agonizing discord between these two polities persists throughout the rest of Samuel and Kings.

If David manages to hold together this political polarity, it is by means of raw force rather than appeal to the nation's interests. Instead of allowing Absalom to rule the people of Israel, whose hearts he had won, David deceptively induces him and "all Israel" to appear on the battlefield. There his smaller army of professional troops, one-third of whom he places under the command of Ittai the Gittite, performs a massive slaughter, wiping out 20,000 members of the nation. Then, after reconsolidating his kingdom with the help of his professional troops, he commissions his servants along with foreign mercenaries (the Cherethites and Pelethites) to quash another rebellion (see discussion in the following chapter).

Perhaps Israel (once) loved David, and perhaps such extraordinarily violent actions were needed to prevent the disunion of Israel and Judah. But David is no Abraham Lincoln. We are never told that he harbored deep anxiety or remorse about the excessive Israelite bloodshed his actions caused during these civil wars. He wages battle only for his own interests. The book concludes by presenting him choosing a plague of death for the entire land instead of an enemy who would pursue him alone. Ultimately 70,000 souls must perish.

The mature David is the personification of an effective yet ruthless leader, and his success is due to the proficient use of private troops rather than any capacity to persuade the people. By registering the names of David's warriors and recalling his exploits with them, the texts surrounding David's final words suggest that this leader's greatest moments in life were the early days that he enjoyed in the camp with this corps of fighters.[13] As the narrative forges ahead in the first chapters of Kings, Solomon succeeds in assuming the throne not least because he has David's "warriors" and elite units of foreign mercenaries on his side. In all these tales we witness how David, in keeping with the behavior of many rulers from the ancient world, willingly subjects his people to death for *raisons d'état*, with the *état* being identical to his own rule.

David's biography – from his glorious early years that he spent as a soldier fighting alongside his men, to his days when he no longer marches out with the others – replicates Israel's history in the biblical narrative. The transition in polity to centralized statehood – from "a people without a state" to "a state with a people" – coincides with the shift in military organization. In the biblical construction of Israel's history, the nation flourished as a people when all of its members were directly contributing to their collective war efforts. This "citizen's army" of Israel's early history was, however, gradually supplanted by the conscripted forces and professional troops who fight *the king's wars*.

As noted earlier, political philosophies are often elaborated via models of military organization. It is therefore not surprising that biblical history, written after the catastrophic collapse of the state and with an interest in the survival of the nation, focuses so much of its attention on this tension between citizen-soldiers and standing armies.

Conclusions

As a foreign mercenary who swears loyalty to the person of the king, to protect him in both death and life, Ittai the Gittite is emblematic of the type of unmitigated allegiance that successful statehood demands.

Kings and their royal guards (representing the state in its most fundamental form) often behave at odds with the interests of the people whom they are obliged to protect. While the biblical authors recognized that the relationship between state and nation is inevitably a vexed one, their writings repeatedly demand that the state serve the interests of the nation.

The state's role is to protect the nation and ensure that justice dwells in its midst. The state is not an end in itself, but a means to an end. The extent to which it defies this subservient role, it is tyrannical. Herein the biblical authors anticipate the nationalist principles of modernity, while departing from the political norms of antiquity, both in ancient Israel/Judah and elsewhere.

By imagining the emergence of a centralized state, the Book of Samuel presents an alternative. Saul's kingdom, with its national army of "all Israel," is characterized by internal unity yet also insecurity on its borders. In contrast, David's kingdom, which relies on a standing army and foreign mercenaries, is characterized by foreign security yet also deep internal divisions.

The final form of the Enneateuch (Genesis-Kings) identifies in the history of Israel a deep tension between a vibrant sense of peoplehood, on the one hand, and a strong, secure state, on the other. Instead of seeking to resolve this tension, the biblical authors present it as a problem for their readers to confront as they endeavor to create a sustainable form of self-governance – both before the catastrophe of 586 BCE and thereafter.

In their account of Ittai the Gittite, the nonnative warrior who swears to protect the king in death and life, the biblical authors commemorate the loyalty of devoted foreign mercenaries. Likewise, they affirm that statehood often demands formal pledges of allegiance and undying fidelity, both of which are embodied by Ittai.

8

David in Exile

Priests, Statehood, and the Benjaminites

Following the Ittai episode, the narrative plods along slowly, as David and his followers exit Jerusalem and escape to the Transjordan. Painting a poignant scene of forced migration, the narrator reports that the whole country wept in a loud voice when they witnessed the king and his entourage leaving the capital city and entering the wilderness.

Each stage of the itinerary is punctuated by a discrete episode – often introduced by the transitional marker *wehinnê*, "and behold" – from the edge of the city, over the Kidron Valley, up the Mount of Olives, arriving at the summit, a little past the summit, on to the town of Bahurim, at the edge of the Jordan River, and finally to the Transjordanian town of Mahanaim, where David and his followers take up temporary residence as refugees.

The growth of this complex itinerary resembles the expansion of other biblical travel narratives, such as the wilderness wanderings in the Pentateuch or Ezra's return from Babylon, both of which furnished a framework for redactors to insert supplementary material.

In this and the following chapter, I examine how the Absalom account gradually evolved from a simple tale of an attempted putsch into a complex literary war memorial depicting how various political actors worked for and against David. I begin by looking at the way David's individual fate anticipates Israel's collective exile.

David's Exile and Israel's Exile

The first episode in David's itinerary, after the exchange with Ittai, relates to the priest Zadok and to the Levites. We are told that they set down the "Ark of God" until the cavalcade had exited the city.

The reference to the Ark is strange here. It may have been added to explain how David later "prostrated himself before God" on the summit of the Mount of Olives. Yet it also brings to the fore how all that David had once achieved is now forfeited: At the culmination of his triumphal days, David relocates the Ark to Jerusalem. Staging an elaborate public performance, David whirls and dances "before the Lord with all his might, amid shouts and the sound of trumpets." Now, however, his life has taken a radical turn. He and the Ark are forced to leave Jerusalem, and this time what is heard are not triumphal trumpets but the entire country weeping.

When David finally speaks, he commands Zadok to return with the Ark to the city (2 Sam 15:23–37). If the authors do not report that Zadok insisted that he accompany David into exile, as they do for Ittai the Gittite in the preceding passage, it is because a subsequent episode presupposes the priest's presence in the city.

Later the narrative will portray Zadok, along with another priest named Abiathar, and each of their sons, endangering their lives to engage in espionage on David's behalf. David arranges that Hushai the Arkite, his "friend," would inform the priests Zadok and Abiathar of Absalom's plans. The priests should pass along all relevant intelligence to their sons (Ahimaaz and Jonathan), who in turn relay it to David. The covert communications expose all involved to great risks:

> Jonathan and Ahimaaz [the sons of Zadok and Abiathar] would wait at En-rogel, where a servant girl used to go and tell them news from King

David and vice versa – for they could not risk being seen entering the city. But this time a boy saw them, and told Absalom.

So both of them went away quickly, and came to the house of a man at Bahurim, who had a well in his courtyard, and they went down into it. The man's wife took a covering, stretched it over the well's mouth, and spread out grain on it, and thereby concealed it.

When Absalom's servants came to the woman at the house, they said, "Where are Ahimaaz and Jonathan?"

The woman said to them, "They crossed over the brook of water."

When they had searched and could not find them, they returned to Jerusalem. After they were gone, [the two sons] came up out of the well and went and informed King David [the secret intelligence from Absalom's court]. (2 Sam 17:17–21[1])

The episode shares many features with the tale of Rahab's valorous efforts on behalf of the Israelite spies (Josh 2). In both cases, a woman who belongs to the other side in an armed conflict hides two spies by covering them with flax/grain. She misinforms the pursuers so that they cannot "find them." In the end, the spies bring their intelligence to the leader (either Joshua or David).

Yet there is also a divergence to be noted. The Rahab story relates to the people of Israel and their crossing to the Jordan from the east to conquer the Promised Land. Our episode, in contrast, relates to a king who is forced to cross back over the Jordan and thereby leave Israel's homeland.

David is the paradigmatic refugee. So much of his life, as depicted in the Book of Samuel, is spent on the run, chased out, and forced to sojourn far from any place he can call home. Think here of the many scenes in which he makes his escape from Saul with the help of Michal or Jonathan, or the lengthy episodes in which he is running from Saul in the wilderness. Now, after establishing a powerful state and enjoying impressive triumphs, he must relinquish all he has and abandon his land.

David's life here again anticipates the exile that his people will later suffer collectively. This feature contributes much to the poignancy of his biography. It also reveals the extent to which Judah's exilic experience shaped the story.[2]

Zadokites, Levites, and Royal Guards

The biblical account pays tribute to various groups – for example, the town of Bahurim. As we've seen, one passage depicts the bravery of an anonymous woman who resides in this Benjaminite town and who places her life in peril during a precarious period in the life of David.[3]

The episodes devote even more attention to the priests' contributions. It is easy to imagine how influential Temple circles would have disseminated such legends of bravery and sacrifice as a way of defending their sanctioned claims to high cultic offices. By claiming that the progenitors of their priestly lines lived at the same time as the great King David, and by recounting how they assisted him against his opponents during a time of civil war, the representatives of these guilds could respond to any doubts that may have arisen about their loyalties to the palace. After 586 BCE, such legends would have served the priestly guilds well, as they sought to fill the void left by the palace and as they traced their origins to this golden age in Judah's history. Such is precisely what they do in the Book of Chronicles.

Priestly guilds often promoted themselves over their competitors by drafting or expanding biblical texts. The Book of Kings (chap. 11), for example, tells at length how the priest Jehoiada, with the help of elite guards, deposed Queen Athaliah and reinstated a Davidic descendant on the throne.

In Chronicles we can witness how priestly guilds (Aaronites, Zadokites, and Levites) revised passages from the Book of Kings with the aim of exonerating themselves from any wrongdoing. For instance, Kings depicts how the Judahite ruler Joash summons the priests and demands to know why they were not repairing the temple with the funds that had been donated. In the parallel passage from Chronicles, the monarch petitions not the priests but "the chief," and he asks why he had not required the Levites to collect the funds.

Similarly, Kings presents Ahaz sending a model of an altar at Damascus to the priest Uriah, who promptly builds a replica of the pagan prototype in Jerusalem. Chronicles deletes the embarrassing episode entirely. Other unfavorable memories, such as Josiah's act of deposing idolatrous priests, are likewise eliminated. One can cite similar cases of such "historical revisionism" in Chronicles, one of which we have already examined in Chapter 5.[4]

In the Book of Ezra-Nehemiah, as in Chronicles, members of the Levitical cultic guild insert themselves into the history of Jerusalem at every possible occasion. In many of the texts, one can see how the Levites are vying with their priestly competitors for status. Ezra-Nehemiah attributes the Levites' rank and position in Judah to the role they performed during the building of the Temple and to the reforms of two leading post-exilic figures, Ezra and Nehemiah. Chronicles makes none other than King David responsible for their honorable positions.

The account of Solomon's accession, found in 1 Kings 2, is a place where we can witness the efforts of the Zadokite priests to legitimate the special prerogatives that they later enjoyed at the Jerusalem Temple. The priest Abiathar had sided with Adonijah, Solomon's competitor whom David had designated as his heir. With a pronounced polemical tone, they explain why Zadok's line, not Abiathar's, succeeded in assuming the high-priestly office. When Solomon decides not to execute Abiathar for his treasonous activities, it is because he remembers Abiathar's loyalty and service to his father during his wars with Saul and Absalom: "You carried the Ark of YHWH my God before my father David and shared all the hardships that my father endured."[5] This passage illustrates how early readers appreciated the political utility of the war commemoration found in the earlier David narratives.

We should note here how war commemoration is applied to the history of the Cherethites and Pelethites. These foreign royal guards are mentioned in the scene with Ittai leaving with David (2 Sam 15:18), the account of the war against Absalom (2 Sam 20:7), and the account of Solomon's accession (1 Kings 1:38, 44). Moreover, one of the groups (often translated as "Carites") plays a key role in placing a Davidic king back on the throne in Judah, under the direction of Jehoida the priest. The account of that putsch bears many similarities to the report of Solomon's accession, with both a priest (Zadok) and a specific unit of soldiers assisting him. All these texts suggest that their authors were consciously commemorating the loyalty of Cherethites and Pelethites to the Davidic dynasty, claiming that they already faithfully served David and Solomon. Such commemoration would have been acutely needed as a riposte to the resentment many would have felt toward these professional (and originally foreign) mercenaries who were there to do the king's bidding, even against the will of the people.

Competing War Counselors

Closely linked to the part played by the priests is the role of Hushai the Arkite. At the summit of the Mount of Olives, he comes out to meet David with a torn tunic and earth upon his head. David urges him, as he has done already to two others, to return to the city. If he could serve as a counselor to David's opponent, he could use his position to defeat the advice offered by a competing figure, Ahithophel the Gilonite (2 Sam 15:32–37).

In espionage parlance, Hushai was to serve as "an agent of influence." The biblical story is, curiously, the subject of an official "secret" CIA file that was released in 1994. According to the report, the case of Hushai and Ahithophel not only is of "historical and human interest" but also "reminds us of the efficacy of simplicity, audacity, speed, and the exploitation of human frailties in this kind of enterprise."

The introduction of Hushai and Ahithophel at this point prepares the reader for the subsequent duel between the two war counselors. In its original form, the account of that showdown was probably much more concise. It's even possible that the scenes with them are late additions. If so, an earlier version might have presented Absalom chasing David across the Jordan, instead of first entering Jerusalem.[6] Whatever the case may be, the episodes not only augment the story's suspense but also provide a context for the authors to expound on a unifying theme of the Absalom account – loyalty.

Ahithophel the Gilonite, we are told, had once served as David's counselor. In what may represent the oldest reference to this figure, his son is identified as one David's warriors (2 Sam 15:12 and 23:34). Numerous legends have grown up around his name in later Jewish lore, and they ascribe to him unparalleled erudition and inspiration.[7] These legends take their point of departure from the biblical comparison of his counsel to a divine oracle:

> In those days the counsel of Ahithophel was accepted like an oracle sought from god; that is how all his advice was esteemed, both by David and Absalom. (2 Sam 16:23)

After Absalom establishes control of Jerusalem, he requests Ahithophel's advice. The sage offers to handpick an army that he himself would conduct into battle. With these select troops, he would be able to eliminate David alone and bring back the rest of the people to Absalom, "as a bride comes to her husband":

> Ahithophel said to Absalom, "Let me choose twelve thousand men, and I will set out and pursue David tonight. I will come upon him while he is weary and discouraged, and throw him into a panic. Then all the people who are with him will flee. I will strike down only the king. All the people I will bring back to you as a bride comes home to her husband. You seek the life of only one man, and all the people will be at peace."
>
> The advice pleased Absalom and all the elders of Israel. (2 Sam 17:1–4)

Absalom and the elders of Israel initially accept the recommendation. Yet they jettison it once his competitor and David's devious ally, Hushai, suggests a different course of action: Absalom should muster *the entire nation* ("all Israel") and personally lead them against David. Hushai's objective is to give David time to escape. (The levy of the militia was time consuming; see 2 Sam 20:4–5.)

This plan also serves David's larger strategic objective, one that he ruthlessly pursues. His aim is to inflict a resounding blow on the people of Israel after they had joined Absalom's insurrection. With the whole nation called to arms and assembled on the battlefield, they would be vulnerable to David's mercenaries and professional fighters – the source of so much uneasiness for the biblical authors. Such is precisely how the narrator presents this harrowing episode of David's late life. In the bloodbath perpetrated by his warriors, 20,000 souls perish – all for the sake of reestablishing David's centralized control.

Everywhere one turns in these chapters there is death. Absalom's acceptance of Hushai's advice devastates Ahithophel. He saddles his donkey, returns to his hometown, and, after putting his affairs in order, hangs himself. "He died and was buried in his ancestral grave."

While we know of Ahithophel's tomb solely from this text, Jewish pilgrims since the eighteenth century CE claimed that a medieval sepulcher in the northern Druze village of Yirka – the *maqam* of al-Nabi Siddik – is the burial site of Hushai the Arkite.[8] This honor bestowed on Hushai – and the extensive castigation of Ahithophel in later Jewish literature – stands in continuity to the original function of the Absalom account. Just as the Yirka memorial assumed new meanings over time, the Absalom account evolved into a complex literary monument as later readers added their interpretations to it.

What would the figures of Ahithophel and Hushai have meant to the earliest readers? It is possible that these two names represented contemporaneous clans. But it is more likely that they serve didactic purposes, exemplifying character traits and types of loyalties. If so, we may compare the Absalom account to a "mirror for princes" (*speculum principum*), a popular genre of didactic court literature from premodern times.

The name of Ahithophel means "brother of insipidity/impiety" in Hebrew. In Syriac *'aḥitōpēlājā* came to signify "traitorous." Even though Hushai is the real colluder in our story, the name has similar connotations elsewhere. For centuries Ahithophel (or Achitophel) was a synonym in England for a wicked and perfidious counselor or politician. A widely distributed political cartoon, published in London in 1830, presents the Duke of Wellington (Arthur Wellesley) – a celebrated military officer and statesman who opposed Jewish emancipation reforms in Great Britain – on a donkey, with a saddle resembling a mayoral gown, approaching the gallows. The donkey and gown relate to Sir John Key, Lord Mayor of London. Underneath both cartoons, the biblical text is quoted with allusions to the lampooned personalities: "And when Ahithophel saw that his counsel was not followed he Saddled his Don-key and arose and went out and hanged himself" (sic).

In his landmark political satire, *Absalom and Achitophel* (1681), John Dryden drew on the biblical tale to treat the bloody succession of Charles II. David stands for Charles, Absalom for the Duke of Monmouth, Absalom's wife Annabel (an invented character) for the Countess of Buccleuch, Ahithophel for the Earl of Shaftesbury, Zion for London, and so on.

Dryden's poem is a remarkably insightful reading of the biblical account. Yet whereas it and the political cartoons address the internal political conflicts that often plague monarchic succession, the biblical tale offers a sapiential parable on the nature of statehood as a whole. Contrasting Ahithophel's plan to avoid bloodshed with the atrocious slaughter perpetrated by David's professional fighters, the biblical authors portray – without any simplistic dualism of good guy versus bad guy – the brutal costs imposed by centralized rule, even while acknowledging its utilitarian value.

The Territory of Benjamin

Ahithophel and Hushai belong together as a contrasting pair. The first is one of the "conspirators," while the second is David's "friend." Embedded in this account is a narrative strand that involves other pairs of personalities. The issue they pose concerns not statehood but rather the territory of Benjamin.[9]

Once David passes "a little beyond the summit" of the Mount of Olives, he encounters Ziba. This servant of Mephibosheth, Saul's descendant, comes out to meet the departing king with saddled donkeys bearing rich provisions. The supply of provisions – for example, by vassals to a ruler on a military campaign or by allies to each other – is a conventional form of wartime contributions. Biblical literature is replete with such accounts.

Whereas Ziba demonstrates his support, his master does not. According to Ziba, Mephibosheth is staying in Jerusalem because he thinks that in David's absence, the "house of Israel" will give him back Saul's kingdom:

> When David had passed a little beyond the summit, Ziba the servant of Mephibosheth met him. He came with a couple of donkeys saddled, carrying two hundred loaves of bread, one hundred bunches of raisins, one hundred summer fruits, and a skin of wine.
>
> The king said to Ziba, "Why have you brought these?"
>
> Ziba answered, "The donkeys are for the king's household to ride on, the bread and summer fruit for the young men to eat, and the wine is for those to drink who faint in the wilderness."
>
> The king said, "Where is your master's son?"
>
> Ziba said to the king, "He [Mephibosheth] remains in Jerusalem, for he said, 'Today the house of Israel will give me back my grandfather's kingdom.'"
>
> Then the king said to Ziba, "All that belonged to Mephibosheth is now yours."
>
> Ziba said, "I do obeisance. Let me find favor in your sight, my lord the king." (2 Sam 16:1–4)

In response David issues a decree that simultaneously punishes Mephibosheth for his disloyalty and rewards Ziba for his solidarity, transferring the property of the former to the latter.

On David's way back to Jerusalem after the death of Absalom, Ziba goes to the Jordan, with a large retinue of sons and servants to welcome the king home. Mephibosheth is also present on the occasion, and he explains to David that his servant Ziba had lied. The reason he did not accompany the king into exile was because he was lame and because Ziba, who sought to impugn his good intentions, had refused to saddle a donkey for him. As a testimony to his genuine solidarity, Mephibosheth had not pared his toenails, trimmed his mustache, or washed his clothes for as many days as David's absence. One now understands why we are told earlier about Mephibosheth's handicap (2 Sam 4:4). The reader surmises that Ziba should have saddled the donkeys for his master rather than bring them to David and present them as a gift in his own name.

When David hears Mephibosheth's side of the story, he is convinced that something is amiss. Yet instead of deciding clearly in the favor of the plaintiff or defendant, he rules that the two would share Saul's estate. Lending credibility to his allegations, Mephibosheth renounces his entitlement to the land: "Let him take it all, for my lord the king has returned home safely." In this way, he exonerates himself from any wrongdoing (2 Sam 19:18–19, 25–31; 21:7–9).

Another episode, earlier in the narrative, provides a basis for Mephibosheth's accusation (2 Sam 9). We are told that Ziba, a high-ranking minister in Saul's palace, helped David find Mephibosheth so that he could show favor to this descendant of Saul. Yet David fails to reward Ziba for his assistance. Instead he makes him, together with his fifteen sons and twenty slaves, the vassal of Mephibosheth, managing Saul's estates and delivering its yield to Mephibosheth. Having been treated in this manner by David, Ziba would have a good motive for behaving as accused.

Here again we see how the authors of Samuel have constructed complex characters without simple black-white moralistic dualities. If anyone is consistently culpable, it is David, who owes his troubles in great part to a pattern of his own imprudent decision making.

In contrast to Mephibosheth, Shimei ben Gera changes his tune according to the shifting direction of the political winds. The account of his actions is set within the frame formed by the Ziba-Mephibosheth episodes. When David enters the town of Bahurim on his departure from Jerusalem, this member of Saul's house comes out to meet him. Yet instead of bringing food and drink to the king, he casts stones at him and his entourage. The insults he hurls carry bits of truth:

> Get out! Get out! You man of blood! You scoundrel! YHWH has brought on you the blood of the house of Saul, in whose place you have reigned. YHWH has given the kingdom into the hand of your son Absalom. See, disaster has overtaken you, for you are a man of blood. (2 Sam 16:7–8)

There is no disputing the fact that David, as depicted in the Book of Samuel, has bloody hands. Yet when David's guard, Abishai ben Zeruiah, offers to go over and lop off Shimei's head, David rebukes him for his ferocity (2 Sam 16:5–13, 19:9b–24).

As the royal cavalcade finally makes its return to Jerusalem, Shimei hurries down with the Judahites to greet David and to bring him across the Jordan. Now instead of stones, he casts himself down before the king and offers an elaborate apology, identifying himself as "the first of all the house of Joseph to come down and meet the lord my king." Once again Abishai ben Zeruiah offers to dispose of him by cutting off his head – a recurring theme in the David narratives. The authors here and elsewhere draw attention to the violence of "the sons of Zeruiah" as a way of justifying their elimination from their high military office.

The account of David on his deathbed in the first chapters of Kings presents David putting his house in order and thinking back upon the major moments of his life. The scene bears similarities to the opening chapters of Deuteronomy, in which Moses reflects on Israel's experiences in the wilderness. In both instances the protagonists devote much of their attention to memories of wartime events. In the case of David, the moribund monarch instructs his son Solomon to finish his business by conferring favors on those who had helped him in times of trouble and by punishing those who had wronged him. This passage from Kings reveals much about the political agendas that motivated the war commemoration we find in the Book of Samuel.

David reminds Solomon of the crimes of Joab, another son of Zeruiah. In murdering two other contenders for his office, Joab "shed the blood of war in peacetime." Solomon must see to it that the bloody general's "white hair does not go down to Sheol in peace" (1 Kings 2:5–6, 28–35).

Instead of punishing Shimei on his way back to the throne, David had pardoned him. Now on his deathbed, he rescinds the clemency and orders Solomon to attend to the punishment of "the Benjaminite from Bahurim." The authors of this passage find a way to reconcile Shimei's execution by interpreting David's oath as binding only for the duration of David's reign:

> There is also with you Shimei ben Gera, the Benjaminite from Bahurim, who cursed me with a terrible curse on the day when I went to Mahanaim. When he came down to meet me at the Jordan, I swore to him by YHWH, "I will not put you to death with the sword." Therefore do not hold him guiltless, for you are a wise man and will know what you ought to do to him. You must bring his gray head down with blood to Sheol. (1 Kings 2:8–9)

What motivates the composition of this text is not the actual death of a historical figure named Shimei. More likely the author of this passage wanted to add ignominy to the population Shimei represents – the Benjaminite town of Bahurim – by reporting that David never forgot Shimei's misdeeds and couldn't live with the prospect of his wellbeing. When Solomon eventually puts Shimei to death, he reminds him of all the wrong he had done to his father in a time of crisis:

> The king [Solomon] said to Shimei: "You know in your own heart all the evil that you did to my father David. YHWH will bring back your evil on your own head. But King Solomon shall be blessed, and the throne of David shall be established before YHWH forever."
>
> Then the king commanded Benaiah son of Jehoiada, and he went out and struck him down, and he died. (1 Kings 2:44–46)

This account illustrates the political purpose of war commemoration. In both the case of Shimei and that of "the sons of Zeruiah," the memory of wartime actions determines belonging, or in this case, elimination.[10]

That our texts likely have a territory or population in their is demonstrated by the fact the narrator repeatedly draws attention to Shimei's origins – he is "the Benjaminite (from Bahurim)." Likewise, Sheba ben Bichri, who will immediately hereafter initiate a new insurrection of Israel against David, is described as "a Benjaminite" (see the following chapter). Association with Shimei impugns the Benjaminite town of Bahurim, especially as it is the place where this adversary hurls stones and insults at the iconic king. Several passages seem to respond to these texts and thereby construct countermemories that pay tribute to Benjamin.

Conclusions

We saw here how David as a refugee (*gōleh*) prefigures Israel's exilic fate. I devoted considerable space to Ahithophel, its message about statehood, and its reception history in later political satire. In addition, I demonstrated how war commemoration was used in the struggles between priestly guilds, such as the Zadokites.

In the context of the latter discussion, we witnessed how an anonymous woman from Bahurim risks her life to conceal the spies from Absalom's men. This legend may represent a commemorative rejoinder to the disgrace brought by Shimei's actions on the name of the town. Furthermore, the reader is told that when Shimei came out to welcome David home, a thousand Benjaminites accompanied him. The statement relativizes the actions not only of Shimei but also of the insurrectionist Sheba insofar as his coup is situated in the context of David's return from exile.

Another episode that merits mention in this context is the assassination of Saul's son Ishbosheth/Ishbaal, told in 2 Samuel 4. The two perpetrators, Baanah and Rechab, sneak into his house, slay their target while he is in bed, and travel with his head all night long so that they can present it to David at Hebron as proof of their loyalty. Yet instead of conferring honors on the assassins, David orders them to be dismembered and hung ignominiously for all to see. Their hands and feet are cut off – the hands with which they beheaded Ishbosheth and the feet with which they ran to bring the head to David.[11]

This account, like others in the Book of Samuel, emphasizes David's solicitude for Saul's household. But it is more than just an *apologia pro vita sua*. The authors repeatedly identify the two assassins as Beerothites from Benjamin and report that the inhabitants of Beeroth, a Gibeonite town, had fled to Gittaim (in Benjamin) and remained resident-aliens "until this day."[12]

Beginning with a tale of how Gibeonites duped Joshua and Israel, several biblical texts witness to a polemical interest in this population, identifying them as outsiders who secure a protected place in Israelite society through an act of pusillanimous subterfuge during the days of the conquest of Canaan. We therefore have good reason to compare this account to the ones treated in this chapter, inasmuch as it exploits the figure of David to censure representative inhabitants of a Benjaminite town by constructing memories of wartime conduct.

9

Territorial Transitions

The Transjordan, Israel, and Judah

The preceding chapter treated several passages related to David's exile to the Transjordan and his return to Jerusalem after the death of Absalom. One of the points at issue in those passages is the territory of Benjamin. The present chapter examines a series of texts that relates to other territories, both within and beyond the borders of Israel. I will begin with a discussion of the Transjordan and then turn my attention to the deep and abiding tensions between Israel and Judah.

Issues Posed by the East Bank

Upon arriving at the Transjordanian town of Mahanaim, David and his entourage are greeted by a delegation of three dignitaries. As Saul's servant Ziba had done before, they deliver food for David and for the people who accompany him. Along with an extraordinary assortment of victuals, they bear gifts of vessels, basins, and beds/couches.

When David reached Mahanaim, Shobi son of Nahash from Rabbath-ammon, Machir son of Ammiel from Lo-debar, and Barzillai the Gileadite from Rogelim presented couches, basins, and earthenware; also wheat, barley, flour, parched grain, beans, lentils, parched grain, honey, curds, a flock, and cheese from the herd for David and the troops with him to eat. For they knew that the troops must have grown hungry, faint, and thirsty in the wilderness. (2 Sam 17:27–29)

The furniture has an obvious utilitarian value. The narrator draws attention, three times, to the "weary" condition of the people. Yet beds and couches were also coveted prestige objects, often possessed by monarchs. They appear frequently as war spoils or tribute in display inscriptions and reliefs. For instance, an inscription of the Assyrian ruler Sennacherib claims that the Judahite king Hezekiah was forced to pay the Assyrian throne not only an exorbitant sum of gold and silver but also various exotic items, such as beds with ivory insets.[1]

The depiction of David's people in the wilderness evokes the image of the children of Israel during their wilderness wanderings. Deuteronomy denies Ammonites and Moabites various communal privileges because they failed to meet Israel with bread and water on their exodus from Egypt. Similarly, Israel is commanded to blot out the memory of the Amalekites because they "surprised you on the march, when you were famished and weary, and cut down all the stragglers in your rear." The parallels to our passage, in both depicted situation and commemorative function, are obvious (see Deut 23:4–7, 25: 17–19).

Another narrative framework we have studied in this book – the account of David's flight from Saul – devotes a lengthy episode to the food and drink David receives from an ally. That episode links the act of provisioning to a political marriage.

The woman whom David eventually marries is the spouse of Nabal, a wealthy man from the Calebite clan. While enjoying a harvest feast, he refuses to provision David's men, which provokes David's retaliation. Nabal's clever wife Abigail saves herself by demonstrating her allegiance. She surreptitiously conveys a generous selection to David. Her gesture placates the anger of this unforgiving warlord. After Nabal learns how Abigail saved his skin, he has a stroke and eventually dies, leaving Abigail to marry David.

The Absalom account does not tell of a political marriage. But we do witness the display of solidarity or allegiance through provisions.

Shobi ben Nahash and Machir

The first figure from the welcoming entourage is Shobi ben Nahash. Coming from Rabbah, the Ammonite capital, his presence poses a problem: In the account that directly precedes the Absalom story, David subjugates another son of Nahash and occupies the city of Rabbah (2 Sam 10). What is more, Shobi is accompanied here by a Gileadite, even though the Gileadites and the Ammonites were incessantly at war with each other. To explain these incongruities, we must first examine the setting of the events as well as the identity of the two other members of the group.

With respect to the setting, David could have easily sought sanctuary in the desert and caves of Judah or in Moab or the region of Gath, as he did when he was running from Saul. Yet instead he seeks asylum in Mahanaim. The choice of this place likely has to do with the authors' interest in casting favorable light on a leading Gileadite town.

The Gilead was a latecomer to the fold of Israel, and it long remained disputed territory. Yet in time, it came to be appreciated as an important place in Israel's (not Judah's) history. Several texts from Joshua present Mahanaim as a city of Israel. And a lengthy account in Genesis traces the name of this town back to the pivotal moment in the life of Israel's leading patriarch, when his name is changed from Jacob to Israel. As a town of Israel, Mahanaim was not viewed favorably by many Judahites. Thus, after Saul's death, his general Abner takes Ishbosheth (Ishbaal) to this place with the intent of making him Saul's successor. From here Israel wages war against David and Judah.[2]

All these texts help us appreciate what motivated the composition of our passage from the Absalom account. By reporting that Mahanaim offered protection to David in his war with Absalom and Israel, it affirms for Judahite readers that Mahanaim – and by extension, the region of the Gilead – played a pivotal role in the earliest days of the Davidic kingdom. Therefore Judahite contemporaries should hold it in great respect. A similar point is made in the Keilah account (see Chapter 4).

This concern with the Transjordan produced the curious constellation of dignitaries in our passage. The second figure in the group is same person who protected Mephibosheth after the death of his father Saul (2 Sam 9). His name, Machir, appears elsewhere as the designation for a central Gileadite region. The Song of Deborah commemorates how Machir contributed to one of Israel's major war efforts – although the song may identify Machir as a Cisjordanian territory. Biblical texts graft the eponymous ancestor of Machir into Israel's genealogies.[3] By reporting that Machir accompanied Shobi in bringing provisions to Mahanaim, the biblical passage removes any doubt that this ruler, and the Transjordanian region he represents, was ultimately loyal to Judah's beloved king despite the favor he showed to Saul's son.

Barzillai the Gileadite

Barzillai is the third member of the group. The earliest portrayal of this figure is likely to be found in the account of David's return to Jerusalem after Absalom's death.

Various clues suggest that this passage predates the account of the three Transjordanian figures coming out to welcome David with provisions. Since we had already met Barzillai two chapters earlier, we would not expect to have here a descriptive – and in some ways superfluous – introduction to him. This text also tells how the Gileadite notable had been provisioning David during his entire time at Mahanaim. If the other account uses imagery reminiscent of the Exodus tradition ("the people were hungry, weary, and thirsty in the desert"), it must have something to do with the prominent position that an Ammonite occupies in that passage. Here such imagery is absent. We hear nothing about the people who accompany David. Acting alone, Barzillai focuses his attention solely on the king.

To reward his generosity, David offers to "provide" for him at his court, just as Barzillai "provided" for the king. Barzillai declines the offer, claiming that he, as an octogenarian, couldn't enjoy the fine food and music of the palace. He agrees to accompany David over the Jordan, but requests that the king take his servant in his stead.[4]

On his deathbed, David instructs Solomon:

> Show favor to the sons of Barzillai the Gileadite and let them be among those who eat at thy table; for so they came to me when I fled from Absalom thy brother. (1 Kings 2:7)

Here again we see how the biblical narratives use memories of exemplary deeds to negotiate status, honor, and belonging.[5]

The disproportionate amount of space devoted to Barzillai in the David traditions was likely occasioned by political controversies in the post-exilic period. Although not noticed by most biblical scholars, the descendants of "Barzillai the Gileadite" make an appearance in the Book of Ezra–Nehemiah. Various population groups, some of whom relocated to the Transjordan, could not prove "that they belonged to Israel." In addition, several of the priests are reported to have "married the female descendants of Barzillai the Gileadite and were called by [i.e., registered under] his name." After searching unsuccessfully for their names in the genealogical records, they were forbidden to eat the holy food of the priests and "were excluded from the priesthood as 'unclean'" (see Ezra 2:61–63).[6] The name of Barzillai the Gileadite, in other words, discredits Judahite priests (and perhaps other persons) who bear it.

This unusually suggestive text from a post-exilic biblical book reveals one context in which to situate the formation of biblical passages, such as the account of Barzillai. Many in the post-exilic period would have dissented from the exclusivist, Judah-centric approach to the boundaries of Israel, which is promoted by these texts from Ezra–Nehemiah. By constructing and transmitting alternative memories, influential families and clans could defend their place in Jerusalemite society. Thus, Barzillai's family, or the priests who had married into it, could claim that their ancestor came to David's aid in a time of war and that the king rewarded the solidarity of this "very great man" by commanding Solomon to make a place for his descendants at his table in Jerusalem. For members of Judahite society and history, it would be difficult to imagine a more enviable honor to report about their ancestors.[7]

From Ezra-Nehemiah to Samuel

With the help of these findings, we can now finally address the incongruities noted earlier with regard to Shobi the Ammonite. The Nehemiah Memoir is a first-person report transmitted in the Book of Ezra–Nehemiah. It refers to an incident with an important Ammonite official named Tobiah, who possessed a pied-à-terre in Jerusalem's Temple precincts. Appalled by the close relations between Jerusalem's priests and this figure, Nehemiah orders the expulsion of Tobiah's property and thereby denies this influential figure a place in Judahite politics (Neh 13:4–9; see also 6:17–19).[8]

The book's authors justify Nehemiah's actions by appealing to the Torah. In the preface to Nehemiah's report, they tell how the community discovered the law in Deuteronomy that denies membership to Ammonites and Moabites because they failed to meet the Israelites in the wilderness with bread and water. By pointing to such pentateuchal memories, circles in the post-exilic period claim historical and legal precedent for decisions about membership within Judah.

The authors of the Shobi account provided readers with a historical precedent to defend a more inclusive policy than what is found in the Torah. As a representative of the Ammonites, Shobi brings David's people in the wilderness not just bread and water but also a wide assortment of fine viands. By appealing to competing memories – ones related to the greatest figure in Judah's history during his wartime trials and tribulations – readers could circumvent the canonical pentateuchal traditions.

The figure of David generated in the Persian and Hellenistic periods many new legends, as we can see in Chronicles, Psalms,

Ruth, and the widely diverging versions of the Book of Samuel in the Septuagint and the Qumran manuscripts. The reason for this flourishing of activity around David's name is obvious: He is *the* most renowned figure in Judahite collective memory. (Similarly, lore about ancient Near Eastern heroes – such as Gilgamesh, Naram-Sin, and Sargon I – evolved for centuries, if not millennia, after their deaths.)

The David traditions in the Book of Samuel are packed with such diverse material because they, more than the Pentateuch, served as the context in which various circles could address issues specific to Judah (as opposed to the people of Israel more generally). It stands to reason, then, that the Judah-centric Book of Ezra–Nehemiah would have given rise to supplements in the Book of Samuel.

Judah vis-à-vis Israel

Within the Succession Narrative, the lines of division initially do not run between Israel and Judah. Absalom wins the heart of "Israel," which appears to include the population of Judah as well. He is made king in Hebron, the erstwhile capital of the Judahite kingdom, before finally assuming the throne in Jerusalem. David's supporters are called his "people" (sometimes with the meaning "army") rather than "Judah." Although this story is clearly told from a Judahite perspective, we do not hear the name Judah until Absalom is dead and David prepares for his return to Jerusalem (2 Sam 19:10–15, 42–44).

That the authors introduce tensions between Israel and Judah into the story at the very end of the Absalom account must be related to the immediately following episode, which describes how Israel, with the help of Sheba ben Bichri, secedes from David's rule, leaving Judah "cleaving to their king" (2 Sam 20).

As for this second insurrection, one can still see how the text originally had nothing to do with the Absalom story. The statements about David's homecoming and his treatment of his ten concubines (20:3–4) are easy to isolate as a portion of the Absalom narrative that has been inserted into this account.[9]

Weaving the originally separate accounts of Absalom's and Sheba's rebellions into a continuous narrative, the redactors depicted growing tensions between Israel and Judah during David's journey back to Jerusalem. In this way, they constructed a new context for understanding Israel's secession under Sheba.

According to the older narrative, Israel breaks away from David and Judah. Sheba motivates Israel with the same dissident rhetoric Jeroboam later uses at the pivotal schism that, in the Book of Kings, cleaves Israel and Judah into two competing states: "We have no share in David, and no inheritance in the son of Jesse. To your tents, O Israel!"

In a farcical squabble over the honor of bringing David across the Jordan, Israel responds to Judah's claim that David is their "relative" (*qārôb*) by protesting that they possess a greater claim to him: "We have ten parts in the king." (The authors responsible for the reworking of the Absalom account interpret the imagery of "share/portion/parts" literally.) Yet Judah ultimately prevails over Israel in this dispute. Immediately thereafter Sheba delivers his speech, inciting Israel to break away from David.

As is obvious from this survey, the story of Judah's and Israel's tussle over the privilege to escort David back to Jerusalem is only partially suited as a prelude to the older Sheba account. At one moment, the people of Israel wish to be close to David, and then suddenly they express their complete disaffiliation from him. This transition remains abrupt, despite the adept work of the later editors to smooth it over.

Supplements to the Absalom story ascribe culpability to David for the bad blood that fuels the insurrection. Whereas the Sheba account makes a Benjaminite opponent responsible for Israel's secession, the secondary preface depicts David, newly reinstated as king, inciting a rivalry between Israel and Judah.

After Absalom's death, Israel rediscovers its allegiance to David and decides to bring him back (2 Sam 19:9–44). The exiled leader should be elated by Israel's restored favor. But he is not. When he learns of Israel's plans, he orders his allied priests Zadok and Abiathar to persuade Judah to take the initiative to escort him to Jerusalem. He also appoints Amasa to the position of general in the place of Joab, and Amasa then is said to have "swayed the hearts of all the people of Judah as one" so that they act in David's interest (2 Sam 19:12–15). By robbing Israel of this honor, Judah rekindles an antagonism that results in Sheba's insurrection. And ultimately it is all David's fault.[10]

Compositional Considerations

According to the Book of Samuel, David bears the blame for Israel's secession from Judah, just as he, at an earlier point in his career, creates a kingdom in Judah by ripping southern territories away from the unified kingdom that Saul established. All Israel may love David (1 Sam 18:16), but his actions tear the nation asunder.

As we shall see in the next chapter, Chronicles differs drastically from Samuel by presenting David as a catalyst of unity. This contrast in portrait corresponds to the book's very different agendas: Whereas Chronicles seeks to present "greater Israel" rallying around a ruler who directs the attention of the people to the centrality of Jerusalem and its temple, Samuel portrays the benefits and costs of centralized statehood for the people of Israel.

In Chapter 3 I argued that the accounts of Saul and David must have been originally separate histories – the one with the Benjaminite Saul as king of Israel (HSR) and the other with David as king of Judah (HDR). As later authors began to address the relationship of Judah to Israel, they synthesized – and amplified – these two independent histories, presenting David as the successor to throne of Israel that Saul established. In the narratives created by this group of authors, Saul represents Israel (or in some places just Benjamin), while David represents the kingdom of Judah. What drives the composition history at this stage is the conflict between Israel and Judah. The same point of contention lies at the heart of the Book of Kings, which describe the incessant conflict between these two states.

With the inclusion of other material, the final form of the Book of Samuel moves beyond the relationship of Israel and

Judah to address questions of a broader political-philosophical nature: One of these larger questions concerns the tension caused by centralized statehood for the people of Israel.

A growing scholarly consensus recognizes that originally Samuel–Kings formed a *Monarchic History*. This work presents David's royal line as the divinely chosen, eternal dynasty, which Israel had wrongly deserted. It imagines an original unity between Israel and Judah that was severed in a catastrophic "original sin." A different history is found in Genesis–Joshua. The core of this *People's History* emerged in Israel (both before and after 722 BCE), while most of the Monarchic History is a Judahite product.

The People's History goes further than the Monarchic History, positing not a *political* unity between two states but a *national* unity of the people of Israel. By joining the two histories to form the "Enneateuch" (or "Primary History"), later authors relativized the monarchy to a late chapter in Israel's long national history.[11]

Judah as Part of Israel

In this final section of the chapter, I turn to a historical question: How did Judah come to see itself as belonging to the people of Israel?

The responses to this question are wide-ranging. On one side of the spectrum, there are those who begin on the premise that the inhabitants of the kingdoms of Israel and Judah saw themselves as one people already at an early point in their history. Some would even claim that the inhabitants of Israel and Judah share common ethnic origins that predate "the emergence of the monarchy" and continued to figure prominently in the consciousness of the population for centuries thereafter. Such assumptions fail, however, to distinguish between biblical Israel and historical Israel. The two are not the same.

On the other end of the spectrum are those who search for the origins of the "pan-Israelite ideology" in the post-exilic period among powerful groups who were concerned to expand

and defend their land claims. While biblical texts were likely used for this purpose from an early point, the evidence suggests a much more complex development. A similar approach identifies the courts of Judah's leading kings as the architects of the pan-Israelite ideology. In viewing this identity as a whole-cloth invention, both approaches fail to do justice to the diversity of the evidence.

My own approach to the origins of the pan-Israelite identity, and of the demotic purview that so thoroughly animates biblical writings, emphasizes the experience of *defeat* and the responses to it. Nevertheless, I would also draw attention to a range of antecedents, which may be aligned into several historical phases.

We must begin with the natural conditions in the Samarian and Judahite highlands. By this I mean the common climate and physical features of the central hill country, which demarcate it from the Shephelah and coastal plain to the west, the Jezreel Valley in the north, the Jordan Valley to the east, and the Negev to the south. As expected, the populations of the highlands developed similar material cultures and survival strategies. Because the physical border in the hill country between north and south is not pronounced, the populations were not sharply segregated. Hence, language, culture, marriage pools, and cultic practices were subject to a high degree of exchange.[12]

At this early stage, a pan-Israelite identity had yet to emerge. In the late thirteenth century, the Egyptian ruler Merenptah claims to have annihilated a people called "Israel." (Whatever he may have achieved, history belies his exaggeration.) We don't know where this population was located. The designation "Israel" most likely did not refer to all the inhabitants of the highlands, in both the north and the south.

It would therefore be naïve to assume that, centuries later, a charismatic personality, such as Saul, could easily form a large all-embracing kingdom by appealing to a common "national" identity. Such theories are informed less by the Bible than by the influence of European nationalist ideologies of "one people, one land, one state."

The historical data leave no room for doubt that the kingdoms that formed in the north were more powerful than that of Judah in the south. The rulers of Samaria gradually expanded into the Jezreel Valley, then into Galilee and the Transjordan, and finally began to exert direct influence over Judah. The formative phases of this expansion were the work of Ahab and the Omride dynasty as well as Jehu and the Nimshide dynasty.

With the expansion, Israel's monarchs inevitably faced resistance from subjugated populations. In response, circles at the court asserted a larger unifying identity under the name "Israel" and perhaps under the sovereignty of one deity – YHWH. Here we may situate the first appreciable impulse for an "Israelite" national identity.

The Mesha Stele furnishes us with an invaluable illustration of this strategy of social-political consolidation. Mesha, a ninth-century Moabite king, ruled a heterogenous population. To unify the rival groups, he appeals to their identity as the people of "Moab" (a designation that appears at least six times in the inscription) and this people's deity Mesha.

A similar strategy likely stands behind the rise of the name Israel and its deity YHWH. Yet in the case of the Mesha Stele, it is the royal house that directly promulgates the Moabite "national" identity. In contrast, biblical literature radically demotes the role of the king. To account for this distinctive feature of biblical writings, we must therefore consider other developments.[13]

The fact that Samaria succeeded in exerting a sustained influence on the political life and culture of not only territories in the Transjordan but also its southern neighbor – much more than on Moab, Ammon, or Edom – goes a long way toward explaining why it is Judah that later inherited Israel's cultural and literary heritage. The many years of Samaria's hegemony over Jerusalem inevitably predisposed the Judahites to thinking of themselves as closely affiliated to Israel. As to be expected, Judahite elites embraced and cribbed Israel's culture as a way of currying favor with the court. (Anthropologists study this phenomenon under the rubrics of "mimesis" and "cultural appropriation.")

Yet while some Judahites would have been eager to adopt northern ideologies and cultic practices, others would have sharply rejected these influences in the process of creating and maintaining a distinct Judean identity. Within the prophetic literary tradition, we see a great number of Judahite texts that censure Samaria (or "Ephraim," "Israel," etc.) and prophesy doom against it. In many cases, these texts belong to the oldest strata of their respective books.

The next formative phase is *the period from the defeat of Samaria (722* BCE*) to the defeat of Jerusalem (586* BCE*)*, what has been called "the long seventh century." After Assyrian armies had destroyed Samaria, various circles preserved the literary monuments created under official state patronage (e.g., legends of patriarchs and heroes, cultic songs and poetry, as well as prophetic writings). Because writings in antiquity were valuable, they were rescued from the flames and safeguarded. Eventually they were copied and expanded with new layers of interpretation, as their readers sought to come to terms with the catastrophic collapse of the state. The histories they produced shifted attention from their kings and states to the *people* of Israel.[14]

Meanwhile, in Judah, few would have mourned the fate of their northern neighbor. Long years of conflict with Israel would have elicited a sense of gleeful vindication, as Judah strove to assume the position of its erstwhile competitor. Now Judahites and especially Judahite rulers had greater reason to embrace the Israelite identity that Samaria's kings had propagated. The political and cultural hegemony that Samaria had exerted over Jerusalem paved the way for the latter to become the primary heir to Israel's illustrious heritage.

The reason the Bible has so little to say about the Galilee in contrast to Judah is that the former was annexed to other states at an early point, while Judah maintained a degree of autonomy and survived for another 135 years after Israel's conquest.

During the years leading up to the Babylonian assault, circles in Judah appropriated Israel's literary legacy and radically revised it. To affirm continuities from their own time to the earliest origins of Israel, they reworked a number of texts and positioned Judah in a place of prominence among all the other tribes.[15]

In the process of centralization, the Judahite state undertook ambitious construction projects and developed an ideology that emphasized the sacred singularity of Jerusalem. The Assyrians gave a push to this centralization by cutting off the southern Shephelah from Judah in the reign of Hezekiah and reducing Jerusalem to little more than a city-state. In time, Judahite centralization became linked closely to the discourse of Israelite peoplehood: one nation, one god, one dynasty, one temple.

At this time, priests at the Jerusalem Temple declared the YHWHs in Samaria, Jerusalem, and elsewhere to be one and the same deity. Presupposing this theological development, authors of the Monarchic History declared David's royal line to be the divinely chosen, eternal dynasty from which the house of Israel had broken away.

Following Hezekiah's reign (c. 715–686 BCE), Judah's hopes repeatedly rose to great heights only to plummet again. While many insisted on resistance and believed that they could successfully repel imperial encroachment, others were much less sanguine. The increasing anticipation of cataclysmic defeat appears to have bolstered reflection on Judah's special relationship to not only YHWH but also to Israel as the people of YHWH.

The evidence of the prophetic writings lends support to this supposition. These writings reflect a growing consciousness of a collective identity, one that is shaped by a common experience of judgment at the hands of "YHWH, the God of Israel." The older prophecies of doom against Israel were now reinterpreted to include Judah.

The final, and by far most formative, phase is *the time after Judah's defeat* (586 BCE). It was in this context that Israel's discourse on peoplehood began to resonate with wider audiences. Modest kernels of texts now blossomed into the massive bodies of literature that are preserved in the Hebrew Bible.

For much of this period, an Israelite national consciousness was surprisingly weak. Various clues – from the Nehemiah Memoir and Aramaic sources in Ezra to epigraphic evidence on the ground – reveal that average inhabitants of Judah rarely thought of themselves as the people of Israel. This fact agrees with the testimony of diaspora communities in Achaemenid Egypt and Babylon, who identified themselves solely as descendants of the former state (and later province) of Judah and did not even use the name Israel in relation to their homeland. If Israel survived in the first centuries after the exile, it was above all in the literary legacy that was preserved, amplified, and passed on to new generations.[16]

So in seeking to account for the way Judah came to regard itself as part of Israel, I would point to this project of peoplehood among some circles who sought to find a common identity uniting first the territories of Israel, and then later the states of Israel and Judah. Although Judahites significantly shaped this discourse on peoplehood, they did not invent it. Rather it emerged in the kingdom of Israel and after its destruction. If Samaria had not exerted influence over Judah for many years, and if Judah had not been interested in the "Israelite" traditions after 722 BCE, the name Israel, and the discourse on peoplehood that grew up around it, would likely have been completely lost or preserved solely among the Samaritans.[17]

Conclusions

Since first being propagated as part of a state strategy to consolidate and confer a common identity on its subjects, the name Israel had been closely associated with a large and heterogenous collectivity. As such, the designation naturally lent itself to images of an expansive and flourishing people ("all Israel"), as communities from the Diaspora returned to their homeland. The name became widely used in prophetic writings to express the hope of national restoration from all corners of the earth.

As Judah, Samaria, and other communities began to thrive again in the late Persian and Hellenistic periods, issues of "belonging" were hotly debated – not only on the ground but also in the prophetic writing and some of the texts we have examined in this book. (Of course, many of the other texts we have treated in these chapters emerged before the exile, as part of the political battles of belonging that were waged in the society of the Judahite state.)

According to the political theorist John Hutchinson, nations may be viewed as "zones of conflict." Without major areas and issues of contestation, the question of national identity is of little concern.[18] In the post-exilic period, we can witness a lively debate over questions of belonging with respect to not only smaller clans and individuals but also larger groups and regions, such as the Transjordan and the Samaritans.

Some circles in Judah refused to think in latitudinarian terms. For example, the Book of Ezra–Nehemiah must have assumed final shape at roughly the same time as the Book of Chronicles, the subject of the following chapter. But whereas Chronicles is pan-Israelite in its purview and identifies communities far in the north and in the Transjordan as legitimate members of the people of Israel, Ezra–Nehemiah confines the name Israel to the populations of Judah (and Benjamin).

Such political disputes reinvigorated interest in the name of Israel. These disputes were conducted often in the commemoration of (real and fictive) battles and wars, as we have seen in the account of David's contest with Absalom.

10

Chronicles

David as a Catalyst of National Unity

Chronicles presents a very different account of David's life from what we have seen so far in the books of Samuel and Kings. For example, it does not include the tales of his conflicts with Saul. We are told about neither his affair with Bathsheba nor his civil wars, first with Absalom and then with Sheba ben Bichri. By omitting these and many other inglorious episodes, the authors of this revisionist history not only presented a much more innocent image of David; they also eliminated the texts that negotiate belonging in Judah and Israel via war commemoration. As a result, most of the accounts studied in the preceding chapters are not found in this work. Yet its authors still engage in war commemoration, even if the way they do so differs substantially from what we have seen so far in Samuel and Kings. This chapter is a consequential one, as it builds upon and integrates all the findings up to this point.

David and All Israel

In what follows I undertake a literary probe, focusing on just two chapters: 1 Chronicles 11–12. A short paragraph, depicting joyful feasting, demarcates this section from the surrounding narrative (see 12:39–41). The section as a whole appears to have grown up gradually around the theme of "assistance" or "support" for David.

The authors of the book's principal narrative were keen to erase all memories of a gradual transition between the reigns of David and Saul. Their revisionist history begins with the nation assembling to install David as *king of Israel*. This happens at one time – after Saul's death. Even so, various groups do gradually defect to David already before Saul's death.

Although creating a tension within the narrative, the authors of these passages aimed to correct the historical record. They achieved this goal by a radical reversal: Where the Book of Samuel depicts groups betraying David to Saul, Chronicles reports that groups deserted Saul's ranks to join forces with David.

The transmitted shape of Samuel presents David creating the kingdom of Judah by severing it from the kingdom of Israel. Throughout the remainder of the book, Judah and Israel are repeatedly at war with each other. Whereas Saul unifies Israel, David brings division and conflict to the nation. In stark contrast to this history, Chronicles begins with the death of the unworthy Saul, setting the stage for David as the ruler who unifies "all Israel" and emerges as their beloved monarch.

The memory of David's rise to power – dividing the nation by creating a kingdom that competes (militarily) with Israel – was a cause of great embarrassment for the authors of Chronicles. When constructing a counterhistory, they dealt with this difficulty by excising the prehistory. Likewise, they conspicuously ignored all the accounts of the tumult accompanying Saul's death and David's accession, as well as the material related to the secession of Israel and civil wars during the time of Absalom and Sheba ben Bichri. In this way, they radically transformed the image of David into a magnetic figure who unifies Israel.

In Chapter 3, we saw how the authors of Samuel depict "David and his men" going up to capture Jerusalem, while the corresponding passage in Chronicles has "David and all Israel" undertaking this feat. This is a parade example of the pan-Israelite perspective that pervades Chronicles.[1]

What immediately follows the account of Jerusalem's conquest are rosters of David's warriors, which appear as appendices in the Book of Samuel. "These are the heads of David's warriors who strongly supported him in his kingdom, together with all Israel, to make him king, according to the word of YHWH to Israel" (1 Chr 11:10). This heading, absent from Samuel, reveals how the authors of Chronicles intend for their readers to interpret the rosters – namely, as evidence of the wide support and assistance that David enjoyed.

One roster names the warriors who "came to David during his time at Ziklag, while he could not move about freely because of Saul ben Kish; they were mighty warriors who helped him in war" (1 Chr 12:1). The verb *'azar* "help," along with synonymous terms, forms a leitmotif that unifies this section. The point is: David received liberal assistance from the entire nation of Israel. (The lexeme *'azar* appears also in many of the personal names.)

Notice the reference to Ziklag in the line quoted in the preceding paragraph. Insofar as the warriors come to David while he is still residing at the town that the Philistine ruler Achish assigned him, they join him before Saul's death. In other words, they enlist in David's army not because they have to, but because they choose to. By abandoning Saul's army to join David, they undertake significant risks.

The ambidextrous fighters are identified as "Saul's kin from Benjamin." Accordingly, they abandon not only their own army, but even their own flesh and blood. In Greek political language, their solidarity with the new *polis* (David's kingdom) transcends ancient affiliations with their ancestral *oikoi* (their Benjaminite clans).[2]

Tribal Corps

The second group that joins David consists of Gadites from the Transjordan. One wonders why are they included here together with the kin of Saul. The reason likely has to do with the close affiliation between Saul and the Transjordan. By recording a substantial Transjordanian presence in David's army, the authors took a decisive side in the contentious issues surrounding the "Israelite" populations of those regions.

As we saw in foregoing chapters, the Book of Samuel presents Saul becoming king by rescuing the representative city of Jabesh-gilead, which remains long beholden to him. Yet according to Chronicles, troops from Gad "separated themselves [to go over] to David at the stronghold in the wilderness." This passage commemorates the Transjordanians' allegiance to David by reporting that their most formidable warriors defected, once again, while Saul was alive.

The authors wax poetic in their tribute of the Gadites, describing them "as fierce as lions and as agile as gazelles." Able to cross the Jordan even during flood season, "the least of them was equal to a hundred men, while the greatest was equal to a thousand." The exceptionally favorable description of the Transjordanian warriors counters reservations among some groups in Judah regarding the identity and status of Transjordanian communities.[3]

As we witnessed in Chapter 5, the retelling of Saul's death in Chronicles devalues the heroism of Jabesh-gilead, a prominent Transjordanian city. Yet when read against the backdrop of the Gadites' defection to David here, the account of Jabesh-gilead's mission to recover the bones of Saul must be interpreted as referring solely to that city, and not to the region it represents. Other than the inhabitants of Jabesh-gilead, the tribe of Gad boasted, according to this passage, many valiant warriors who eagerly seceded to the side of David.

Surprisingly, this text presents Benjaminites and Judahites – the core of the post-exilic community that produced the Bible – much more ambivalently. When they approach the fortress, David goes out to confront them:

> If you have come to me in peace, to offer aid to me, then my heart will be knit to yours. But if you have come to betray me to my adversaries, though my hands have done no violence, then may the God of our ancestors see and recompense. (1 Chr 12:18)

The warning provokes the leader of the corps, a figure named Amasai, to affirm the tribes' fidelity with greater force. "Clothed in the spirit," he declares,

> We are yours, O David,
> And with you, O son of Jesse!
> Peace, peace to you,
> And peace to those who aid
> and abet you!
> For your God assists you.
> (1 Chr 12:19)

This unequivocal expression of allegiance underscores the nexus between assistance and reward. Their offer of aid engenders deep solidarity, a union of hearts (*yihyeh-lî ʿalêkem lēbāb leyāḥad*). The terminology here and elsewhere in the account is political, referring to the formation of an alliance. Only after they make this formal declaration does David receive the Benjaminite and Judahite soldiers, and make them officers of his troops.[4]

The Book of Samuel depicts several instances of Judahite groups betraying David to Saul. But we would expect the same warning to be issued to Saul's kin (1 Chr 12:1–8), who would have more reason to betray David than his own Judahite kindred. How should we explain the incongruity?

I suggest that this odd account relativizes the pride of place enjoyed by Judah and Benjamin.[5] To be accepted, to be called David's kin, the representatives of the tribes that constitute much of post-exilic Judah had first to voice their willingness to "assist and abet" in the same way as all the other tribes of Israel. In other words, belonging and status are determined by the principle of equality and allegiance, not personal propinquity.

The next paragraph depicts members of the tribe of Manasseh defecting to David (1 Chr 12:20–22). It identifies all as military commanders. Manasseh, along with Ephraim, often represents in Chronicles the northern tribes. As in the case of Saul's elite warriors mentioned earlier in this section, the men of Manasseh go over to David's side while Saul is still alive.

The occasion to which the authors date the Manassehite defection is noteworthy: "when [David] came with the Philistines to make war against Saul." What the authors have in mind here is the depiction of David serving with his men in the Philistine ranks on the eve of Saul's death:

> Now the Philistines mustered all their forces at Aphek, while the Israelites were encamped by the fountain that is in Jezreel. The Philistine lords were lining up in formations of hundreds and by thousands, and David and his men marched in the rear with Achish. (1 Sam 29:1–2 [see 28:1–2])

The narrator goes on to report that the Philistines prohibited David and his men from taking part in their campaign out of fear that David would reconcile himself with Saul and become an adversary to the Philistines in the midst of battle.

The entire account constitutes, as suggested in Chapter 3, a late narrative construct that harmonizes the independent Saul and David accounts (the HSR and HDR). If the Philistines slay Saul, and if David serves as a Philistine mercenary, readers might wonder whether David had a hand in Saul's death. To obviate this inference, the authors of Samuel composed an account in which the Philistines send David home just as their forces assemble to establish their battle order at Aphek.

It is precisely here that the authors of Chronicles supplement the historical record that they inherited. According to their "new and improved" account, prominent military commanders from Manasseh join David and his men *before* they are sent home. In this way, Chronicles can portray the tribe of Manasseh as ready and willing to fight against Saul. Although the tribe's commanders did not see any action during the Philistine campaign, they are able to "assist" David later when he fights against "the raiders" (i.e., the Amalekites who plunder the town of Ziklag).[6]

A National Army

The authors of Chronicles corrected not only the extent of support David boasted but also – and what is more important – the constitution of Israel's fighting forces. In Samuel, David commands a private army. The soldiers, many of whom are not even

Israelite, are called "David's men/servants." Chronicles transforms this mercenary band into a national army.

After Chronicles describes all the Israelites who defected to David, the reader must revise the meaning of "David and his men." They are no longer a small retinue of soldiers of fortune who fight in David's ranks. Rather, they constitute a representative selection of Israel's tribes, whose finest fighters and commanders come from far and wide to volunteer for service.

Just as Chronicles transforms a band of mercenaries into a "people-in-arms," it radically alters the size of David's army. According to the Book of Samuel, David's private force ranged from four to six hundred men. Conversely, Chronicles reports,

> From day to day troops kept coming to the aid of David until there was a vast war camp, like the camp of God. (1 Chr 12:23)

The following paragraph adds substance to this claim by providing numbers for each of the tribal contingents that joined David at Hebron after Saul's death. The register begins with Judah and continues with the other eleven of Israel's phratries.

Even the Levites are included among these armed troops. They are otherwise exempted from military assignments so that they can perform cultic duties. Their participation here reveals the extent to which these chapters negotiate belonging in Israel via memories of wartime contributions. In addition, they identify the eponymous ancestor of the Zadokite priests as a young *warrior* who conveys officers from his own house.

Although Judah appears first, the more remote regions or tribes contribute greater numbers. Zebulon contributes 50,000 seasoned troops, and the contested Transjordanian tribes dispatch 120,000, the largest number of all. The grand total for the tribes of Judah, Simeon, Levi, and Benjamin do not even match the single contribution of Dan, located on the northernmost border. The more remote the tribe, the larger its delegation. Ralph Klein describes the principle well:

> All the tribes supported [David], and the tribes that were most distant, were far and away the most supportive. The tribes of Judah, Benjamin,

and Levi at the time of the Chronicler needed no special justification to be part of Israel, nor did the small community of Yehud exhaust what might be meant by "Israel." The Chronicler gives significant importance to the tribes other than Judah and expresses thereby a broader hope for what Israel might become.[7]

The authors thus set forth a vision of "greater Israel" by highlighting the contributions of the tribes farthest away from the divinely chosen center of Israel's world. Inspired by memories of the past, they reimagine an Israel that includes a much more diverse population than solely the people of Judah (and Benjamin).

From Deborah to David

The culmination of the section reports that everyone – including the three northernmost tribes of Issachar, Zebulun, and Naphtali – brought "food on donkeys, camels, mules, and oxen, as well as abundant comestibles of meal, cakes of figs, clusters of raisins, wine, oil, oxen, and sheep." Although the occasion is David's coronation, all these men are rallying to David arrayed in battle order.

The fine viands they convey are a type of wartime contribution, corresponding to the conventional duty of alliance partners and vassals to provision a campaigning army. By means of these provisions, civilians or a people without an army can contribute to a military campaign and demonstrate their allegiance.[8] The wider civilian population is indeed the focus of this concluding paragraph, which reports that "all the rest of Israel" (not just the warriors) came to Hebron and "were of one mind to make David king."

Interspersed throughout this chapter are comments that underscore the participants' purpose: "they were registered by name to come to establish David as king" or "they were equipped for battle to assist [or: "to take formation"] with a singleness of purpose."

The authors not only draw attention to the intentionality. They also assign unique features to each of the tribes. For example, the two hundred chiefs of Issachar who come with "all their kin under their command" are said to "understand the times to know what Israel ought to do."

These features bring to mind the Song of Deborah from the Book of Judges, and specifically its "catalogue of tribes." While praising "the people who offer themselves willingly" for the campaign against the Canaanites, the song rebukes a number of the tribes for dodging their national duty to furnish troops and to contribute to Deborah's war effort.

> From Ephraim came they whose roots are in Amalek;
> After you, your kin Benjamin;
> From Machir came down leaders,
> From Zebulun such as hold the marshal's staff.
> And Issachar's chiefs were with Deborah;
> As Barak, so was Issachar
> Rushing after him into the valley.
> Among the clans of Reuben
> Were great decisions of heart.
> Why then did you stay among the sheepfolds?
> And listen as they pipe for the flocks?
> Among the clans of Reuben
> Were great searchings of heart!
> Gilead tarried beyond the Jordan;
> And Dan – why did he linger by the ships?
> Asher remained at the seacoast
> And tarried at his landings.
> Zebulun is a people that mocked at death,
> Naphtali – on the open heights.
>
> (Judg 5:14–18)

The song resembles Homer's "Catalogue of Ships" and a number of other (literary) monuments from the Aegean world that commemorate the wartime sacrifices and contributions of cities, tribes, regions, and classes. Both biblical and extrabiblical texts demonstrate that war commemoration is a natural context for interpreting the type of historiography displayed in these passages from Chronicles.[9]

We can observe both conspicuous similarities and differences between our texts: Deborah's song and our tribal register refer to characteristic features of the tribes. Whereas the song only refers to ten tribes and chides several for shirking their duties, Chronicles presents all of Israel's twelve tribes proving their solidarity by supplying military officers and valiant troops.

In the song, the tribes from the northern periphery and the Transjordan are those most reproached. This is much different from Chronicles. As I noted, the more remote the tribe is from David, the more it contributes.

The song pronounces a curse on those who failed to "come to the help of YHWH" (*'ezrat yhwh*). Likewise, the term "help" (or synonyms thereof) appears as leitmotif throughout the descriptions of the tribes that assist David.

In the song, the tribes send their troops to the battle under the aegis of "a mother in Israel" and Israel's God. No (human) king leads these armies. Yet the enemies they fight are the kings of Canaan. Chronicles, however, depicts the tribes coming together not to wage battle but to make David their king (see especially 1 Chr 12:39).

A Nation in Arms

So if tribal corps in Chronicles are not mobilizing for battle, why do they appear in Hebron "arrayed in battle order" and armed with all their weapons? The reason is that the authors conceive the national unity that David elicits as a unified people-in-arms, similar to what we witness in the Pentateuch and in the Book of Joshua. Gary Knoppers, a celebrated Chronicles commentator, draws attention to this point: "Inasmuch as the roster of tribal detachments also resembles the census lists in Numbers, its presence here marks the unity of Israel at a new moment in its history like the inaugural moment at Sinai."[10]

The participation in David's coronation is voluntary military service. Throughout the "Enneateuch" or "Primary History" (Genesis–Kings), war efforts are the means by which the members of Israel participate in public life and demonstrate their national belonging. To demonstrate solidarity, communities are expected to offer each other succor and to fight collectively against common enemies.

In keeping with this ideal of nationhood, the narrative in Genesis–Kings depicts a gradual transition. It begins with a unified people who conquer the land (Joshua) and offer military assistance to neighboring tribes (the Song of Deborah and the rest of Judges). This society is slowly replaced by a centralized state with a monarch who conscripts his subjects (or pays others) to fight *his* wars (Samuel–Kings).

For much of this wide-ranging account of history, the collective nation is at the center of attention, living a robust life of its own. It and its God play the primary roles. By the end of the narrative, though, the people have been smothered out of existence. All that remains is the king and the elites surrounding him.

The final chapter of Kings depicts a resounding defeat of Judahite state, in all facets of its existence: the execution of Zedekiah's sons; the deportation of this ruler together with the royal family and administrative elite; the destruction of the Temple, palace, and the surrounding city; and the despoliation of Jerusalem's wealth. These themes express the book's overriding interest in narrating both the rise and demise of the states of Israel and Judah.

The conclusion has astonishingly little to say about the nation as a whole. The Babylonians deport professional soldiers, weapons manufacturers, and royal officials, leaving only some of the peasants to till the soil. The narrator concludes, "and thus Judah was exiled from its land." The cursory statement takes us by surprise after so much of the narrative treated the nation and its God as the primary protagonists (2 Kings 24:14–16, 25:11–12).[11]

For the biblical writers, a strong centralized kingdom undeniably has many advantages. Yet it also constitutes a grave danger inasmuch as it threatens to eclipse the nation. The advantages of statehood are illustrated by the way in which David and Solomon bring tranquility and welfare to the people from the enemies who encompass them. Conversely, the dangers of statehood are illustrated by the way in which a "people's army" or a force of "citizen-soldiers," who fight voluntarily for their country, clans, and national deity, is gradually superseded by a professional army consisting of impressed subjects and foreign mercenaries. In the end, the kingdoms of Israel and Judah are destroyed, and little remains of this greater people of Israel.

Within the narrative of Genesis–Kings, the Book of Samuel marks a transition. What was once a nation without a centralized state is now a centralized state with a severely enervated nation.

The pivot point in this development is the reign of David. Whereas Saul mobilizes the nation in a manner similar to Joshua and the Judges, with farmers going to war to defend collective national interests, David prefers to make use of his own servants and private troops. By the end of his life, as we have seen for both Absalom and Sheba ben Bichri, the troops are fighting solely for David and slaughtering many members of the nation.

The authors of Chronicles radically revise this older history. They present David not as a ruler with a private army, but rather as a catalyst of national unity – as one whom all Israel is eager to assist. In this book, "David does not make Israel; Israel makes David."[12]

From Battles to Building

The first projects for which the David of Chronicles mobilizes the nation are not military campaigns. Instead they have to do with Jerusalem and the Temple. Immediately after assuming the throne, David consults with Israel's commanders about "bringing up the Ark of our God" (1 Chr 13:1–5). This task will occupy the attention of much of the remaining chapters.

The most substantial portion of Chronicles' extra material relates to David's efforts to prepare for the Temple's construction and to organize its cult. To underscore the centrality of Jerusalem, the authors present David occupying and building this city as his very first action. Although they follow the Book of

Samuel in presenting Solomon as the one who actually constructs the Temple, they identify David as the one who undertakes all the necessary preparations and who commands all the leaders of Israel to "help" his son in building the Temple just as they "helped" him (see 1 Chr 22:17–19). To borrow a metaphor used by Julius Wellhausen, David makes the dough and kneads it, so that his son just has to shove the loaf into the oven.

When recounting the nation's history, the authors of Chronicles take particular delight in telling how several of Judah's rulers mobilized the nation around the Temple cult and construction projects in Jerusalem. While confining themselves to the most salient details of the Babylonian destruction, they conclude with the Persian ruler Cyrus declaring his divine commission to build YHWH's house in Jerusalem.

Ezra–Nehemiah as a book has many features in common with Chronicles and was likely composed at the same time. In telling the history of the post-exilic period, it replaces war efforts with *construction projects* in Jerusalem (the Temple and the municipal wall). One still proves belonging through participation, yet now in building rather than in battles.

Ezra–Nehemiah is much more selective than Chronicles when defining Israel. Whereas Chronicles presents David as a catalyst who unites Israel's remote communities, Ezra–Nehemiah confines Israel to Judah (and in some places includes Benjamin as well). When rebuilding the Temple and Jerusalem's wall, the Judahite protagonists rebuff offers from others to participate in these construction projects.

Despite its more discriminatory attitude, Ezra–Nehemiah pays tribute to the contributions of various groups to Judah's restitution, while accusing others of attempting to thwart their building activities (see especially Ezra 4:1–5 and Neh 2:19–20). In this way, it uses the memory of construction projects in Jerusalem to negotiate belonging and status in a very similar manner to the way the authors of Genesis-Kings use military conflicts.

Ezra–Nehemiah commemorates various groups by name: (1) those who leave Babylon to rebuild the Temple, (2) those who contribute to the building of the wall, (3) those who pledge to support the cult and its personnel, and (4) those who move to Jerusalem and reside there (see the lists in Ezra 2, 8; Neh 3, 7, 10).

The correspondence to wartime contributions is here undeniable. The lists resemble the tribal registers in the Song of Deborah as well as the census in Numbers, which counts those who take part in the wars of conquest. What's more, the people in Ezra–Nehemiah "bless" those who "volunteer themselves" (*hammitnadebîm*) to reside in Jerusalem, just as the Song of Deborah pronounces a blessing on those who "volunteer themselves" to contribute to a war effort.

Here we can observe again how building replaces battles as the sphere of public participation and the performance of peoplehood. The shift marks the beginning of what was to become (and remain until the present) a centerpiece of Jewish communal life: collective building projects and individual philanthropy, with the names of the sponsors and contributors publicly displayed and commemorated (compare Neh 11:2 with Judg 5:2, 9).

Scholarship in the wake of Julius Wellhausen (d. 1918) and his predecessor Wilhelm de Wette (d. 1849) has often viewed Chronicles and Ezra–Nehemiah as evidence that Israel gave up its *political-national* identity and reinvented itself as a *religious* community. This paradigm does not bear the burden of the evidence. Both histories present their protagonists prepared to take part in both fighting and building.

One of the most striking examples illustrating this point is when Nehemiah arms the population of Judah in preparation for the onslaught of their enemies. He recalls how later they continued building with one hand while bearing their weapons in the other hand. The rhetoric of his battle speech incorporates standard themes from biblical war traditions: "Have no fear of them. Remember the Lord, the great and awesome one, and fight for your kin, sons, daughters, wives, and houses" (Neh 4:8).

A similar juxtaposition of building and battles is found in Chronicles. Various themes, which scholars refer to as *topoi*, recur at high points in its account of Judah's history. They include not only solicitude for the Temple and cult but also building military fortifications in Jerusalem and throughout Judah, provisioning troops with weapons, and defeating the nation's enemies in battle.

Even after Israel and Judah had forfeited their political autonomy to imperial powers, the authors of biblical literature are remembering – or constructing memories of – battles, warfare, and territorial sovereignty. This commemoration is the historiographical correlate to the new nonmartial contexts in which individuals could contribute to public life. In both the memories of the past and in the activities of the present (above all, community construction projects), the biblical writers adapted the political potential of war efforts to the conditions of foreign rule.[13]

The New David of Chronicles

A final question remains: Why did the authors of Chronicles, in these and other chapters of the book, so radically alter David's image? Did they wish to make him into a more saintly figure, in line with the image he assumes in the Psalms? Or was it something else?

Most scholars assume that the authors sought to purge David's portrait of its unsavory moments in order to make him a more qualified founder of the Jerusalem Temple cult. This approach, again, takes its point of departure from the writings of de Wette and Wellhausen. Expressing his predilection for heroic individualism and his disdain for the herd instinct of the clergy, Wellhausen wrote,

> See what Chronicles has made out of David! The founder of the kingdom has become the founder of the temple and the public worship, the king and hero at the head of his companions in arms has become the singer and master of ceremonies at the head of a swarm of priests and Levites; his clearly cut figure has become a feeble holy picture, seen through a cloud of incense.[14]

Wellhausen's claim – that the authors sought to transform David into a pious sponsor of Jerusalem's cult – poses a problem:

One has to explain why Chronicles disqualifies him for the role of Temple builder on the grounds that he had shed too much blood (1 Chr 22:8, 28:3).

More recently scholars have assumed a deliberate antipathy for Saul among some circles from the Persian period. While this may be the case, it is more likely that the Saul of Chronicles serves as a literary foil to David. Chronicles tells about David's sin and the punishment in taking a census of Israel. Why, then, does it omit the accounts of David's sin with Bathsheba and the ensuing chaos in David's house, especially since these stories are nicely suited to the book's conception of direct retribution/reward?

The shortcomings of past explanations require us to seek an alternative. As noted, the very first thing David does in Chronicles is to occupy Jerusalem. He subsequently works to establish a centralized cult and to build a temple in the city. By depicting how this figure unifies Israel, and by eliminating the older material that reports how certain towns and clans in Judah betrayed him, the authors show how the entire nation, by virtue of its solidarity with David, contributes to the construction of Jerusalem and to the cult at the Temple.

From this perspective, we can understand how David's radically modified image goes hand-in-glove with Chronicles' pan-Israelite emphases. This work promotes the Jerusalemite Temple as the center of all Israelite communities in the land – not only in the province of Judah but also in the north and in the Transjordan. It portrays communities from beyond Judah's borders uniting around David to support the construction of Jerusalem and make pilgrimages to the Temple.

Chronicles presents Judah's greatest monarch as a magnet who attracted the broadest possible national "support/assistance." By deleting the accounts of David's wars with Saul, Absalom, and Sheba, its authors transformed this complex figure into a catalyst of national unity, with all Israel joining him to make Jerusalem and its Temple the center of Israel. As we have seen, Absalom's and Sheba's *coups d'état* are presented by the authors of Samuel as the direct retribution for David's sin with Bathsheba. The authors of Chronicles rightly understood that they could not expurgate the former accounts without the latter.

So the desire to make David into a more saintly figure was not what motivated the authors of Chronicles to delete these accounts. What prompted their revisionist history was an interest in showing how the Temple, and Jerusalem as a whole, benefit from the support of very remote communities. The authors depict an expansive and diverse people ("Greater Israel"). At the instigation of great leaders who follow in David's footsteps (such as Solomon, Jehoshaphat, Hezekiah, and Josiah), the communities that identify with Israel come together to support the Temple and affirm Jerusalem's centrality.

Conclusions

This chapter focused on a pivotal passage from Chronicles. We saw that the authors of this revisionist history, when dispensing with much of the material they inherited, did not seek to make David a saintly figure, as often assumed. Their concern was rather to depict the unity that Israel once enjoyed, a unity that they attribute to the figure of David.[15] To transform this emblematic Judahite ruler into a catalyst of Israelite national unity, they had to dispense with precisely those texts from the Book of Samuel that we have studied in the preceding chapters.

In the Samuel account, David resembles the patriarch Joseph. He charms those around him. Yet his dreams of glory provoke jealousy and inflict pain. In one of the first scenes of his life story, we hear his brother berating him for his "impertinence and impudence." Family troubles plague him throughout his life. Three of his wives he takes from other men. In a heart-wrenching scene, one husband cries as he is forced to give up his cherished spouse. That same wife, Michal, criticizes David's behavior when he brings the Ark to Jerusalem, and he upbraids her in the most demeaning fashion. Later his sin brings death to one of his children. Thereafter one of his sons rapes his sister, and another of his sons kills the guilty brother. The son who slew his brother then steals the throne from his father David and forces him to flee for his life.

Beyond the friction and dissension within his house, David brings division and bloodshed to the nation. He carves out a kingdom for himself by ripping the southern territories from the united kingdom that Saul reigned. Throughout his career, many prove disloyal and seek his demise. And at each step of the way, he and those closest to him resort to shocking violence.

A large portion of his biography, as portrayed in Samuel, treats the period during which he is exiled from Israel. Eventually his armies eliminate his son who occupied his throne, together with the thousands of Israelites who supported him. Immediately after these events – on his way back from exile! – his actions precipitate another civil war. Later he responds to a famine by ordering the execution of seven of Saul's descendants. This incident is followed by another during he which chooses to save his own life yet allow a pestilence to wipe out 70,000 members of the nation. Finally, on his deathbed, he orders his son to execute vengeance for him, even in a case in which he had sworn to spare someone's life.

Chronicles erases (or revises) all these episodes. Its authors needed David for a different purpose. In their retelling of history, the golden age is not that of the Patriarchs and Matriarchs, or of Moses and Joshua. It is the time when the Temple is built. Naturally, the first great king in Israel's history must be one who concerns himself with the construction of this sacred place and all matters that pertain thereto. He must also consolidate the entire nation around the building project and galvanize their support for the Temple cult. For this reason, the authors of Chronicles had no other choice than to compose a revisionist history, one that discards the many depictions of the strife and discord that follow David wherever he goes.

Nevertheless, Chronicles follows Samuel in negotiating status and belonging via commemoration. As we saw, several chapters depict Israel's tribes joining David and supporting him, even before Saul's death. These texts, which introduce the names of numerous new representative figures, bear a striking resemblance to the Song of Deborah, the monumental exemplar of war commemoration in the Hebrew Bible. The differences have to do, I noted, with a shift "from battles to building": Chronicles and Ezra–Nehemiah commemorate contributions to *building* projects, whereas texts from Genesis–Kings commemorate contributions to *war* efforts. This is not a hard rule: Occasionally we do encounter commemoration of building projects in the latter, and commemoration of war efforts in the former.

11

Caleb and the Conquest

Inventing a New Judahite Hero

Having now spent the preceding ten chapters investigating King David and the minor figures who surround him, I will pivot here and turn my attention in the next three chapters to a Judahite hero who lived long before David but who is nevertheless closely related to him: Caleb ben Jephunneh. In probing the biblical memories of Caleb's exemplary deeds, we will see how they evolved in competition with the veneration of King David.

A series of biblical passages (from Numbers and Deuteronomy) ascribe to this figure exemplary deeds during the conquest of Canaan. Most importantly, Caleb is remembered as the one who opposed the spies who discouraged Israel from undertaking an invasion of the land. In other accounts (from Joshua and Judges), Caleb dispossesses the formidable Anakites who occupy Hebron, a central place in the kingdom of Judah.

In the process of transforming Calebite identity, the biblical authors integrated Caleb into Judahite history. The means they adopted to achieve this integration was war commemoration. By inserting texts in the canonical narrative of Israel's history of conquest, they amplified this war memory to include tales of the Calebites' ancestor performing indispensable deeds of valor on the behalf of Judah and of all Israel. As such, this literary supplementation illustrates the relationship between commemoration and national integration that I am exploring in this book.

Various lines of evidence point to the possibility that the legends of Caleb's stoutheartedness and great military feats emerged in response to questions regarding the membership and status of Caleb's clan in the society of Judah and among the people of Israel. We will see that it is unwarranted to think in terms of the Calebites' assimilation into an already unified Judah. Not only it is likely that Judah coalesced very late and remained for a long time only loosely consolidated; also the issue posed by the Calebites may have been less about belonging than about privilege and honored status. That is, rather than being outsiders, the Calebites may represent a noble clan whose distinctiveness the biblical authors acknowledge and seek to explain by means of war commemoration.

The story of the Calebites is a not story of integrating the other. It is, indeed, the opposite: resistance to complete integration, whether it be in the context of the Judahite state or after the destruction of the state, as Edomites/Idumeans occupied their territory.

Was Caleb an Israelite?

The name "Caleb" is etymologically related to "dog" (*keleb*), a self-deprecating designation that servants and subjects often applied to themselves when communicating with their superiors.[1] The root appears in many Akkadian and Phoenician names. In each instance, it is joined to a theophoric element, expressing thereby devotion to the named deity (e.g., *Kalbi-Marduk*, *Kalbi-Sin*, *Kalbi-Šamaš* or *Klb'lm*). It is therefore likely that "Caleb" is the shortened form of a longer name beginning with "*Kalb-*" and continuing with a name of a god. In other words: dog + god.[2]

Several biblical texts refer to Caleb's father, Jephunneh, as "the Kenizzite" (Num 32:12; Josh 14:6, 14.). Elsewhere the Bible applies this ethnonym to a *non*-Israelite people. Thus YHWH makes a covenant with Abra(ha)m at Mamre, promising that his descendants would inherit the land and dispossess its inhabitants, including the Kenizzites. Another text assigns Kenaz, the eponymous ancestor of the Kenizzites, to the descendants of Jacob's twin-brother Esau (Gen 15:17–21, 35:11, 15, 42; see also

1 Chr 1:36, 53). The two texts are difficult to harmonize since, according to the second one, the Kenizzites wouldn't have come into existence until long after Abraham.

While incongruous, these texts agree that the Kenizzites are not Israelites. This fact would seem to warrant the opinion, long-held by scholars, that Caleb must originally have been an alien to Israel and only later became a "member of the tribe." Representing this popular view, the noted pentateuchal scholar Jacob Milgrom concluded: "That Caleb was not an Israelite is indicated by his ethnic designation as Kenizzite."[3]

There are, however, problems with this scholarly consensus. What does it mean that Caleb "was not an Israelite"? If we were talking about a historical figure, we would have to agree that the designation "Israelite" is anachronistic. The clans that resided in Judah before the establishment of a Judahite kingdom – and perhaps even long after – would not have easily embraced a Judahite identity, let alone an Israelite one.

It would be grossly simplistic to view the demographic situation in Judah during the early Iron Age in terms of an "Israelite ethnicity." Instead of imagining a population neatly demarcated from all others, we must reckon with a long process of "nation-building" in which diverse groups in Judah came to see themselves as Judahites – and an even longer process for a pan-Israelite identity to take hold. The early stages of biblical literature do not yet presuppose the notion that the populations of Israel and Judah are direct descendants from a single progenitor, the patriarch Jacob.

Now if we are talking about the *literary* figure of Caleb, then there can be no disputing the fact the biblical texts present him as full-fledged Israelite. While Jethro, Rahab, and Jael are all explicitly identified as outsiders in biblical texts, the first introduction to Caleb in the Spy Account (Num 13–14) presents this figure as the scout Moses selected to represent Judah. The honorable assignment confers on him high status. He even bears the title of *nasi* "prince" of Judah. The reader then assumes that Caleb enjoyed an impeccable Judahite pedigree.

The same goes for all the other biblical texts in which Caleb makes an appearance, even those in which his father is called "the Kenizzite." Taken together, the biblical accounts present this figure in the same category as Moses or Joshua, so that the unsuspecting reader of the biblical material would have no reason to question that Caleb was an Israelite.

Additional considerations gainsay the identification of Caleb as a non-Israelite. The references to the Kenizzites in the two passages from Genesis discussed above are likely late. Long identified as a fragment of an older Elohist (E) source, Genesis 15 is now increasingly seen as an exilic/post-exilic supplement that emerged in its present literary setting. As for Genesis 36, this chapter, usually attributed to the Priestly (P) source, refers to Kenaz in *supplemental* portions of the Edomite genealogy according to many scholars.

Taken together, the composition and reworking of these texts in Genesis likely reflects political developments after the Babylonian conquest of Jerusalem in 586 BCE. At that time the site of Mamre/Hebron, along with the tribal holdings of various Kenizzite clans, passed from Judahite to Edomite control.[4] In the process Kenizzites came to be identified as an Edomite group (which explains the late composition/editing of Gen 36). Prior to this shift of Judah's border, the Kenizzites would likely have been considered no differently than the other clans that constituted Judah's diverse population.[5]

The three texts that add "the Kenizzite" to the name of Caleb's father are even more problematic (Num 32:12; Josh 14:6, 14). If these texts were composed or edited at a late point (see the following chapter) and if they present Caleb as one of the most illustrious figures in Judahite history, we have all the more reason to doubt that their authors wished to identify Caleb as a descendant of Esau or part of populace that Abraham encountered when he first entered Canaan.

Othniel, the Younger Brother

A set of texts describes Caleb as the "brother" of Othniel son of Kenaz. Yet how can Caleb be Othniel's brother if his father is "Jephunneh the Kenizzite"? Perhaps the term "brother" (*'aḥî*) should be understood loosely as "kin," so that "son of" may bear the more general sense of "descendant," as it does in many other biblical texts.[6] The problem with this approach is that two texts add "the younger one" to Othniel, when describing him as Caleb's brother (Judg 1:13, 3:9); this description implies that Othniel and Caleb are brothers in the most basic sense.

Alternatively, we could understand Caleb and Othniel as half-brothers – with the same mother but different fathers. Such was the approach of Raba as well as Rashi, Radak, and other medieval Jewish commentators.[7] The difficulty presented by this option is explaining how Othniel could be the younger brother if Kenaz is his father. Caleb would have to belong to at least one generation *after* Othniel if his father Jephunneh, "the Kenizzite," is not even Kenaz's direct son.

It is difficult to escape the impression that the confusion and contradiction are due to the conflation of disparate traditions so that Caleb and Jephunneh were originally unrelated. Several late texts link Caleb to the Kenizzites by referring to his father as "the Kenizzite" (Num 32:12; Josh 14:6, 14). In doing so, they created a tension with earlier texts that tell of interactions between Caleb and Othniel, the son of Kenaz. Whereas the older texts subsume the history of the Kenizzites to that of the Calebites, the younger texts conflate the two by making Caleb a Kenizzite.

Both sets of texts reflect a situation in which Kenizzites inhabit the region around Hebron. Abraham receives his promise in this same region. But in contrast to Genesis 15, all these texts do not deny that the Kenizzites belong to Israel. Hence, instead of distinguishing between two (or more) unrelated groups of Kenizzites, we should reckon with competing literary traditions.

With respect to Othniel being Caleb's *younger* brother, only texts in the Book of Judges assert this. The authors of this work apparently wanted to ensure that Othniel, as Israel's first Judge, does not belong to the generation of Joshua. In this way, the authors could harmonize the narrative with the book's historiographical scheme according to which Othniel is Israel's first judge after the death of Joshua and his generation, which includes Caleb.

The addition of "the younger one" reinterprets the meaning of *'aḥî*. Instead of referring generally to "kin," it must now mean brother, so that Caleb and Othniel would share at least one parent. This would explain why Caleb is not called "the Kenizzite" in passages that refer to Caleb together with Othniel ben Kenaz.[8]

The development of these traditions is admittedly complex. Yet our findings lay the foundation for the impending investigation.

The Calebites as Judahite Aristocracy

The Book of Samuel describes an encounter between David and an individual designated as a "Calebite." It also depicts the Amalekites, one of David's main opponents, making a raid on "the Negeb of the Cherethites, on [the territories] that belong to Judah, and on *the Negeb of Caleb*" (my italics). Another text distinguishes the Negeb of Judah, the Negeb of the Jerahmeelites, and the Negeb of the Kenites/Kenizzites.[9]

Perhaps Judah differs here as a class from the Jerahmeelites and Kenites/Kenizzites (as 1 Sam 30:26–31 does). But then how does "the Negeb of Caleb" relate to these three territories?

The problem is that we have multiple authors composing and editing these texts so that we shouldn't expect consistent terminology. What is a Calebite for one may be a Judahite, a Kenite, or a Kenizzite for others. Be that as it may, it appears that the name Judah was originally on par categorically with the names of neighboring regions, like "Jerahmeel" and "Caleb," before they were subsumed to "greater Judah."[10]

The genealogies in Chronicles, which likely originated in the post-exilic period, construct these political developments and territorial relationships in familial terms, either of father/son or brothers. They conceive Judah as the oldest ancestor of the plurality of regions and cities that comprised the Judahite state.

The genealogists make great efforts to graft the Calebites' eponymous ancestor into the Judahite family tree. In what appears to be an older text, Kenaz and Caleb appear in the lineage of Judah (1 Chr 4:13 and 15). The problem is that the text does not provide the names of the fathers of Kenaz and Jephunneh, leaving unresolved questions regarding the exact relationship of these figures to the Judahite line.

In order to implant Caleb more securely within Judah's line, another text eliminates Jephunneh as Caleb's father and replaces him with none other than Hezron, the son of Perez and grandson of Judah. In this way, Caleb (or "Chelubai") becomes one of three primary ancestors of all Judah, the other two being Jerahmeel and Ram, the ancestor of David.[11]

The same text organizes Judah's ethnography into three Hezronite clans: Jerahmeel, Ram, and Caleb (1 Chr 2:9; cf. 1 Sam 27:10, 30:29). This system, which also appears in the appendix to the story of Ruth, identifies Ram as the ancestor of David. The Chronicler is, to be sure, very interested in all matters related to David.

Later hands appear to have reworked this system so as to make Caleb the ancestor of most of the clans and towns in Judah. His descendants include such important towns as Mareshah, Hebron (and its dependencies), Maon, and Beth-Zur. With the help of his concubines, he becomes the father of many other places. Later he takes on a second wife, Ephrath, and their son Hur is identified as the ancestor of Kiriath-Jearim, Bethlehem, and Bethgader, three cities in the north of Judah that were originally not included in Calebite territory.[12]

The Aristocratic Calebites and the Davidides

Why did the genealogist of Chronicles expand Caleb's progeny to this extent? According to Jon Levenson and Baruch Halpern, the reason was David's assumption of kingship in the very capital of the Calebite patrimony, Hebron:

> 1 Chr 2:50–51 reflects a process by which the Calebites came to see David as one of theirs, a process which his assumption of their late chieftain's lady [Abigail] would surely have facilitated, and probably necessitated.[13]

There are serious problems with this proposal. It seems unlikely that the redactions of the genealogies were completed so early, long before the composition of Chronicles in the Hellenistic Period. For example, the designation of Mareshah as the father of Hebron in this context is conceivable only in the late Persian Period and thereafter, when it became an important city that left behind very rich remains in the archeological record.[14] We must view the genealogies not as the point of departure but rather as the culmination of efforts by the Judahite kings to consolidate various clans and cities into the "House of Judah."

In the coming chapters we will observe how the figure of Caleb evolved in competition with that of David. Given the rivalry between the two Judahite heroes, it is remarkable that the genealogists of Chronicles, from the Hellenistic Age, would want to graft David and many others in Judah into Caleb's lineage. What precipitated this turnabout is, as we shall see, the war commemoration that made Caleb into a stalwart, noble warrior with a name eclipsing all others in Judah.

Scholars often express surprise at the fact that the Calebites remain an issue and maintain their distinctive identity for such a long time after other groups had thoroughly assimilated a Judahite identity. Why don't we have comparable legends about other figures, such as Jerahmeel? How do the Calebites differ from the Jerahmeelites and from other clans that coalesced to become Judah?

The distinctiveness of the Calebites is likely due to their own efforts to maintain separation from other Judahite populations. The legends of Caleb's singular valorous deeds resemble the battle legends that nobility tell about themselves in order to affirm the honor of their name and their rights to patrimonial estates. The way the epic tales celebrate Caleb's courage is consistent with the tendency in many cultures to define aristocratic courage as a distinguishing (inheritable) character trait.

In European history many of monarchs and rulers were known as "lionhearted," appealing thereby to their exceptional soldierly bravery as their primary qualification for rule. Likewise, in his blessings on the twelve sons, Jacob honors Judah, the ancestor of David's tribe, as *gûr 'aryêh*, "young lion" (Gen 49:8–10). And the roaring lion appears as the iconographic symbol for Judah/Yehud in numerous official stamps dating to the Persian

Period (although in many cases the animal looks more like a nauseous cat).

The Calebites therefore may have identified themselves as a distinctive elite clan within Judah. If so, the assumption in past scholarship that the Calebites did not belong to Israel would be the result of the texts' interest to protect this clan's noble status and aristocratic honor. In this case, the Calebites and Davidides would have been mutually interested in affiliating their lineages.

Even so, one must not lose sight of the evidence that the Calebites shaped the memories of their eponymous ancestor in opposition to and competition with the figure of David that the royal court in Hebron (and later Jerusalem) promulgated. This evidence is the subject of the coming chapters.

Caleb in Jewish, Christian, and Muslim Traditions

After procuring a prominent place in the halls of Judah's heroes, Caleb donned a mantle of honor in Jewish, Christian, and Muslim traditions. Across these traditions we can discern both similarities and important differences in what Caleb represents. Let's begin with the Jewish tradition.

The Septuagint strives to eliminate any questions about Caleb's identity raised by the fact that Genesis portrays Kenizzites as a population that inhabited Canaan before Abraham's advent. Hence the Greek translators interpreted the designation "Kenizzite" following Caleb's name to mean "the one set apart" (*diakechōrismenos*), as if this name were a nonethnic designation (like "Nazirite").

At a later point, the Jewish sages embellished Caleb's profile in creative ways. I will cite here a few examples: The discrepancy between "they went up by the south and came [singular] unto Hebron" (Num 13:22) is interpreted as meaning that Caleb left the other spies in order to pray at the graves of the patriarchs in Hebron (b. Sotah 34b). His wife Azubah (1 Chr 2:18) is identified with Miriam, who has this name because all men "forsook her" (*'azabûha*) at first (b. Sotah 12a). The names of their sons are read as expressions of their father's loyalty when all the spies were intent on transgression: "Jesher" because he set himself right (*yiššēr*); "Shobab" because he turned his inclination aside (*šībbēb*); "Ardon" because he disciplined (*radâ*) his inclination. As a reward for his irreproachable conduct, he (and Joshua) receives the shares of the other spies.[15]

The rabbis carry on the war commemoration of the biblical authors by claiming that Caleb was the one who, with Phineas, rescued Rahab and her family from the destruction of Jericho. He was rewarded with the hand of Miriam, and with her he fathered Hur, whose valor is also rewarded.[16] What sustains this rabbinic myth-making is the conviction that good deeds will eventually be recognized, even if it is not in one's lifetime. Within the world of the ancient Near East, these principles have their origins not only in wisdom traditions but also in a "military meritocracy."

Jewish texts from the Hellenistic Period emphasize Caleb's boldness in voicing dissent in the public forum.[17] For example, First Maccabees, written at a time of renewed Jewish sovereignty, depicts Mattathias on his deathbed exhorting his sons to "give their lives for the covenant of our ancestors." Commemorating these ancestors' heroic deeds, the father points to the example of Caleb: "Because he testified (*martyrasthai*) in the assembly, Caleb received an inheritance in the land" (2:56).

The same quid pro quo theology and emphasis on public dissent informs Ben Sira's presentation of Caleb. This sapiential work from the early second century BCE identifies the Judahite hero, together with Joshua, as a team who:

> Opposed the congregation,
> Restrained the people from sin,
> And stilled their wicked grumbling.
> And these two alone were spared
> Out of six hundred thousand infantry,
> To lead the people into their inheritance,
> The land flowing with milk and honey.
> The Lord gave Caleb strength,
> Which remained with him in his old age,
> So that he went up to the hill country,
> And his children obtained it for an inheritance,
> So that all the Israelites might see
> How good it is to follow the Lord.
>
> – (Ben Sira 46:6–10)

These emphases on deed and reward continue not only in later Jewish writings (e.g., Josephus and Philo) but also in early Christian and Muslim teachings. The difference between the two is that where the Jewish writings hold up Caleb's actions of dissent and defiance in the political community, Christian and Muslim writings draw attention to faith and belief.

Thus John Chrysostom, the Archbishop of Constantinople (fourth century CE), uses Caleb as an illustration in a sermon on the New Testament book of Hebrews, contending that he and Joshua escaped punishment and entered the Land of Promise because they believed:

> Now what he [the author of Hebrews] says is to this effect. They also heard, as we hear: but no profit came to them. Do not suppose then that by hearing what is proclaimed ye will be profited; seeing that they also heard, but derived no benefit because they did not believe. Caleb then and Joshua, because they agreed not with those who did not believe, escaped the vengeance that was sent forth against them. And see how admirably he said, not, They did not agree, but, they were not mixed – that is, they stood apart, but not factiously when all the others had one and the same mind. Here it seems to me that a faction too is hinted at. (John Chrysostom, Sixth Homily on "Hebrews"[18])

Citing a line from Hebrews, "there is still a 'rest' for the people of God," Chrysostom concludes that the land of promise cannot refer to the territory conquered by the Jews. Here we witness how the political and territorial dimensions of the biblical and Jewish writings have been abandoned in favor of a disembodied spiritual theological doctrine.

A similar point about belief is made in the Quran. Providing instructions on how to preach to Jews and Christians, Sura 5 presents Caleb and Joshua, albeit not by name, contending with the obstinate "people of God" who refuse to enter the Holy Land:

> O people of the scripture [i.e., Jews and Christians], our messenger has come to you, to explain things to you, after a period of time without messengers, lest you say, "We did not receive any preacher or warner." A preacher and warner has now come to you. GOD is Omnipotent. Recall that Moses said to his people, "O my people, remember GOD's blessings upon you: He appointed prophets from among you, made you kings, and granted you what He never granted any other people. O my people, enter the holy land that GOD has decreed for you, and

do not rebel, lest you become losers." They said, "O Moses, there are powerful people in it, and we will not enter it, unless they get out of it. If they get out, we are entering." *Two men who were reverent and blessed by GOD said, "Just enter the gate. If you just enter it, you will surely prevail. You must trust in GOD, if you are believers."* They said, "O Moses, we will never enter it, so long as they are in it. Therefore, go – you and your Lord – and fight. We are sitting right here." He said, "My Lord, I can only control myself and my brother. So allow us to part company with the wicked people." He said, "Henceforth, it is forbidden them for forty years, during which they will roam the earth aimlessly. Do not grieve over such wicked people." (Quran, Sura 5:19–26)[19]

The authors of these strikingly similar texts draw attention to what is, as we shall see, Caleb's most distinctive attribute: his defiance and boldness, displayed for example in the stand he takes over against the other spies and the people in the public assembly.

Yet these texts diverge on a fundamental point. The Christian and Muslim writings, expressing the perspective of emerging transnational religious communities, spiritualize the land and make its acquisition contingent upon "belief" or "faith." In contrast, the Jewish writings follow the course that was, as we shall see in the following chapters, charted by the evolution of the biblical texts: This composition history embellishes the character of Caleb with pious traits. Yet it does not supplant his original character as a warrior.

We can observe a greater degree of continuity between these later Jewish writings and their biblical forebears inasmuch as they are much more national and political and less disembodied in character. Just as a concrete physical territory remains central, so does Caleb embody qualities – courage, valor, public dissent, obedience to the command of YHWH, a desire to dwell in the land, and genealogical descent – that many biblical and later Jewish writers deemed to be indispensable to the survival of their people.

Faith, Descent, and the Land

A standard contemporary theological lexicon suggests that the Calebites may have been able to become members of Judah and

Israel because they were YHWH-worshippers.[20] This understanding of ethnic integration is echoed throughout the guild of biblical scholarship, yet it is most pronounced – and with an unmistakably Protestant accent – in a recent 700-page German tome on the Book of Numbers. According to the volume's author, Reinhard Achenbach, a "Hexateuch-Redactor" seized on the Kenizzite figure of Caleb in order to portray how solely a non-Israelite merited the privilege of entering the Promised Land. Not originally reckoned as a Jew, Caleb represents a true *Jahwegläubiger* ("believer in YHWH"), one who *am Bekenntniss zu Jahwe festhält* ("holds firm to his confession of YHWH"). He is the prototype of the proselyte and serves to remind the reader of the degree to which faithful Israel is a *Mischvolk* ("mixed people"). In Achenbach's understanding, what is decisive for this tradition is not genealogical descent but rather solely *unverbrüchlichen Glaube an Jahwe* ("unfaltering faith in YHWH").[21]

Such interpretations stand in line with the importance Christian and Muslim theologies attach to creedal confession. The statements of dissent and protest that Caleb utters in the assembly are understood as some sort of religious testimony, in keeping with faith more than meritorious deed. In minimizing genealogical descent and conduct (especially wartime contributions), one runs roughshod over the biblical accounts.

Admittedly the Book of Numbers devotes considerable space to relations with nonnatives.[22] Yet the account of the spies provides no basis for doubting that Caleb ben Jephunneh is any less of an Israelite than Joshua bin Nun.[23] Even if we could show that the oldest texts do not identify Caleb as a member of Israel, we must avoid reading that knowledge into the narrative world of biblical texts that portray Caleb as a full Israelite. Rahab, Jael, Uriah the Hittite, Ittai the Gittite, and a host of other aliens in the Bible demonstrate their allegiance to Israel through wartime service, yet they still maintain their otherness. Not so with Caleb. The biblical texts consistently identify him as a full-fledged Israelite. As we shall see in the following chapters, the commemoration of Caleb's martial valor is part of his clan's defense of their territorial claims. It has little if anything to do with questions of membership among the people of Israel.

The emergence of Caleb's pious character does not expunge or eclipse his martial courage and prowess. Rather, the two sides germinate in a natural symbiosis: as he becomes more devout, he becomes more valorous. In the Book of Judges, his brother Othniel goes from the daring Kenizzite who leads the attack on a certain city to Judah's first "deliverer/judge" whom the spirit of YHWH empowers to subjugate an Aramean ruler.[24]

In like fashion, the tradition transformed Caleb into a warrior who leads the tribe of Judah in the reconnaissance of Canaan and distinguishes himself by his confidence in Israel's deity, which he expresses in elaborate speeches. What characterizes him, as well as Othniel and his daughter Achsah, is an earnest desire to take possession of a piece of the land, both by force and through the arts of persuasion.

Divine approbation for Caleb's piety and loyalty is affirmed in the extraordinary title that YHWH confers upon him ("my servant") and in the declaration of Caleb's distinctiveness ("he possesses a different spirit and has been loyal to me"). In return for his faithfulness, the deity exempts him from a punitive plague and grants him a portion in the land.[25]

With respect to this final reward, the passages from Joshua and Judges describe territories that Caleb and his descendants acquired within Judah. Whereas these texts address issues of belonging and status within Judahite history, the Pentateuch conceives the award for Caleb's valor and loyalty in terms of entering or seeing Israel's Promised Land as a whole. Caleb functions here as a paradigm of the virtues held up for the people of Israel: obedience to YHWH's command, indomitable courage, and irrepressible fervor to take possession of (a piece of) the land.

Conclusions

What prompted the embellishment of Caleb's character with such pronounced pious traits? The strongest stimulus was likely the loss of native sovereignty. After Judah and her neighbors were administratively reorganized as provinces of the Persian Empire, the battlefield and ongoing war efforts were no longer the primary contexts in which communities and individuals could negotiate their belonging/status among the people of Israel. What replaced martial prowess and wartime contributions were genealogical descent, fidelity to Israel's God, and a proficiency in Torah-study – all three qualities incarnated in the post-exilic figure of Ezra.[26]

Although Jewish communities in the Persian Period rarely if ever fought native wars, one could still engage in war *commemoration*. This fact explains why memories and traditions about earlier wars and warriors multiplied in very late stages of the Bible's composition history. Thus the Calebites constructed memories of their ancestor's role in the conquest of Canaan by portraying him as a Judahite of the finest extraction and by underscoring his unwavering devotion to Israel's God.

With respect to the way the biblical authors flesh out Caleb's martial portrait with pious traits, a close analogy may be found in the account of the Israelite tribes from the Transjordan (Num 32; see also Deut 3; Josh 1 and 22). Many wondered if these tribes, living beyond the Jordan River that marks the border to the Promised Land in the Book of Joshua, really belonged to Israel. Responding to the question, biblical authors portrayed representative members of these tribes agreeing to contribute to the nation's war effort in an extraordinary fashion: by marching in the most dangerous vanguard position of Israel's armies and thereby risking their lives to conquer territories that were not their own (see discussion in Chapter 5).

At a later point, however, service and sacrifice in wartime were deemed to be an insufficient basis for affirming membership in the national community. In keeping with these changes, later readers reworked the texts to present the Transjordanian tribes fighting with a new incentive. Instead of merely expressing their fraternal solidarity in order to affirm their national belonging, they now contribute to Israel's war effort in accord with the word of YHWH and the teaching of Moses. In this way, acceptance of and adherence to the Torah, understood as Israel's constitution, becomes the criterion for membership in the political community.

This shift resembles the redactions of the Caleb legends, which supplement the attention devoted to his prowess in battle with an accentuation of his allegiance to YHWH. In the next chapter, we turn our attention to these legends.

12

Caleb the Warrior

The Evolution of Legends

Writing in 1869, the Dutch biblical scholar Abraham Kuenen drew conclusions from his study of Caleb for the critical-historical investigation of the Bible, which at the time was still in its infancy:

> If Caleb . . . is transformed by tradition into one of the spies sent out by Moses, and even into a prince of Judah; if his exploits are attributed by the same tradition to the tribe of Judah or to the whole of Israel, fighting under the leadership of Joshua – then, if we want to get at the truth, we must not follow that tradition without restriction; then we must keep its character continually in view during our investigations, and in preference form our idea of the course of events from the minor traits which do not harmonize with its system.[1]

Kuenen's formulation of the task of critical biblical investigation still shimmers with methodological perspicacity. In this chapter and the next one, I follow him in focusing on "minor traits which do not harmonize with its system."

The Bible contains an array of legends commemorating Caleb's exceptional valor. While some of the legends are very late, others may derive from early oral tradition. Together they witness to the kinds of lore Calebites promulgated about their eponymous ancestor in order to hold high their family name and claim for themselves a special role in Judah's history.

I will begin my investigation with the material in the Book of Joshua. As we shall see, this material contains the earliest exemplars of Calebite war commemoration. In the second half of the chapter, I examine the composition of the spy account in the Book of Numbers, where Caleb makes his first appearance in the biblical narrative. Caleb does not seem to be an original protagonist in this story. Which poses the question: Why would later biblical authors have decided to insert Caleb into the Pentateuch at this point?

Early Calebite War Commemoration

Nestled within the lists in the second half of the Book of Joshua is a passage that reports that Caleb received "a portion among the Judahites in keeping with the command of YHWH to Joshua." This portion of land includes an important city:

> And to Caleb ben Jephunneh he gave a portion among the Judahites, in keeping with the command of YHWH to Joshua – namely Kiriath-Arba (Arba is the father of the Anakites) which is Hebron. And Caleb drove out from there the three sons of the Anak: Sheshai, Ahiman, and Talmai, the children of the Anak. (Josh 15:13–14)

This account and the immediately following passage in 15:15–19 (see the following section) are also found in the first chapter of Judges. They may be the oldest Caleb traditions in the Bible (aside from the references to the Calebite territories in the Book of Samuel). They both certainly seem to antedate the lengthier passage in the immediately preceding chapter:

> Then the Judahites came to Joshua at Gilgal, and Caleb son of Jephunneh the Kenizzite said to him, "You know what YHWH said to Moses the man of God in Kadesh-barnea concerning you and me. I was forty years old when Moses the servant of YHWH sent me from Kadesh-barnea to spy out the land. I brought him an honest report. While my brothers who went up with me made the heart of the people melt, I was loyal to YHWH my God. And Moses swore on that day, saying, 'Surely the land on which your foot has trodden shall be an inheritance for you and your children forever, because you have been loyal to YHWH my God.'

"And now, as you see, YHWH has kept me alive, as he said, these forty-five years since the time that YHWH spoke this word to Moses, while Israel was journeying through the wilderness; and here I am today, eighty-five years old. I am still as strong today as I was on the day that Moses sent me; my strength now is as my strength was then, for war, and for going and coming.

"So now give me this hill of which YHWH spoke on that day. You heard on that day how the Anakim were there, with great fortified cities. It may be that YHWH will be with me, and I shall drive them out, as YHWH said."

So Joshua blessed him, and gave Hebron to Caleb son of Jephunneh for an inheritance. Therefore Hebron became the portion of Caleb ben Jephunneh the Kenizzite unto this day because he was loyal to YHWH, the God of Israel. The name of Hebron was formerly Kiriath-Arba, the great man among the Anakites. And the Land had rest from war. (Josh 14:6–15[2])

The information provided in this account from chapter 14 overlaps with the passage in chapter 15 cited earlier. The reader is now told in two contiguous texts (1) that Joshua "gave" Kiriath-Arba to Caleb; (2) that Kiriath-Arba and Hebron are the same places; and (3) that Arba represents the Anakites.[3]

The texts are also tension with each other in multiple respects. In the preceding chapter of this book I noted the incongruity with respect to the description of Caleb's father as "the Kenizzite," which appears twice in chapter 14. To it I can add other observations. The statement in 15:13 contains a secondary explanatory note that equates Kiriath-Arba with Hebron. The gloss resembles countless others that identify a range of locales with Hebron, one of the most important cities in Judahite history. The account in chapter 14 mentions Hebron first and proceeds to tell the reader that "the name of Hebron was *formerly* Kiriath-Arba" (Josh 14:13–15; see also Judg 1:10, 20). That "formerly" (*l*[e]*pānîm*) refers to a time in which texts such as Joshua 15:13 (see also 15:54) were drafted. Such clues allow us to conclude that the account in chapter 14 most likely postdates the one in chapter 15 and presupposes its gloss.

Whereas chapter 14 refers to Caleb's activities during the reconnaissance of the land, the version in 15:13–14 can be understood without knowledge of any preceding texts. Its *raison d'être* is to explain and legitimize the control of Kiriath-Arba/Hebron by the Calebites, whom the text distinguishes from other Judahites: Joshua grants Caleb not a piece of Judahite land, or a traditional "partrimony/inheritance" (*naḥ^a lâ*, see 14:13–14), but rather "a portion (*ḥēleq*) *among* the children of Judah." This line implies that Caleb and his clan somehow differ from other Judahites.[4]

The region of Kiriath-arba/Hebron lies at the very center of Judah, similar to the location of Paris in relation to the rest of France. The city of Hebron itself was likely home to an ancient sanctuary of YHWH, as it is there that David makes a covenant "before YHWH" and that Absalom asks permission to "worship/serve YHWH" (2 Sam 5:3, 15:8–9). Archeological excavations at Tel Rumeida (located adjacent to the modern city of Hebron) reveal that it was an important Canaanite city already in the Early Bronze Age (3300–2200 BCE). It was also where major routes intersected. For such reasons it was likely selected to be the first capital of the Judahite kingdom.

What, then, was so special about Caleb and his descendants that they deserved to occupy Judah's centermost territory? Produced in response to this question, the account in chapter 15 defends the Calebites' landholdings in three ways. First, it contends that the clan received their land long ago – at the same time Joshua assigned Judah its territories. Second, it affirms that this land grant complied with a direct command by YHWH to Joshua (*'el-pî* YHWH *lîhôšua'*). Third, it portrays Caleb as worthy of occupying Hebron insofar as it commemorates how he courageously vanquished the Anakites who formerly resided there.[5]

Caleb's Daughter Achsah

The continuation of the passage from chapter 15, cited earlier, describes how Caleb, after conquering Kiriath-Arba/Hebron, marches up against the inhabitants of Kiriath-Sepher/Debir.[6] Yet instead of fighting himself, he offers his daughter Achsah to the warrior who captures Kiriath-Sepher. The one who achieves this feat is Othniel ben Kenaz, and as promised, Caleb gives him Achsah as wife:

> From there [Caleb] marched against the inhabitants of Debir – the name of Debir was formerly Kiriath-sepher – and Caleb announced, "I will give my daughter Achsah in marriage to the man who attacks and captures Kiriath-sepher." Othniel ben Kenaz, brother of Caleb, captured it. So he gave him his daughter Achsah in marriage.
>
> When she came [to him], she induced him to ask her father for some property. She dismounted from her donkey, and Caleb asked her, "What is the matter?" She replied, "Give me a present [or: pool]. You have given me away as Negeb-land, so give me springs of water." And he gave her Upper and Lower Gulloth. (Josh 15:15–19)

For making this pledge, Caleb is censured by the rabbis: If a slave had succeeded in taking the city, he would have been required to demote his daughter's status (*Gen. Rab.* 60.3). Yet instead of censuring Caleb in the way that the author of Judges censures Jephthah for his rash vow, the legend explains that the Kenizzites came to possess land near Hebron because the Calebites' eponymous ancestor granted it to them. Whereas the Calebites received Hebron in keeping with a command of YHWH, the Kenizzites owe their possession of Debir to the Calebites since Caleb had originally possessed it and had offered it to anyone who had the martial prowess to capture it.

The composition of rest of the passage is perplexing and has left many gaps for later commentators to fill. First Achsah "induces" her husband to ask her father for a field. But apparently, as the Jewish commentator Radak (d. 1235) observed, Othniel did not rise to the occasion. Whereas the preceding paragraph commemorates the martial prowess and valor of this Kenizzites' ancestor, this sequel presents him in a more ambivalent light. Achsah must take control and dismounts from her donkey. Evidently this act was a gesture of entreaty, since Caleb immediately inquires about what was bothering her. Achsah responds by boldly demanding a water source to go along with the lands she possessed: "Give me a present. Since you have already given me the land of the Negeb, give me now *gullōt māyim*." What she requests are literally "bowls of water," probably referring to the name of well-known pools. The account concludes by reporting that Caleb accedes to her demand, granting her both "the upper *gullōt*" and "the lower *gullōt*."[7]

Whatever one is to make of the details, the general gist of the legend seems obvious enough: It addresses water rights to what was known as "the upper *gullōt*" and "the lower *gullōt*." The author contends that these resources, which would have been especially precious in the arid Negeb, passed from Calebite to Kenizzite hands thanks to the assertive Calebite Achsah and her wealth that she brought into the marriage with Othniel.[8]

The first chapter of Judges, which is widely acknowledged as a preface to late editions of the book, includes a version of this account. Yet, as an increasing number of scholars agree, this version represents a tendentious retelling of the Joshua account. It ascribes the conquest of Hebron to Judah as a whole, instead of specifically to Caleb. (It tells how Judah first took Jerusalem then Hebron.) Dwelling at Hebron are Canaanites, not Anakites. Similarly, Judah goes up collectively against Debir, and when Caleb and Othniel act, they do so not on their own but rather as members of the *Judahite* tribe. The chapter does not introduce the three sons of Arba, apparently assuming knowledge of them from Joshua 15. Finally, if the Judges version were older, it would be difficult to explain why Joshua 15:14 changes the verb from *n-k-h* ("struck/defeated"), which is used consistently in Judges 1, to *y-r-š* ("dispossess"). It is more conceivable that the Judges version modified the language of its sources in keeping with its unified scheme.

Now what can one say about our passage in chapter 15 in its context? The legend of Othniel and Achsah describes a different method of land allocation than what we encounter in this section of the book (Josh 12–22). It is also curious that the first line lacks a subject: "To Caleb ben Jephunneh he gave a portion among the children of Judah." The phrase that follows, "in keeping with the commandment of YHWH to Joshua," disconnects the predicate and looks like a redactional *retouche*; it may have been conceived to remedy the problem of the missing subject. Few scholars would deny that much of the material separating our account from the older half of the book (ch. 1–11) consists of very late supplements. It is remarkable in this regard that the final line of chapter 14 repeats the final line of chapter 11 ("So the land had rest from war"). Such repetitions – what redaction-critics call *Wiederaufnahmen* – often indicate interpolations. We have then all the more reason to conclude that the Caleb-Achsah-Othniel legend in chapter 15 has been either transposed or gradually isolated from its original setting as a consequence of successive supplements.[9]

Caleb the Spy and Aristocratic Courage

So why does the Book of Joshua contain two separate accounts pertaining to Caleb? Does the duplication reflect two discrete sources that told the same story in different ways, as some claim? Probably not. Notice that the first passage only presents Joshua *assigning* Hebron to Caleb as his inheritance. In contrast to the second passage, it does not report that Caleb actually conquered and took possession of the city. The two texts do overlap in some respects (see, for instance, the use of "gave" in 14:13 and 15:13). Yet they are not exact duplicates or "doublets." Instead, the former serves as a preface to the latter, and this fact speaks in favor of supplementation, not source division.

The much longer preface introduces numerous features that are missing in chapter 15, the older account. Most of these features amplify Caleb's image with characteristics corresponding to his new role: a spy in the first reconnaissance mission carried out during the days of Moses. Caleb recalls how he alone brought a good report and was loyal to YHWH, "my God." He receives his inheritance as a reward for his martial valor and especially for his fidelity to YHWH. And he remains committed to execute the divine war plans crafted more than forty years earlier: Against the fearsome Anakites who dwell in "great, fortified cities," he affirms his eagerness to engage in battle in order to dispossess them "as YHWH had spoken/commanded."[10]

We can witness here how devotion to YHWH and his command (ch. 14) begins to trump raw military valor (ch. 15). Yet this development does not sever loyalty to YHWH from martial action. To the contrary, the two aspects go hand-in-hand: Caleb's piety grows with his soldierly prowess. This piety should be conceived as a kind of wartime allegiance to the deity – even if this time it means taking sides *against* the nation.

The later passage, chapter 14, devotes a significant amount of space to the issue of Caleb's age. He stands ready and eager to conquer his territory, even though he is now an octogenarian. What generated the authors' attention to this issue was the composition of new texts. The older legend, chapter 15, presents Caleb fighting formidable foes. This fearsome warrior was not likely an old man. Yet after authors inserted Caleb into the Spy Account from Numbers (see the following), his age had to be adjusted: If Caleb was at least forty years old at the time he served as a scout, and he survived forty years in the wilderness, he had to be at least eighty by the time he was ready to take possession of his land.[11]

Caleb's reward is more than mere survival for forty years in the wilderness; it also includes the irrevocable title to a piece of the Promised Land. Yet when we turn to Deuteronomy, we notice a different accent: His faithfulness is recompensed with the privilege of *seeing* the "good land" as well as receiving familial rights to a portion of it. Moses recalls how YHWH, in response to the faintheartedness of the people, swore in his anger:

> Not one of these, from among this evil generation, shall see the good land that I swore to your ancestors. Except Caleb ben Jephunneh; he shall see it. And to him I will give the land on which he set foot, and to his descendants, because of his complete fidelity to YHWH. (Deut 1:34–35)

The reference to viewing the land is undoubtedly related to Deuteronomy's broader rhetorical strategies. Thus YHWH is said to have conferred on Moses the honor of *seeing* the land even if he did not set his foot upon it.[12]

Notice a remarkable shift in the passage from Deuteronomy quoted here: That passage is an excerpt of the prebattle speech that frames the book's law code. In that speech, Moses reviews Israel's history, highlighting aspects that serve his pedagogical-rhetorical purposes. As he strives to embolden his audience for their struggles that will attend their collective future, he holds up the example of Caleb. Israel must demonstrate the courage and fidelity displayed by Caleb alone so that they could avoid the fate of the Exodus generation.

Earlier we saw how the oldest Calebite legends give prominence to the lionhearted courage of Caleb (as well as of his daughter Achsah and of his son-in-law Othniel). Such appeals to fearlessness and valor are common means by which aristocratic clans throughout history have distinguished themselves from nonnobility, defending their prerogative to rule and their entitlement to precious estates. The shift in our passage from Deuteronomy can be witnessed in the way the authors take this aristocratic hallmark and "democratize" it. No longer is bravery the unique possession of noble warriors such as Caleb and his clan. It is instead a quality to which all members of the nation should aspire – and that is indeed critical to their future as a corporate body. Thus Caleb has become here a paragon of national virtue, and this didactic use of his character paved the way for his exemplary role in the later writings we examined in the preceding chapter.[13]

Composition of the Spy Account

Given the dynamics of war commemoration that we are exploring in this book, it makes sense that the biblical memory-makers would have selected a pivotal moment in Israel's conquest narratives to depict Caleb's meritorious deeds. But why did they choose to place him specifically in the Spy Account of Numbers 13–14?

The tale begins with Moses sending twelve men on a reconnaissance mission to inspect Canaan. The man chosen for Judah is none other than Caleb ben Jephunneh. Later in the book, YHWH tells Moses the name of each tribal leader whom he had selected for the honorable task of apportioning the land after the conquest. He begins with the tribe of Judah, and he names Caleb (not Nahshon) as its chieftain (Num 34:16–29; compare 1:7; 2:3; 7:12, 17; 10:14; 13:6). The Judahite hero has come a long way from the oldest legend related to this figure (Josh 15). Instead of just staking a claim to prime real estate in the territory of Judah, Caleb is now the paramount leader of the tribe of Judah. According to later interpreters, the promotion of Judah from third place to first place was the reward for Caleb's deeds during the scouting expedition.

One has often read the Spy Account as betraying a pro-Judahite bias. Just as Moses names Judah first when transmitting the divine instructions for the division of the land, Caleb here stands alone in the public assembly and voices his confidence in Israel's ability to vanquish the enemy (13:30; see also 14:24, 34:19, Deut 1:36, and Josh 14:6–14). Such partiality to Judah is noticeable elsewhere: In the Book of Joshua, the allocation of territories in Canaan begins with this tribe. Likewise, in the final form of Judges, Judah is chosen to "go up first" and Othniel the Kenizzite represents Judah as Israel's first "judge/savior."

Yet while the Spy Account is clearly written from a Judahite perspective, it is not a Judahite apologia. Nowhere are we told that the *tribe* of Judah collectively broke away from the rest of the Israelites as the assembly proclaimed its desire to give up the fight and return to Egypt. There is only one Judahite who voices dissent, and it is Caleb. The story makes better sense when read instead as an attempt to account for the place of the *Calebite clan* within Judahite society and history. More specifically, it explains why the deity later grants Caleb and his descendants a "possession among the Judahites" (Josh 15:13).

The authors point to a decisive moment in Israel's history when Caleb displayed dauntless courage in preparation for a military campaign. In challenging the assembly, and by standing on the side of Moses and Aaron, he and Joshua expose themselves to mortal danger: "and the whole congregation threatened to stone them." Later YHWH singles Caleb out in approbation: "But Caleb, my servant, has a different spirit and has been loyal to me. Hence I will bring him into the land into which he went, and his descendants shall possess it forever." By designating him "my servant," the deity places Caleb in a very exclusive club, consisting solely of Moses and Joshua.[14] In the end, a plague takes the lives of all the spies with the exception of Caleb and Joshua (14:36–38).[15]

In its transmitted form, this unusually lengthy account ascribes a major sin to Israel and describes Moses's efforts to mitigate the divine wrath. In both content and language, the account overlaps and competes with the pericope in which Israel sins in worshiping a golden calf (Exod 32–34). As in that theologically profound pericope, Moses succeeds here in persuading YHWH to pronounce a less severe punishment. Instead of being consigned to oblivion, Israel would eventually enter the land. Yet with the exception of Caleb (and Joshua), all the adults would have to live out the rest of their days wandering in the wilderness.

Most biblical scholars agree that this unusually lengthy account can be divided into at least two layers, one deriving from the Priestly source (or from a Priestly-influenced circle of authors) and another from a non-Priestly source. Yet is the non-Priestly material older or younger than the Priestly narrative? This question divides the traditional documentary hypothesis (JEDP) from the "supplementary approach," which has introduced thorough modifications to the documentary hypothesis. Supplementarians view the biblical text as a product of gradual accretions (or "supplements") by successive generations of authors. In contrast, adherents to the documentary hypothesis align the text into running sources or "documents." They usually attribute the non-Priestly material to the "Jahwist" (J), which is said to be the oldest document.[16]

I would agree that it is possible to distinguish separable strands, as it is otherwise difficult to explain the overlap and "doublets." These separable strands may correspond to competing versions of the story, which would have developed in the history of the literary tradition. The problem arises when one moves immediately to press the isolated strands into one of the four standard pentateuchal JEDP documents. We must reckon instead with the possibility that redactors, in the aim of preserving competing literary witnesses, endeavored to integrate multiple late versions that emerged as the text assumed authority and spawned polemical substitutes at very advanced stages in the formation of the Pentateuch. The existence of these late versions would account for the numerous repetitions, which are difficult to interpret merely as expansions or supplements. Similar to what we find in Jubilees and others exemplars of "Rewritten Bible," these retellings of the biblical accounts proliferated *after* the Pentateuch began to assume an authoritative status.[17]

The synthesis of parallel versions explains the unusual length of the pericope, which in the case of our text is due primarily to two overlapping passages.[18] Yet the length is also due to many supplements that these recensions accumulated over the course of their transmission histories (both prior to and after being combined to form a unified account).

Invasion from the South

In addition to the evidence for two or more versions and numerous supplements, one can detect remnants of a much more basic substratum of the Spy Account. Its objective is to explain why Israel invades from the *east* rather than from the *south* – the most direct route for a convoy traveling from Egypt.

Older literary traditions constrained the historians responsible for the account in Exodus–Joshua to depict Israel entering Canaan from the east. In these early texts, found in the core of the Book of Joshua, Israel crosses the Jordan River and gradually establishes territorial sovereignty in the central hill country and in proximity to the Jordan. When an early generation of authors used these texts to construct an elaborate narrative of the exodus and conquest, they faced a problem. They had to explain why the older literary traditions do not present Israel first establishing hegemony in the *south* from which they could advance northwards, as this route would make the best sense if Israel were coming up from Egypt.

The oldest traditions in the Book of Joshua must have originated in Israel, not Judah. They attribute Israel's conquests to a non-king (Joshua), who with the help of Israel's national deity slays Canaanite monarchs. The northern provenance of the oldest Joshua tales explains why they do not tell about military campaigns in the south. The deliberate circumvention of Judah and conscious evasion of any references to the south reflect competition with the kingdom of Judah. Rulers and priests in Jerusalem presented their city as the one and only place toward which the people of Israel should orient themselves – both politically and religiously. This Jerusalemite doctrine is however not espoused in early versions of the exodus-conquest saga. Moreover, tradents of the older exodus-conquest account may have reckoned with an Israel that originated in the Transjordan and that crossed the Jordan to establish hegemony in the Samarian hill country.[19]

While this exodus-conquest saga has its origins in Israel, it assumed its final shape in Judah. In a southern context, the depiction of Israel entering Canaan from the eastern side of the Jordan would have agitated readers. History told from a Judahite perspective would have presented Israel leaving Egypt and immediately marching up to Hebron or Jerusalem in order establish it as the seat of YHWH's and Israel's sovereignty. Fragments from Hellenistic authors leave no doubt that such histories were actually written.

Yet instead of starting from scratch and fashioning a history in its own image, the Judahite circles responsible for the contours of our Bible appropriated Israel's literary traditions and *reshaped* them. With respect to Israel's first entrance into the land, they realigned the account in two ways.

The first way, which occupies the most space, was to present the eastern invasion as a consequence of Israel's sin. This story is found in the Spy Account from the Book of Numbers. Moses sends out scouts to reconnoiter Canaan. They go up from the south into the Negeb, reaching Hebron and the Wadi Eshcol. They then return to the camp of Israel with a foretaste of the land in hand. But their report demoralizes Israel: "We are not able to go up against this people, for they are stronger than we!" In his anger, YHWH wipes out the scouts with a plague and decrees that the entire generation would die in the wilderness. Their wanderings take them up from the wilderness to the territories of the Transjordan, whence they enter the Promised Land after 40 years.

The second, and older, explanation for the eastern invasion is found in the Book of Exodus. It takes up much less space. According to it, the deity feared that his people, if led directly northwards through the land of the Philistines, would witness war and then desire to return to Egypt. "So God turned the people *by the way of the wilderness to the Red Sea*" (Exod 13:17–18, my italics).

Within the Spy Account, we can isolate a similar explanation, which is easy to miss given the mass of material devoted to Israel's sin and punishment. At one point YHWH commands Israel: "Now, since the Amalekites and the Canaanites live in the valleys, tomorrow turn and set out for *the wilderness by the way of Red Sea*" (Num 14:25, my italics). The isolated position of this statement has flummoxed scholars since H. Holzinger, Bruno Baentsch, and Julius Wellhausen. Although separated now by the lengthy negotiations between Moses and YHWH, it may well have originally continued the passage in which the scouts report that the land is both fecund and home to formidable inhabitants (13:27, 33). Because their report provokes the people to despair, YHWH directs the people into the wilderness. Notably, Deuteronomy harmonizes the text by deleting the line "now, since the Amalekites and Canaanites live in the valleys" so that it cannot be confused with the later punitive rationale for the prolonged wilderness itinerary.[20]

The passage that follows the Exodus passage quoted here refers to the pillar of cloud and fire, similar to the description of the cloud in Numbers (9:15–10:36). Insofar as the earliest versions of the Spy Account appear to continue the description of the cloud in Numbers 9:15–10:36, it would seem that what we have here are two parallel explanations – which cannot be easily assigned to conventional sources – as to why Israel did not launch an invasion from the south. What Exodus reports summarily, early versions of the narrative in Numbers portray at greater length, in story form, and with different emphases.[21]

In the confines of this chapter I cannot afford to engage the scholarship on the vexing problems posed by this pericope. Setting aside a more detailed defense of my suggestions for another context, I turn now to the question of what prompted authors to insert the figure of Caleb into this account.

Caleb's Absence from the Spy Account

One of the strands of the Spy Account, which is most likely older than the others, presents Moses "sending men to spy out the land of Canaan" (see Num 13:1a, 3). They are described as heads of the children of Israel. But their names are not listed. As most scholars agree, the register, which identifies one scout per tribe, is a secondary interpolation. It appears too late, since Moses had *already* sent the selected men in the preceding verse. Its insertion necessitated a *Wiederaufnahme* or "redactional repetition."[22] Without the register, Moses sends out an anonymous group of men. At the other end of the pericope, we are told that the deity executed all "*the men* whom Moses *sent out to spy out the land*" as punishment for the evil report they brought to Israel (14:36–37, my italics). The language here differs from much of that used throughout the story, yet it corresponds precisely to the introduction in 13:1a, 3. Based solely on its formulation, the reader would have to conclude that all the spies died. Correcting this impression, the next line (14:38), easy to identify as an addition, reports that Joshua and Caleb remained alive.[23]

Without the secondarily interpolated register of names, the older account would have failed to introduce Caleb to the reader. According to the conventional JEDP theory, the first time that Caleb appears in the older strand of the narrative is the reference to him hushing the people before Moses (13:30). The line is obviously out of place, since we have yet to be told about Israel's reaction. It may well be linked to 14:24, where YHWH singles out his servant Caleb and rewards his descendants with possession of the land. Yet proponents of the JEDP theory have trouble explaining how the reader would have known who Caleb is.

Nothing in this version would have indicated that he had served as a spy. What's more, if this is the first time that he appeared in the narrative, why didn't the author introduce him with his patronymic ("ben Jephunneh")? Its absence is highly unusual in biblical narrative. It seems then more likely that we have here a late supplement, which presupposes the insertion of the register of names.

Now if the register has been interpolated, one must search for another introduction to Caleb. A good candidate is found in 14:6, which presents him alongside Joshua. This line includes not only patronymics for the two figures but also a statement that they participated in the reconnaissance mission, information that is superfluous if they had been introduced earlier. The line is a part of short paragraph (14:6–10) that interrupts the surrounding narrative pertaining to Moses's negotiations with YHWH on the behalf of Israel. The supplement goes together with the reward for Caleb and Joshua in 14:30b and 38. I have already discussed 14:38 and noted that it is easy to identify as a supplement. As for 14:30b, the speeches of the deity stress that no one would enter/see the land. By eliminating the exceptions made for Caleb and Joshua in 14:30b, the reader can better appreciate the contrast between the present generation and their children: "None of you shall come into the land . . . ; however your little ones I shall bring in and they shall know the land that you have despised."

We have therefore good reasons to suspect that early versions of the account presented an anonymous group of men being sent to scout out the land and then later dying altogether as punishment for the report they bring back to camp. If so, Caleb would have been introduced secondarily. The question, then, is: Why?

Hebron and the Anakites

According to my thesis, early versions of the account endeavored to explain the circuitous route taken by Israel. This rationale resembles the one found in Exodus inasmuch as the deity conducts Israel into the wilderness in order to avoid premature engagement with the enemy. Yet there are the differences between these early versions. For example, Exodus identifies the enemy as the Philistines. Surprisingly, the account in Numbers never mentions this population. In their place, one line refers to five different peoples, assigning each to a geographical region. This line appears to be an ethnographic gloss, so that the older versions would refer to a single population: the Anakites.[24]

Other references to Anakites in the Bible likely postdate our Caleb texts. Deuteronomy presents all the inhabitants of Canaan as "larger and mightier than you" and "a strong and tall people," and then proceeds to identify them as "the descendants of the Anakim" (Deut 9:2). Similarly, Joshua is portrayed as exterminating the Anakites, beginning in Hebron and then in the hill country of Judah, and then in the hill country of Samaria and in the Philistine coastal territories. This text belongs to a redaction that presents Joshua as the one who subjugates the entire land, ascribing to him the feats of other biblical heroes (see Josh 10:40–42, 11:23). Thus, it attributes to his name the conquest of Hebron and Debir, which older accounts attribute to Caleb (and Othniel).

In amplifying the identity of the Anakites to include the entirety of Israel's foes, these texts differ from the older ones that confine the Anakites to the region around Kiriath-Arba/Hebron. By asserting that Joshua, in keeping with Deuteronomistic stipulations, completely wiped out this population, the text creates a glaring contradiction: If the Anakites had been eradicated, there would have been none left for Caleb to dispossess.

Why are the Anakites so closely linked to the city of Kiriath-Arba/Hebron and the name of Caleb? A central reason, I propose, was the need to attribute an extraordinary feat to the eponymous ancestor of the Calebites in order to legitimate the presence of this clan in the important city of Hebron. The authors of Joshua 15 identified the former denizens of this city and its environs as the giant Anakites. (The Book of Genesis describes, in contrast, Hittite nobility residing in Hebron.) In this way, the earliest explanation for the Calebite presence in Judah made Caleb into an intrepid giant-slayer. By taking possession of his divinely granted territory, he demonstrated outstanding bravery, a traditional justification for aristocratic privilege.

By identifying the Anakites as the populace whom Caleb vanquished, the authors availed themselves of an already notorious enemy. Deuteronomy quotes what was apparently an old saying: "You have heard it said, 'Who can stand up to the Anakites?'" (Deut 9:2). In the Book of Joshua, the population residing at Hebron/Kiriath-arba are descendants of man named Arba, who is called "the Anak." The word "Anak" may be linked etymologically to the Greek *anax*, "lord, leader," which in turn derives from Linear B *wa-na-ka* (although there are problems with this suggestion). Anak accordingly originated as the title for the rulers of what was originally an Aegean population. One may compare them to the Philistines and to their title *seren*, "lord, commander."[25]

These considerations assist us in laying our finger on what likely prompted the authors to interpolate Caleb into the Spy Story. Early versions of the story, which seek to explain why Israel did not launch an invasion from the south, describe a reconnaissance expedition focused on the Negeb and (perhaps secondarily) the hill country, which differs from a later supplement that presents the scouts reconnoitering the entire land (Num 13:21; compare Num 13:17, 22–23). In going up into the Negeb, the spies came to the town of Hebron. There they encounter the three sons of Arba "the Anak," whom Caleb later vanquishes in what we have identified as the oldest Caleb legend.[26]

Now one might argue that the reference to Hebron and the Anakites is a late insertion that presupposes the introduction of Caleb into the Spy Account. Yet even without the reference, the episode relates to the territory of Judah, and as such would have furnished a fitting place in Israel's war memories for Judahite authors to situate Caleb.

Conclusions

The addition of Caleb to the Spy Account constitutes a remarkable act of war commemoration on the behalf Calebite clan. The expanded account tells how this figure alone stood before the political assembly in Israel and urged them, "Let us go up at once and occupy [the land], for we are well able to overcome it!" (Num 13:30). Caleb's courage is expressed not only in his confidence that Israel could conquer Canaan but also in his public dissent with the national consensus. For this exceptional stoutheartedness the Judahite hero is rewarded with permission to live out his days in the Promised Land (14:24).

The redaction has a clear message: Had Israel followed Caleb, an entire generation would not have been doomed to die in the wilderness. They would have marched up from the south and established the seat of sovereignty in Hebron, at the heart of Judah's territory. (The account may allude here to David and Jerusalem.[27]) But because they failed to follow Judah's first great leader, Israel was punished with years of wilderness wanderings and ultimately collective death. The survivors then had to enter Canaan from the Transjordan and their descendants had wait for centuries until Judah, during the days of King David, managed to achieve its ascendancy over Benjamin and Ephraim.

This investigation has revealed that the oldest Caleb legends are found not in the Pentateuch but in the Book of Joshua. One of the passages in that book presupposes Caleb's presence in the Spy Account; the other does not. Among all distinctive aspects of the younger account in Joshua 14, the most important is the great lengths to which it goes in order to defend the Calebites' territorial entitlements. Whereas the older account in chapter 15 simply reports how this clan, along with Kenizzites, came to possess Hebron, the new episode reveals that disputes had arisen over their claims. In response to them, it allows the eponymous ancestor of the Calebites to rehearse the exceptional role he played in Israel's history and to remind others of the land that he received for his loyalty to YHWH.[28]

The conferral of the land is repeatedly declared to be in perpetuity: "to you and your children forever" and "until this day" (14:9, 14; cf. Deut 1:35). The authors are evidently responding here to groups who objected to this claim or perhaps even had already divested the Calebites of their territories. We will see in the following chapter that what occasioned these responses were territorial encroachments of the Judahite state and then the defeat of this state, which resulted in the forfeiture of Hebron to the Edomites. Over against the heroic figure of David, our texts hold up Caleb – both as a venerable Judahite leader and as a champion of the Calebite cause. His impassioned plea for patrimonial properties anticipates the advocacy of later tribal *sharifs* who sally forth to defend their clans' collective assets of territory and water sources.[29]

13

Caleb the Judahite

An Iconic Figure

> When [the Muslims] came to Hebron, they were amazed to see the strong and handsome structures of the walls. Yet they could not find an opening through which to enter. Then the Jews happened to come who lived in the area, and they said to the Muslims: give us [a letter of security] that we may continue to live amongst you and permit us to build a synagogue in front of the city's entrance. If you will do this, we shall show you where you can break in. And it was so.[1]

In this penultimate chapter I turn to the political history of Judah. My objective will be to discern more precisely what might have provoked this war commemoration on the behalf of the Calebites' eponymous ancestor. Why did biblical authors celebrate Caleb's valor? In order to answer this question, I will begin by examining evidence from the independent history of King David that I isolated in the first chapters of this book. From there I will consider other factors that shed light on the historiographical contexts in which the figure of Caleb assumed shape and color.

Abigail, David, and Calebite Territories

The earliest biblical passage to mention Caleb refers not to a person but to a place, namely "the Negeb of Caleb." The passage belongs to the account of David's time in the employ of the Philistine ruler at Gath. In Chapter 3 I situated that passage in relation to the independent history of David's reign over Judah (HDR). A lengthy excerpt from the HDR has often served as the point of departure for previous treatments of David's relationship to the Calebites. Depicting an event from David's time as a warlord prior to his mercenary service at Gath, the excerpt portrays the fate of a wealthy Calebite landowner named Nabal. While this "churlish fellow" refuses to pay for the "protection" afforded by David and his warriors, his brave wife goes out of her way to provision the troops with a generous array of fine foods.[2]

The tale, told in 1 Samuel 25, appears to be relatively unified. While it likely did not belong to the first version of the HDR, it is relatively old. The outer framework integrates the episode into the narrative of the Book of Samuel.[3] In the process of being harmonized with the Saul narrative, the account itself may have undergone slight changes.[4]

The depicted episode takes place at Carmel, a town close to Hebron, during the time of sheep shearing – traditionally an occasion of feasting and generous gift-giving. David sends some of his servants to Nabal in order to ask for a gift in recognition of the security services they had rendered. Quoting their captain, the servants address Nabal:

> As you know, your shepherds have been with us. We did not harm them, and nothing of theirs was missing all the time they were in Carmel. Ask your servants and they will tell you. Therefore, let [David's] young men find favor in your sight. We have come on a festive occasion. Please give your servants and your son David whatever you can. (1 Sam 25:7–8)

The request has much in common with the logic of protection racketeers, who coerce their victims to pay for immunity from the menace they themselves pose. Living up to his name, which is used elsewhere to describe egocentric misfits, Nabal foolishly spurns David: "Should I take my bread and my water, not to mention the meat I have slaughtered for my own shearers, and give them to men who come from I don't know where?" Upon hearing this response, David orders his men to arm themselves, taking 400 with him to slaughter every "wall-pisser" (male member) of Nabal's household. Already here we notice features common to texts that I have included in the earliest versions of the HDR: In addition to David's policies of extermination, he commands 200 men to stay behind with the baggage, just as he does at Ziklag.[5]

David's plans to carry out this brutal retribution are preempted by the prompt and quick-witted action of Nabal's wife, Abigail. With her impudent and imprudent husband in the background drinking himself into a stupor, his servants inform her how David had been brusquely rebuffed, even though he and his men served as "a bulwark for us, both by night and day, all the time we tended the flocks." Conscious of the impending evil, Abigail quickly prepares an array of costly comestibles: 200 loaves of bread, 2 *pithoi* of wine, 5 dressed sheep, 5 seahs of parched corn, 100 raisin cakes, and 200 cakes of pressed figs. Similar to the actions of Jacob when he confronted Esau and 400 of his troops, as depicted in Genesis, Abigail sends the donkeys bearing these gifts ahead of her with the servants. When she intercepts David on the warpath, she demonstrates deference by quickly dismounting, just as Achsah does when she approaches her father Caleb with her petition. Yet David is no Caleb here. Instead of a prince of a noble clan, he is a roaming brigand. And it is at his feet that Abigail, a refined noblewoman, prostrates herself.

The speech Abigail utters at this moment is the longest one uttered by a woman in any biblical narrative.[6] She begins by assuming the blame, while also calling her husband a "wretched fellow" (*'îš b^e^lîa'al*) and mocking his name. Drawing attention to the victuals that she had sent as a token of her support for "the followers of my lord," she assures David that YHWH would grant him an enduring house, in contrast to her husband's. She identifies this divine favor as a reward for fighting "the battles of YHWH," even though the reader knows that David's actions are more akin to those of a mafioso.[7] Finally, she beseeches David to not forget his "maid" when YHWH blesses him.

Abigail's eloquence, which speaks to David's political aspirations, and her liberal provision of viands, which demonstrates her unmitigated support, assuage David's anger. Later when she tells Nabal of the jeopardy he endured during his drunken stupor, he is seized by a heart attack, dying soon thereafter. When David sends messengers to beckon the widowed noblewoman to become his wife, she displays once again exceptional humility for her elevated social status, hastening to bow low, and with her face to the ground, and proclaiming: "Your handmaid is ready to be your maidservant, to wash the feet of my lord's servants." The genteel lady subsequently mounts her donkey and, taking five of her damsels, follows the messengers to join the house of David. (Notice the similarities to the portrait of Caleb's daughter Achsah in Josh 15 and Judg 1.)

The authors juxtapose here the generous, gracious solidarity of Abigail with the coarse ingratitude of her Calebite husband. His behavior and demise resemble that of Sukkoth and Penuel as portrayed in Judges 8. These two cities fail to support Gideon's war effort by refusing to provision his famished troops with bread and water as they pursue the Midianites. In retaliation, Gideon lays the towns to waste. Similarly, Nabal begrudges David and his men bread and water, let alone the anticipated remuneration for the security they provided. He thereby aligns himself with the enemy from whom David had protected him and brings upon himself the retribution described in Abigail's speech. In contrast, Abigail goes to great lengths to demonstrate her support for David.

The Calebites versus the Davidic State

According to an influential interpretation of this text set forth by Jon Levenson and Baruch Halpern, Nabal represents a Calebite chieftain or prince.[8] David's marriage to Abigail is accordingly to be seen as a shrewd move by a Bethlehemite not only to take possession of rich landholdings that he and his men later inhabit but also to assume the throne in the Calebite center of Hebron.[9] Levenson and Halpern explain the biblical authors' interest in

Caleb by appeal to the depiction of Hebron as the place where David is installed as king and rules over Judah. These historical events are said to have prompted scribes in the court of David or Solomon to rework older texts (such as the genealogies in Chronicles) and to transmit legends of Caleb's valor. To quote these two scholars:

> [T]he Caleb-Hebron traditions entered the pentateuchal story under the pressure of David's recent ascent to kingship in Hebron; the event, which took place after the old narratives had been told and retold for generations, was one that the early written sources, especially J, could not and did not want to ignore. After all, assuming the centrality of David's marriage to Abigail in his attaining royal status, David's title to Hebron was only as good as Caleb's. This explains the continual reiteration in Numbers through Judges of the promise to Caleb and its fulfillment. The grant to Caleb prefigures David's reign. The lateness of the Hebron pericope, which Noth remarked, is thus the result of the Judean recension of the old *Heilsgeschichte* materials in the Davidic-Solomonic era.[10]

In the preceding chapter I showed that we have good reason to suspect that Caleb was added to the pentateuchal texts at a very late stage. Even so, one must ask: To what degree was the attention the biblical authors devoted to the figure of Caleb engendered by the political interests of the Davidic court? In the course of this chapter, I will adopt a new approach to this question. Instead of attempting to discern the intentions of the historical David – an endeavor that is severely impeded by the nature of our sources – I will demonstrate the degree to which competing political factions delineated Caleb and David as rival figures that vie with each other for the position of Judah's greatest hero.

To begin, notice how the authors have sandwiched the episode with Nabal and Abigail between the two Ziphite passages (see discussion in Chapter 4), encouraging the reader to view Nabal's behavior as typical of the way a hostile southern clan treated Judah's first king. It is noteworthy in this connection that the royal (LMLK) Judahite jar handles for the late eighth-seventh centuries stem from four places: Hebron, Socoh, Ziph, and MMŠT.

According to a recent study, most of the exemplars for the seventh century bear the name Hebron or Ziph (located several miles to the southeast of Hebron).[11]

There are additional points that deserve consideration. Nabal's suspicion of the Bethlehemite David may reflect the territorial divisions in Judah. An important text that I discussed in earlier chapters distinguishes the Negeb of Caleb from the territories "that belong to Judah." It also juxtaposes the former with the Negeb of the Cherethites, a populace that never became part of Judah, except as members of an elite foreign guard (1 Sam 30:14). The identification of Nabal as a Calebite, the name of Abigail's son (Chileab), and references to Carmel throughout the account suggest that the chapter should be read as part of the disputes over Calebite landholdings that generated the composition of Caleb accounts we studied in the preceding chapter.[12]

All the Calebite texts address the clan's entitlement to specific territories, most prominently Hebron and its environs. It is therefore not surprising that the account of David's move from Ziklag back to Judah sounds so apologetic, insisting that a divine oracle commanded David and his 600 men, with their families, to occupy the towns around Hebron. Instead of spurning David and his massive entourage, the Judahites welcome him with open arms by promptly making him their king:

> After this David inquired of YHWH, "Shall I go up into any of the cities of Judah?" YHWH said to him, "Go up." David said, "To which shall I go up?" He said, "To Hebron." So David went up there, along with his two wives, Ahinoam of Jezreel, and Abigail the widow of Nabal of Carmel. David brought up the men who were with him, every one with his household; and they settled in the towns of Hebron. Then the men of Judah came, and there they anointed David king over the house of Judah. (2 Sam 2:1–4a)

One must bear in mind that David functioned as a representative figure for the Judahite royal court for the *duration* of its existence. If the court defended its policies by projecting them back into the life of David, it may have justified the occupation of Hebron and its surrounding towns by claiming that David and his warriors had already occupied these properties long ago – and with divine authorization. The addition of the Abigail-Nabal account bolsters this polemical defense: It depicts the divine punishment of a brutish Calebite landowner from the region along with the marriage of his widow to David. Later David and his followers move from Ziklag to Calebite territories, and David becomes King of Judah at Hebron.

If the Calebites had already settled in these territories, an expanding Judahite kingdom from its capital at Hebron would have certainly affected them. The earliest legends of their ancestors may be understood as efforts to resist the Judahite kings' expropriation of their territories: Caleb acquired the estates around Hebron long ago, in the presence of all Judah, with divine sanction, and by dispossessing the Anakites that lived there. Likewise, the closely related Kenizzites acquired their lands thanks to Othniel's feats of valor and the initiative of Caleb's daughter.

Some may doubt that Judahite circles would have waged such memory wars in opposition to the state's expropriation of properties, claiming that the conception is anachronistic. Yet in this respect Judahite political negotiations and polemics would have been hardly different from circles in Israel, and for Israel we know that groups did in fact protest against the royal court by accusing it of requisitioning its subjects' patrimonial properties. Such polemics are found most famously in the traditions about Ahab and Naboth's vineyard (1 Kings 21, 2 Kings 9).

Hebron, Calebites, and the Judahite Capital

There are a couple of problems with the approach I have just presented. First, we do not know at what point the Calebites began to occupy Hebron. Second, much of the biblical material related to Caleb may have originated *after* the demise of the Judahite kingdom. Here and in the following sections I address these problems.

Various clues suggest that the Calebites migrated to, or at least staked a claim at, Hebron at a later stage in their history. As noted earlier, the oldest reference to Caleb refers to the southern Negeb, and the Nabal-Abigail episode takes place in Carmel, south of

Hebron. Likewise, the oldest Caleb legend links the conquest of Kiriath-arba/Hebron to that of Kiriath-sepher/Debir, a locale that also lies somewhere to the south of Hebron (see "land of Negeb" in Josh 15:19). It is possible that the northernmost tip of the Calebites' territory included Hebron or that the Calebites gradually migrated northwards toward Hebron (see discussion below). But it is equally possible that the oldest Caleb legend (Josh 15) and the accounts that it spawned represent attempts to assert ownership to the first capital of the Judahite kingdom.

In scrutinizing the oldest Caleb legend, I noted that it begins by referring to Kiriath-arba and then explains, in what seems to be a later gloss, that this city is the same as Hebron. But can the identification be trusted? Are the two places really the same? Or was an editor interested in identifying Kiriath-arba with neighboring capital of Judah? Whatever the case may be, it is certainly strange that the author did not originally refer to Hebron, which was the name of the capital according to the reliable data in the Book of Samuel. Later texts do the opposite, either referring solely to Hebron or clarifying that Hebron "was formerly known as Kiriath-arba." (These texts include Num 13–14, Josh 14, and Judg 1.)

What this means is that the oldest Caleb-legend may have claimed entitlement to a town or properties in the *vicinity* of the ancient Judahite center. In this case, it wouldn't be absolutely necessary to envisage a scenario of Calebite resistance to the Judahite state after the latter began to encroach on the former's ancestral territories.[13]

Ultimately, however, one cannot deny the polemical character that suffuses the Caleb accounts. The contentious quality is unmistakable in the account of the passionate disquisition that Caleb delivers before all the Judahites, calling to mind the exceptional role he played during the first reconnaissance mission. As a reward for his loyalty, YHWH awards him Hebron as a *perpetual* territorial inheritance for his descendants (Josh 14:6–15). This oration provided a rhetorically powerful script for contemporaneous generations of Calebites who needed to make a case for their entitlement to disputed terrain.

As it centralized and bolstered its power, the Judahite court would have faced resistance from large clans and tribes. Based on the comparative history of state-tribal relations, it is safe to assume that the throne would have at least occasionally attempted to break the power of clans and tribes by reducing them to smaller nuclear units and challenging their collective territorial claims.

Evidence for such nation-building programs can be found throughout the Bible, and particularly in some of the war commemoration texts studied in this book. By constructing memories of cities and groups that betrayed David in times of war or that aided and abetted his enemies, the Judahite court could target cities and clans that threatened to obstruct its agendas.[14]

Yet war commemoration also offered a means of resistance by groups who opposed measures of state centralization. Thus the Calebite clan paid homage to the deeds of their eponymous ancestor as Judah's first hero, one who rivals the figure of David constructed by the Judahite court.

This war commemoration could have been performed in the political contexts of the Judahite kingdom. But perhaps to an even to a greater degree, this war commemoration is the product of the circles who struggled to articulate a new political identity for Judah by appeal to the formative periods in Judah's past.

According to the interpretational approach introduced in the preceding chapter, the Caleb accounts affirm that long before David managed to consolidate a kingdom of Judah at Hebron, Caleb had represented Judah during the conquest of Canaan. As a scout commissioned by Moses to reconnoiter the land, he went up to Hebron and returned to the camp with a "good report." David may have been Judah's/Israel's greatest king, but Caleb alone stood against the national assembly, insisting that Israel go up and take possession of the land. If the nation had followed his recommendation, it would have avoided forty years of wandering in the wilderness and marched up promptly from the south into what was later Judahite territory. David may have been a great warrior in his early years, but Caleb was still able to vanquish the fearsome Anakites and take possession of Hebron at the age of 85.[15] More importantly, from the perspective of Judahite readers, if Caleb's courageous counsel had been heeded, it would not have taken so long for Judah to establish its ascendancy and preeminence in relation to the rest of Israel.

In support of this reading, consider a similar competition in the Benjaminite-Ephraimite region between the figures of Joshua and Saul. According to the portrayal in the biblical narratives, Saul becomes king in Israel after heeding the call for help from the town Jabesh-Gilead during a siege, just as Joshua heeds the Gibeonites' call for help from a coalition of Canaanite kings. Like Saul, Joshua marches up straightaway with an army to "save" the beleaguered population. Yet unlike Saul, Joshua does *not* assume a throne. In the narrative sequence of the books of Joshua–Samuel, the actions of Israel's great nonmonarchic hero, who leads Israel in the conquest of Canaan, relativize those of Israel's first king.

The case of Joshua and Saul may be compared to that Caleb and David. By fashioning a figure that could trump the portrait of David, groups could thwart the tendency of Judahite "nation-building" to homogenize the population of its territories, subsume all achievements under the names of the Davidic kings, and thereby neglect the particularity of the ancient clans that occupied these lands for centuries. By recalling the deeds of Caleb and of others like him, populations could combat the amnesic proclivities of the political community.

Such memory wars would have likely been waged within the context of the Judahite kingdom. Yet as we have seen with respect to Barzillai the Gileadite, Shobi the Ammonite, and others, Judahite circles continued to use the figure of David to negotiate politics long *after* the destruction of the kingdom. The same was likely true with respect to Caleb. To this post-exilic context we now turn.

Rivalries, Ancestral Tombs, and Divine Promises

The independent David history (HDR) reflects a loosely consolidated Judahite kingdom in which Hebron serves as the capital.

Jerusalem appears solely as a garrison on the northern periphery. If the HDR had presented Jerusalem as Judah's capital, we would expect to find an elaborate description of YHWH directing David to move to Jerusalem, similar to the account of the relocation to Hebron. But nothing of the sort is to be found in the material that has been transmitted. Instead, all we have is a passage that tells how David conquered Jerusalem and fortified it against foes from the north – which would have included, most directly, Israel! In contrast to this narrative, the much more predictable account in Chronicles portrays David immediately going up to occupy Jerusalem after becoming king.[16] The authors of the HDR, however, made little effort to shift attention from Hebron to Jerusalem.

As noted earlier, Hebron owed its status, not least, to its location at the center of the kingdom. Jerusalem gradually grew in importance because it was located on the border between Israel and Judah. Yet it may have not become the Judahite capital until after the defeat of the kingdom of Israel in 722 BCE. At that time, Judah sought to annex southern territories of the former competitor kingdom. The relocation of the capital to Jerusalem would have faced resistance among factions in Hebron. Rivalry with Jerusalem may be reflected in the depiction of Absalom going to Hebron when he stages an insurrection against David in Jerusalem.

Tensions with Jerusalem undoubtedly would have occasioned efforts by the inhabitants of Hebron – likely for centuries thereafter – to remind the political community of their city's honored place in Judahite history. These efforts include, first, of all of the war commemoration we have studied here: Armed with memories of Caleb's valor, Calebite groups could position their ancestor against the revered figure of the Judahite court, King David.

Another tactic appealed to events in the lives of patriarchs and matriarchs of Israel. The authors responsible for the final shape of the Book of Genesis contend that long before the emergence of the kingdom, this place was the abode of Israel's patriarchs and matriarchs, both during their lifetimes and after. By locating the graves of the nation's ancestors at Hebron, they could trump Jerusalem's honor of being home to the tombs of Judah's kings.

In several passages of Genesis we witness the attempts of later readers to identify southern locales with Hebron. Thus, in the account of Sarah's death, an editorial gloss explains that Kiriath-arba is the same place as Hebron.[17] Another set of texts links Hebron to Mamre: Jacob is said to have visited "his father Isaac at Mamre, or Kiriath-arba (that is, Hebron), where both Abraham and Isaac resided." If the attempts to connect these places can be assigned to glossators who were working at an advanced stage in the composition history of Genesis, we could explain why what is likely the oldest text from the Abraham cycle refers to Mamre without any reference to Hebron.[18]

A similar redactional move can be witnessed with respect to Machpelah, the place Abraham purchased as a burial site. Repeatedly the texts state that it is "east of" or "faces" Mamre. For example, Abraham is said to have "buried Sarah his wife in the cave of the field of Machpelah facing Mamre (that is, Hebron) in the land of Canaan."[19] While an early literary tradition locates Jacob's burial place in the Transjordan, later authors reworked the text so that this Israelite ancestor is also interred in the Judahite site of Machpelah. Due to these identifications, Hebron became known in the Jewish tradition as *'Îr 'Abôt*, "The City of the Patriarchs."[20]

In an influential study from 1953/1954, Alfred Jepsen argued that the Calebites were responsible for promulgating traditions about Abraham in Mamre. Jepsen even maintained that Abraham was a direct ancestor of Caleb. Whereas the patriarch was not able to maintain a permanent hold on the region and was eventually expelled by nomadic groups, Caleb managed to conquer Kiriath-Arba and drive out its inhabitants. In order to defend their rights to the land, the Calebites appealed to a covenant made between Abraham and his God. Later the Calebite clan formed a federation with other Hebrew tribes in the south, which gave rise to the name *Ḥebrôn* – meaning "league, covenant place." This southern federation is the direct predecessor to the grand tribe of

Judah. During the time of David it became a state and adopted YHWH as its god.[21]

Jepsen's hypothesis is too speculative to be sustainable. The Calebite connection to Abraham is more conceivable as the work of later generations. This means that the oldest Abrahamic traditions have little if anything to do with Caleb. Yet one possibility deserves closer consideration: The first Abrahamic covenant, portrayed in Genesis 15, may have originally referred solely to the region of Mamre.

After removing the battle account in the preceding chapter, which most likely represents an interpolation into the narrative, we find Abraham dwelling at "the terebinths of Mamre, which are in Hebron."[22] It is there that YHWH makes a covenant with the patriarch as a pledge that he would indeed take possession of the land promised to him. The description of that land includes two very different conceptions. One is expansive, reaching from the river of Egypt to the Euphrates, populated by "the seven nations" of Deuteronomy. The other conception refers simply to "this land," as if it were the region in the immediate vicinity. Consistent with this much more modest territory, the corresponding nations consist solely of three southern populations: the Kenites, the Kenizzites, and Kadmonites. Othniel, Caleb's son-in-law, is identified as a member of the second group in this triad.

If the Abrahamic covenant originally related solely to the direct environs of Mamre/Hebron before it was expanded with a pan-Israelite purview, then the question needs to be asked: Cui bono? Whose interest did the covenant serve originally? Was it the concerns of Israel as a people? Or did it have in view an ethnically mixed, "ecumenical" group of Abraham's descendants? Perhaps it served the agenda of the Calebites, as they attempted to dispossess the Kenizzites. Alternatively, it could have been in keeping with the designs of the Davidic court. Still another possibility is that the covenant defended Judahite territorial claims after the defeat of the kingdom.

It would take us too far afield to evaluate all these scenarios. But one conclusion is already warranted: This early version of the Abrahamic covenant provides further testimony to the hotly disputed status of the Hebron region. Both it and the accounts of Abraham's purchase of burial grounds line up next to the Calebite legends in attesting to the existence of groups within Judah who laid claim to the territory by appealing to a prior covenant/contract or a divine sanction. While the Calebite legends emphasize martial valor, it is noteworthy that the chapter directly preceding the account of the Mamre covenant portrays Abraham in the role of a brave and noble warrior.[23]

Hebron Irredenta and the Edomites

Earlier I discussed the problems that Judahite state centralization would have posed for the Calebites. In this final section, I examine an external force – friction with a neighboring population – that would have helped shape our texts.

Throughout our passages we repeatedly encounter glosses identifying Mamre, Machpelah, Kiriath-Arba and other places with Hebron. Glosses can rarely be aligned to larger redactions and are hence difficult to date. But it would be surprising if these editorial activities were not related to the incursions of a particular population: the Edomites.

Following the sixth-century onslaught of the Babylonian Empire, the Edomites advanced into the south of Judah, ultimately controlling much of the Negeb, the southern Shephelah, and the hills of Hebron. As to when exactly this migration occurred, Albrecht Alt argued long ago that the Negeb was cut off from Judah in 598/7 BCE, during Judah's first military conflicts with Babylon. More recent studies reckon there was a gradual process of Edomite infiltration that began in the final years of the Judahite kingdom. Once Judah reconstituted itself decades later as a Persian province, its southern border extended only to Bet-Zur, circa four miles north of Hebron.[24] Thus, the case of Hebron must be viewed from the perspective of borderlands and border-towns, which, as I noted in regard to Keilah (Chapter 4), are very often sites of virulent contestation.

Amidst these political-demographic changes, the editorial activities that I identified make good sense. Many in Judah must have found the Edomite occupation of Hebron difficult to countenance. Without the military means to redeem the lost territory, they could only fight for the *memory* of Hebron.

This is where the graves of the patriarchs and matriarchs come into play. Ancestral graves have long served as means by which communities defended territorial claims.[25] The authors portray, with attention to minute details, how Abraham legally purchased the burial grounds at Machpelah. They identify this location with Hebron/Kiriath-arba. And they report that most of Israel's patriarchs and matriarchs (Abraham, Sarah, Isaac, Rebekah, Jacob, and Leah) were buried there.

In these ways, the Priestly source drives home a consequential point: Hebron was not just an important political center for the erstwhile *kingdom* of Judah. Long before the kingdom, it had already served as a central site for the *people* who descended from Abraham – and it can endure as such. As with many of the biblical texts we have examined, the Priestly source might be viewed as "irredentist," a position named after the 19th-century Italian *irredentista* who sought to "redeem" to the Italian homeland all Italian-speaking districts subject to Astro-Hungarian rule. Accordingly, the Priestly authors were asserting a longstanding claim to the territory of Hebron over against the Edomites who actually possessed it.

Recent work on the Priestly source takes a much different approach, one that views the work as inclusivist or "ecumenical." This document supposedly identifies the patriarchal tombs as a sacred center for the various peoples whom Abraham and Isaac begat, not just members of Israel.[26]

While various aspects of the Priestly source speak in favor of this alternative to the irredentism approach, there are also problems with it. The messages of both the Abrahamic and Calebite texts were addressed to the biblical authors' own communities, and many leaders in Judah probably would not have been bashful about asserting these land claims vis-à-vis the Persian satrapal authorities. After all, matters related to borders were ultimately not up to the leaders of the small provinces. The satraps were expected to supervise the provinces within their satrapies and arbitrate border disputes. (In some circumstances, they would consult the central court.) Such being the case, the biblical narratives may reflect the *types* of claims that Judah made to imperial officials and their neighbors in defense of its territorial interests.

Hebron persisted as a contested site in the late Second Temple period and beyond. The Book of Jubilees makes Hebron a territorial focal point in the lives of Israel's ancestors. It also presents some of Jacob's descendants continuing to dwell at Hebron after his death, so that Israel could claim an uninterrupted presence at the site even while the nation was in Egypt (Jub 45:16, 46:11). A register from the Book of Ezra–Nehemiah, dating probably to the Hellenistic period, reports that "some Judahites lived in Kiriath-arba and its villages" (Neh 11:25). The author likely intended to use an antiquated name for Hebron in what is a nostalgic description of Judah's borders. The Book of First Esdras, from the Greco-Roman period, asserts that King Darius of Persia had issued a decree long ago that the Edomites/Idumeans should "give up the villages of the Jews that they held" (1 Esd 4:50).

Earlier polemics against the Edomites are found in the Book of Samuel. It portrays a figure named Doeg the Edomite betraying David and Ahimelech the high priest, and thereby facilitating Saul's atrocious massacre of the village Nob.[27] In a wide range of biblical texts, circles in Judah negotiated their political stance toward the Edomites by "remembering" their opprobrious actions in wartime.[28]

As Judah regained its native military strength, it transformed its polemical-historiographical responses to military campaigns: In their war against the "descendants of Esau," the Maccabees recaptured Hebron, laying it and its villages to waste.[29] In the late first century BCE, King Herod the Great, a Jew of Edomite/Idumean descent, built a beautiful enclosure around the cave of Machpelah.

Since antiquity, a small Jewish community has resided at Hebron. Over the centuries their relations with Muslims (and Christians) were generally harmonious. This changed in 1929 when Arabs, fearing the ramifications of Jewish immigrations, slaughtered sixty-seven Jews. Another massacre occurred in 1994, this time when an Israeli settler opened fire inside the Abraham Mosque at the Cave of the Patriarchs, murdering twenty-nine Muslims. After the Six-Day War (1967), a Jewish group took up residence in an abandoned military base at Hebron. Becoming a harbinger of the "settler movement," they called their new home Kiriath-arba, the oldest biblical name for the town.

Competing political interests in Hebron have long been tied to its ancestral tombs, to the figure of Caleb, and to the memory of David. From a Jewish perspective, the head of the yeshiva at Kiriath-arba affirmed that just as Hebron is the place where David became king first of Judah and then later of all Israel, so its resettlement presaged the redemption of the entire land. Thus, as in biblical days, the modern history of Hebron is situated squarely between the forces of statehood and the impact of defeat.

Conclusions

In my initial survey of the Caleb texts, I noted that a promise to Abraham mentions the Kenizzites among the populations who long inhabited the land, while Esau's genealogy identifies this clan as descendants of Esau and thus Edomites.[30] This reidentification likely took place after the Edomites moved into the region that Othniel is said to have conquered.

So why didn't the biblical authors also reidentify the closely related Calebites as descendants of Esau? The reason is related to the tradition history reconstructed in the present book. If the Calebites preserved their distinctiveness, never becoming fully absorbed into Judah like other clans that we no longer know about, it was because their territories were subject to bitter political disputes. The earliest struggles would have been with competing clans, such as the Kenizzites. Later it was tensions with the court of the Judahite state, which chose Hebron as its first capital. After the capital was relocated to Jerusalem, Hebron would have struggled to maintain its place in Judahite/Israelite collective memory. And still later, the final years of the Judahite kingdom and its defeat witnessed the forfeiture of its southern territories to the Edomites, with Judah's new border running just north of Hebron.

All these contexts posed significant challenges for the Calebites and other clans on Judah's southern periphery. While many clans would have succumbed to these social-demographic changes, the story of the Calebites is one of defiance. Indeed, the varied forms of their resistance in the shifting political contexts of Judah's collective experience gave rise to the much later stories of their *heros eponymos*, his daughter, and their pertinacious personalities.

14

War-Torn David

Conclusions

For many generations, scholars have insisted that the oldest portions of the Bible are the David accounts, especially the so-called Court History or Succession Narrative (2 Sam 9–20 and 1 Kings 1–2). Likewise, some still assert that earliest sources of the Pentateuch were composed in the direct wake of these writings.

The present investigation has severely undermined these claims. I have demonstrated that the Court History likely developed in several stages, and that even its oldest portions are probably late addenda to the earliest account of David's life.

That account, which I have called the History of David's Reign (HDR), has nothing to say about Israel. Instead, it presents David as the youngest of eight sons. Without prospects of a patrimony, he takes the career path of many disadvantaged, making a name for himself as a soldier of fortune and warlord. In the employ of a Philistine potentate, he wins the allegiance of clans in the southern hill country. Eventually these clans come together to anoint him king over "the House of Judah."

David builds his capital at Hebron, located at the center his kingdom and already an important site a thousand years before his reign. Early supplements to this account tell how David captures Jerusalem (the City of David). It serves as a fortress on the northern periphery of the kingdom, in the territory of Benjamin, where Judahite kings later competed with northern states (see, e.g., 1 Kings 15:16–22), and where even the historical David may have staked a claim.

This early account of David's reign relates solely to Judah and has nothing to say (explicitly) about Israel. The Court History, however, depicts various kinds of challenges David faces as ruler of Israel. It therefore cannot be as old as often thought. Rather, its authors presuppose a series of thorough revisions and substantial expansions that tell how David came to occupy the throne of Israel.

These revisions and expansions are the work of circles who combined the older David account with the originally independent history of Saul's reign. The fusing of the two sources radically reshapes the way we read them. David's experiences as a mercenary warlord in the service of a Philistine monarch are now to be understood as the events in his life after he had already made a name for himself in the ranks of Saul's army, won the affection of Saul's son Jonathan, received the hand of Saul's daughter Michal, and aroused the jealousy of Saul himself. Because Saul fears the ambition and success of his soldier, he determines to assassinate him. David therefore takes flight. It is here where the authors splice in the older account of David's adventures as a soldier of fortune. Instead of wandering about, he is running from Saul's spear.

One can imagine the thought process that led to the literary synthesis. If David was truly king of Israel, what should one make of the received account that depicts his years as a mercenary warrior and then as king of Judah? For the circles insisting that he ruled over all Israel, the answer was obvious: That account covers only a brief period in David's life. What is missing are the many episodes related to both his very early and his later years – his anointing by Samuel as king of Israel, his time in the court of Saul, then, later, his wars with Saul's house, his eventual accession to the throne of Israel, his wars with Absalom, and so on.

So if the earliest account of David tells only about his achievements in establishing the kingdom of Judah, and if this qualifies as our most reliable historical information about him, why did later authors go to the trouble of synthesizing his story with Saul's? And why did they make these accounts so complex? Was it really necessary to include so many characters, place names, and details?

I noted that this question has most often been answered in the past on the assumption that narratives were composed soon after David's death or in the court of his son Solomon. Their authors were concerned supposedly with exonerating Judah's great leader from any wrongdoing toward the house of Saul. The problem with this solution is that it fails to explain a whole series of texts that depict David in a less-than-favorable light. No Judahite king would have countenanced such a report of his beloved forefather's life, let alone condoned it or even commissioned it, as argued by so many of my colleagues.

The finest fictional retelling of David's life ever written – Stefan Heym's *The King David Report* (German original in 1972) – displays this insight with brilliance: When Solomon commissions Ethan the Scribe to write the official history of his father, he expects an account that will extol his greatness. But as Ethan undertakes his research, he discovers a long trail of David's crimes. Ethan has to decide whether he will fulfill his debt to truth or deliver a report that conceals David's record.

Heym did not invent this dilemma. He discovered it at the heart of the biblical accounts. As a Jew and as a dissident writer living in East Germany, he viewed his own literary work as the continuation of the unflinching efforts of his biblical forebears, as they set about the task of coming to terms with both the boon and bane of royal power and statehood.

What Heym saw is exactly what generations of readers have appreciated in the David narratives. If the facts did not speak so clearly for themselves, this history of interpretation would suffice to undercut the popular claims that these narratives were drafted in the Judahite royal court as an *apologia pro domo sua*.

In this study I set forth a more nuanced and tenable model of interpretation. The model reckons with three stages of development.

1) The first is the older independent David account that is focused on the kingdom of Judah. It may have been composed quite early, even before the conquest of Israel in 722 BCE.
2) The second stage is the synthesis of this account with the independent Saul account. The authors show how David and his line are the rightful rulers of all Israel. Their work must be dated before the conquest of Judah in 586 BCE.
3) The third stage is post-exilic. The authors now exploit the figure of David in a manner similar to that of Shakespeare's plays. They unmask royal power by revealing the ruthless ambition of Israel's greatest king. Their objective is not to cast aspersions on kingship and centralized statehood altogether. Rather, in keeping with the overarching purpose of Enneateuch or Primary History (Genesis–Kings), they are concerned with setting forth a new model of political community: a *people* (or *nation*) that can survive the loss of statehood and territorial sovereignty. David embodies unalloyed state power, and the account of his reign becomes the pivot in this history.

Thus we must concede that a number of texts portray David in a favorable manner. They present the same prophet who had previously anointed Saul now anointing David as king of Israel. Later, Israel's God affirms his steadfast love to David and to his dynastic line alone. Closely related to these affirmations are the texts in which David outdoes Saul, in both his martial feats and his moral conduct. Saul may have originally only reigned over the territory of Benjamin, but in these texts he represents the kingdom of Israel, just as David embodies Judah. Telling how David spares Saul's life, mourns his death, and performs acts of benefaction for his household, the narratives affirm that Israel's God chose Judah's royal dynasty to rule the nation. The same goes for portions of the accounts of David's wars with Absalom and Sheba ben Bichri.

In these narratives, later readers discerned parables of Israel's and Judah's history (as the biblical authors understood that history). Being the youngest of eight sons, David is an underdog. Even so, Israel's God chooses him to replace Saul. He eventually becomes king of Judah. Yet when he mounts the throne of Israel, it is only after long years of wars with Israel, culminating in the death of Saul and his sons. Likewise, the tales of Absalom's and Sheba's insurrections relate to the historical division between Israel and Judah.

In all these texts, we can hear representatives of David's royal line summoning communities in the north and asserting their authority over "all Israel." Now that Assyria had deported Israel's "secessionist" kings, those who remained in the land could submit themselves to the authority of the divinely chosen dynasty ruling in Jerusalem.

The unification that the biblical authors long for is not a *return* to the political conditions that prevailed under Saul, David, and Solomon. Rather, they create memories of that period of unity in order to define the status quo – the separation of Israel and Judah – as the wicked rupture from a primordial unity. They date the "original sin" that caused the division to the time after Solomon. Yet because this issue is of such great concern to them, they devote many lines of their accounts to the wars between David and Saul, and then David and Saul's households, and then between David and Absalom, and then again between David and Sheba. Israel's political and also national unity consumes the attention of these authors.

Coming now to the unusual complexity of the David narratives – the feature that causes readers the most work – scholars have often interpreted the plethora of details in line with the assumption that the authors were writing with recent events and contemporaneous personalities in view. Yet how are we to explain that the biblical authors found these narratives worthy of preserving, transmitting, and placing at the center of their history? They must have found an abiding significance in their details.

Here again we witness the deficiencies of the popular approach to the David narratives and the need for an altogether different one. The approach that I adopt in this book grew out of my work on war commemoration. According to my claims, the same activity that produced the monuments dotting our national landscapes propelled the Bible's formation. Using representative individuals, the biblical writers appealed to memories of wartime contributions and sacrifice as they addressed issues of belonging – both within the community of Israel and between Israel and other peoples.

In developing this approach, I take issue with the source-critical approach that has witnessed a recent resurgence in pentateuchal studies. Reckoning with self-standing sources and minimum intervention from later editors, practitioners of this approach fail to do justice to the evidence of gradual growth of texts representing a diverse trajectory of agendas and concerns. My own findings substantiate the work of the "supplementary approach" by delineating a comparative social context ("war commemoration") for appreciating the much messier activities by which political communities negotiate belonging.

Many will persist in the effort to press the Bible's competing memories into a single source or to demonstrate that they belong to different sources that emerged separately from each other. But such an endeavor proves naïve in the face of the sheer abundance and heterogeneity of the rival memories. A more tenable and sensitive approach recognizes the extent to which the Tanakh's sources gradually accumulated overlapping layers of accretions. Inasmuch as it is much less tidy, this model of supplementation reflects more faithfully the often contradictory and cluttered character of demotic war commemoration and other decentralized processes of collective social formation. The construction and contestation of memories is well attested in contexts where cultural-political expressions are not monopolized by a single power and where groups can readily challenge each other on issues posed by populations within their societies and on their borders.

In testing this approach on the David narratives, we saw how the accounts of David's flight from Saul and from Absalom served as frameworks for generations of readers to grapple with questions of membership and status in the society of Judah and then among the people of Israel. These readers amplified the narratives with an array of episodes that pursue two basic polemical agendas: Either they pay homage to those who assisted Israel's iconic king during his wars with Saul and Absalom, or they malign the memory of those who betrayed him during his struggles with his nemeses.

I examined a wide range of examples:

- **towns**, such as Keilah, Jabesh-Gilead, Abel Beth-Maacah, Bahurim, and Mahanaim;
- **clans and tribes**, such as the Ziphites, Kenites, and Ephraimites;
- **regions and territories**, such as the Gilead or Benjamin;
- **neighboring peoples**, such as the Ammonites or Edomites; and
- **guilds and professional groups**, such as the temple personnel (Zadokites or Levites) and military guards (the Pelethites and Cherithites).

In three chapters of this book I treated the case of the influential Calebite clan. The earliest legends defend their possession of tribal territories by commemorating the exceptional bravery of their eponymous ancestor Caleb. This figure rivals David in Judahite collective memory. What may have originally given rise to the Caleb legends, I have argued, is the encroachment of the Judahite state on Calebite territories around Hebron. But more than anything, the biblical stories are the product of much later literary circles working with inherited historical narratives. In seeking to come to terms with the loss of all that David and his sons had established, these writers present Caleb as non-royal figure who represents Judah as a mighty warrior centuries prior to Judah's first king.

The biblical authors show that if Israel had followed Caleb's counsel, the nation would not have wandered about for an entire generation and then entered Canaan from the east. Instead it would have marched up directly from the south into the Judahite territory surrounding Hebron that Caleb has inspected on his reconnaissance mission. Whereas David was no longer able to fight in his advanced years, Caleb managed to route the formidable Anakites from Hebron at the age of 85. But more than physical superiority Caleb, as a non-king, had a conquest plan for the entire nation. It ensured that Judah and Hebron would be in a position of preeminence vis-à-vis the rest of Israel long before David founded his throne.

Like his assertive daughter Achsah, Caleb endures in biblical and post-biblical memories as an unusually stouthearted and indefatigable figure. He insists, with unyielding resolve and impressive rhetorical force, on his entitlement to a piece of the Promised Land, one that he, despite his octogenarian age, would seize from the formidable Anakites with his own arms. The final stages of the tradition defend his clan's claim to a central Judahite territory by pointing to his distinctive record of public dissent at a pivotal moment in the nation's history.

Refracted in Caleb's composite portrait, one that resembles the picture of Dorian Gray, is the turbulent history of a southern Levantine clan. It weathered many political challenges – from the territorial consolidation of the Judahite state to the defeat of that state, which permitted Edomite encroachment on its ancestral territories. These challenges elicited creative responses from the Calebites, such as those we have witnessed in our study of the legends of valor propagated around the names of Caleb, his daughter Achsah, and his son-in-law Othniel. If the Calebites were not remembered for resisting centralization efforts of the Judahite state and the incursions of Edomites, such legends would likely not have been created by later biblical historians or been significant enough to merit transmission in the biblical corpus.

By adapting and embellishing the traditions of Caleb's extraordinary courage, the biblical authors promoted this figure as a contender for the unsurpassed esteem and honor that King David boasted in the halls of Judah's history. The genealogists of Chronicles follow suit by making him the noble ancestor of his royal rival. Among early Jewish, Christian, and Muslim communities, he became a model of a courageous defiance that merits inheritance of the land – even if these communities differed widely in their understanding of what that land constituted.

Taken together, the biblical writings may be compared to war monuments that have accumulated new layers of meaning thanks to the many generations and rival groups through whose hands they have passed in their precanonical history. Thus if the Book of Samuel is a monument of triumph, the Book of Kings, which concludes with the Babylonian conquest, is a memorial to defeat.

Yet this bifurcation proves to be untenable. Defeat, as I have argued here and elsewhere, looms large on every page of the history of Israel told in Genesis–Kings. This explains why David's triumphs in the Book of Samuel are depicted so differently from typical monarch monuments. The core of some accounts, even those in the David narratives, may have been very similar to official state inscriptions. But the biblical authors have significantly amplified and reshaped them. And they have done so in the wake of military campaigns that vanquished the kingdom that David founded.

In both the empires of antiquity and the nation-states of modernity, war commemoration has played a key role in Jewish survival. But my work has demonstrated something quite remarkable. It was not only after Israel's "ethnogenesis" was completed, and after Jews had already become a people, that war commemoration began to assume its central role in Jewish history (in empires and nation-states). No, it is the very process by which Israel became Israel. We can therefore trace a line of continuity from modern Jewish culture to the biblical origins of Israel via the activity of war commemoration.

This book has treated many other aspects of the David accounts, such as the way his life anticipates Israel's exile or how contributions to building projects replace participation in war efforts in post-exilic works. But instead of reviewing these points here, I would like to conclude with a question about David the man:

If Saul had taken better aim when he hurled his spear at the young musician playing in his court, how would history have been different?

Anyone who has viewed many television documentaries or read the slew of sensationalistic works on King David, which continue to see the light of day, will have a ready answer to this question: Without David, nothing would be the same. There would be no Jewish people. There would be no Jewish state. There would be no Jerusalem. No Judaism. No Christianity.

I do not wish to speculate here on David's historical impact. But I cannot embrace the "Great Man Theory" of history that Thomas Carlyle popularized in the nineteenth century and that continues to resonate with so many. History is not the work of heroes.

Although the biblical authors, when depicting the lives of Israel's ancestors, ascribe a decisive role to individual action, they consistently shift the spotlight from the one to the many. In the case of David, Israel is hardly his own creation. He may have brought security to the nation, but he also brought great bloodshed. He may have captured Jerusalem and it may have become known as "the City of David." But without the contributions of later kings such as Hezekiah, post-exilic leaders such as Nehemiah, and a host of nameless others, this city would have passed into oblivion long ago.

While David's life and achievements will continue to arouse impassioned debate, there is no room for doubt that the *memories* of David embedded in 3,000 years of literature and art have profoundly shaped our histories, making him – thanks to others – one of the truly greatest figures in our past and in our present.

Notes

Chapter 1: Slings and Arrows

1 Robert Pinsky, *The Life of David* (New York: Schocken, 2005), p. 178. *The Book of J*, trans. David Rosenberg, interpreted by Harold Bloom (New York: Grove Press, 1990), 295.

2 Joseph Heller, *God Knows* (New York: Simon & Schuster, 1984), 5–6.

3 Notice that it is Jonathan's love for David that is celebrated ("your love to me") rather than David's own love. Notice too that, this love notwithstanding, David apparently has no qualms about eliminating the last survivors of Saul's house. I would like to thank here Prof. Tamara Cohn Eskenazi for this observation, and for taking the time to share with me her insights on the David narratives, many of which are included in this chapter. On the love between David and Jonathan, see Susan Ackerman's *When Heroes Love: The Ambiguity of Eros in the Stories of Gilgamesh and David* (New York: Columbia University Press, 2005).

4 Robert Alter, *The David Story: A Translation with Commentary* (New York: W. W. Norton, 1999), ix.

5 See the brilliant work of Baruch Halpern, *David's Secret Demons* (Grand Rapids: Eerdmans, 2001). See also P. Kyle McCarter's important two-volume commentary on the *Book of Samuel* in the Anchor Bible series (New York: Doubleday, 1980 and 1984), as well as his article on the subject: "The Apology of David," *Journal of Biblical Literature* 99 (1980): 489–504; Michael B. Dick, "The 'History of David's Rise to Power' and the Neo-Babylonian Succession Apologies," in *David and Zion: Biblical Studies in Honor*

of J.J.M. Roberts, ed. Bernard F. Batto and Kathryn L. Roberts (Grand Rapids: Eisenbrauns, 2004); and H. Hoffner, Jr., "Propaganda and Political Justification in Hittite Historiography," in *Unity and Diversity: Essays in the History, Literature, and Religion of the Ancient Near East*, ed. H. Goedicke and J.J.M. Roberts (Baltimore: Johns Hopkins University, 1975). For a critique of the apology-approach, as well as a good overview of recent approaches to the David narratives (including David M. Gunn's "serious entertainment" approach), see Nadav Na'aman, "Saul, Benjamin and the Emergence of 'Biblical Israel,' (continued, Part 2)," *Zeitschrift für die Alttestamentliche Wissenschaft* 121 (2009): 335–349.

6 The studies of the David narratives are, as to be expected, profuse. The works I encourage readers to consult, and make a place for in their libraries, include the following: Walter Dietrich's *The Early Monarchy in Israel*, trans. Joachim Vette (Atlanta: Society of Biblical Literature, 2007), which provides a balanced and useful discussion of the texts and the possibilities for interpreting them. My favorite work on David is Jonathan Kirsch's *King David: The Real Life of the Man Who Ruled Israel* (New York: Ballantine, 2001). For a review of recent research on David, see David Bosworth, "Evaluating King David: Old Problems and Recent Scholarship," *Catholic Biblical Quarterly* 68 (2006): 191–210. Also recommended is Steven L. McKenzie's *King David: A Biography* (New York: Oxford University Press, 2000) and Israel Finkelstein and Neil Asher Silberman, *David and Solomon: In Search of the Bible's Sacred Kings and the Roots of the Western Tradition* (New York: Free Press, 2007). Much of the recent research on the David and Saul narratives has been published in German: Klaus-Peter Adam, *Saul und David in der judäischen Geschichtsschreibung: Studien zu 1 Samuel 16–2 Samuel* (Tübingen: Mohr Siebeck, 2007); Reinhard Müller, *Königtum und Gottesherrschaft: Untersuchungen zur alttestamentlichen Monarchiekritik* (Tübingen: Mohr-Siebeck, 2004); André Heinrich, *David und Klio: Historiographische Elemente in der Aufstiegsgeschichte Davids und im Alten Testament* (Berlin/New York: De Gruyter, 2009); Regine Hunziker-Rodewald, "Wo nur ist Sauls Kopf geblieben? Überlegungen zu I Sam 31," in *David und Saul im Widerstreit – Diachronie und Synchronie im Wettstreit: Beiträge zur Auslegung des ersten Samuelbuches*, ed. Walter Dietrich (Fribourg/Göttingen: Vandenhoeck & Ruprecht, 2004), 280–300. I also thank Hannes Bezzel for sending me his essay on "The Numerous Deaths of Saul," which is being prepared for publication.

7 Unfortunately, there are not many works on Caleb to which I can refer the reader. See J. H. Pace, *The Caleb Traditions and the 40 Role of the Calebites in the History of Israel* (Diss. Emory, 1976) and Walter Beltz, *Die Kaleb-Tradition im Alten Testament* (Stuttgart: Kohlhammer, 1974). For the territorial history of Calebite territory, see Avi Ofer, "The Monarchic Period in the Judaean Highland: A Spatial Overview," in *Studies in the Archaeology of the Iron Age in Israel and Jordan*, ed. Amihai Mazar (Sheffield: Sheffield Academic Press, 2001), 14–37.

Chapter 2: Flesh and Stone

1 Num 10:29–32; Judg 1:16, 4:11.
2 See my two articles on the subject: Jacob L. Wright, "War Commemoration and the Interpretation of Judges 5:15b–-17," *Vetus Testamentum* 61 (2011): 1–16, and Jacob L. Wright, "Deborah's War Memorial: The Composition of Judges 4–5 and the Politics of War Commemoration," *Zeitschrift für Alttestamentliche Wissenschaft* 123 (2011): 516–534.
3 See John Hutchinson, *Nations as Zones of Conflict* (London: Sage, 2005) and Benedict Anderson, *Imagined Communities: Reflections on the Origins and Spread of Nationalism* (London: Verso, 1991 [1983]).
4 *Exercises at the Dedication of the Monument of Colonel Robert Gould Shaw* (Boston: Municipal), 1897, p. 24. For the history of the 54th, see Peter Burchard, *One Gallant Rush: Robert Gould Shaw and His Brave Black Regiment* (New York: St. Martin's Press, 1990).
5 *Exercises at the Dedication of the Monument of Colonel Robert Gould Shaw* (Boston: Municipal, 1897), 41.
6 Such monuments continue to appear. A film was released in 2010 that documents the many sacrifices and accomplishments of African American soldiers (*For Love of Country: The Story of America's Black Patriots*). See also Natasha Tretheway's recent Pulitzer Prize-winning *Native Guard: Poems* (New York: Mariner Books, 2007). For a recent look at the case of Hispanic Americans, see PBS's landmark six-hour documentary *Latino Americans*.
7 The first group of texts is Num 32, Deut 3, Josh 1 and 22. The second group includes Judg 5:15–17, 8:5–17, and 21:8–14.
8 See Jonathan Rosen, *The Jewish Confederates* (Columbia: University of South Carolina Press, 2000), ix.
9 Philadelphia: The Levtype Company, 1895.

10 Jacob L. Wright, "Surviving in an Imperial Context: Foreign Military Service and Judean Identity," in *Judah and the Judeans in the Achaemenid Period*, ed. Oded Lipschits et al. (Winona Lake, Indiana: Eisenbrauns, 2011), 505–528.
11 *Heritage and Hellenism: The Reinvention of Jewish Tradition* (Berkeley: University of California Press, 1998), 199.
12 Ibid, 206.
13 See John H. Molyneux, *Simonides: A Historical Study* (Wauconda, Illinois: Bolchazy-Carducucci Publishers, 1992), 183.

Chapter 3: King of Judah

1 The next verse, found in the following chapter, begins with David leaving from somewhere: "David departed from there and escaped to the cave of Adullam and when his brothers and all his father's house heard, they joined him there." The original referent of "from there" is likely not the court of Achish but rather Nob, where David visits the priest Ahimelech (21:1–10). Here we can see how the author neatly inserted this episode with Achish into an existing framework.

On the Philistines in the Bible and Israel's history, see the brilliant article by Peter Machinist, "Biblical Traditions: The Philistines and Israelite History," in *The Sea Peoples and Their World: A Reassessment*, ed. E. D. Oren (Philadelphia: University Museum of the University of Pennsylvania, 2000), 53–83.

2 What I observe here from the perspective of the David narratives has been seen from the perspective of the Saul narratives by W. Lee Humphreys' several articles, which were brought to my attention by Emory PhD student Aubrey Buster (via her seminar paper "Saul and David in 1 Sam 27–2 Sam 1: A New Narrative Analysis"). See W. Lee Humphreys, "The Tragedy of King Saul: A Study of the Structure of 1 Samuel 9–31," *Journal for the Study of the Old Testament* 6 (1978); idem, "The Rise and Fall of King Saul: A Study of an Ancient Narrative Stratum in 1 Samuel," *Journal for the Study of the Old Testament* 18 (1980); idem, "From Tragic Hero to Villain: A Study of the Figure of Saul and the Development of 1 Samuel," *Journal for the Study of the Old Testament* 22 (1982). See also important observations by Baruch Halpern, *The Constitution of the Monarchy in Israel* (Chico: Scholars Press, 1981).

3 See 1 Sam 25; 27:3; 30:3, 5, 18; 2 Sam 2:2. In this older history, David begins with two wives (1 Sam 25:43, 27:3, 30:5, 2 Sam 2:2) and then takes on others (3:2). But he is not yet married to Michal, in contradiction to 1 Sam 18–19! The contradiction is explained redactionally in 1 Sam 25:44 and 2 Sam 3:13ff.

4 The Book of Samuel introduces David to King Saul not just twice but several times, and each in different ways:

- 1 Sam 14:52, 16:19–22 (expanded with 16:14–18, 23);
- 1 Sam 17:12–39*;
- 1 Sam 17:55 – 1 Sam 18:4.

The oldest introduction is likely the third one: Later in this story Saul has no idea who David is and asks his general about him: "When Saul saw David go out against the Philistine, he said to Abner, the commander of the army, 'Abner, whose son is this young man?' Abner said, 'As your soul lives, O king, I do not know.' The king said, 'Inquire whose son the stripling is'" (1 Sam 17:55–56).

5 "The Akkadian Inscription of Idrimi," *JANES* 8 (1976): 59–96.

6 For an overview of this discussion, see H. J. Zobel, "Beiträge zur Geschichte Gross-Judas in früh- und vordavidischer Zeit," in *Congress Volume Edinburgh 1974* (Vetus Testamentum Supplements 28; Leiden: Brill, 1975), 253–77. A related issue in past research is whether the Judahite coalition already saw itself as somehow related to the larger Israelite amphictyony or whether the union of these two groups was David's achievement.

7 Alexander Fischer, "Beutezug und Segensgabe. Zur Redaktionsgeschichte der Liste in 1 Sam. XXX 26–31," *Vetus Testamentum* 53 (2003): 48–64.

8 A somewhat conflicting statement is found in 1 Sam 30:16b. These statements likewise do not match precisely 1 Sam 27:8–10. Even so, it's not necessary to ascribe these differences to multiple authors. The Ziklag episode is likely an early addition to the older HDR. It is closely connected to the insertion of a supplement that tells how David received this town from Achish (1 Sam 27:5–6). The secondary nature of that supplement is reflected not only in the tight connection between vv. 3a and 7 but also in the fact that vv. 7–12 present David returning to Achish and do not presuppose his residence in Ziklag. The Ziklag episode as reconstructed here does not present the town as David's residence (but rather as a town that David rescued, similar to Keilah); as such, it would predate the insertion of 27:5–6.

9 The finds at Khirbet Qeiyafa are discussed widely. One can begin at the official site of the dig: qeiyafa.huji.ac.il (without "www"). The momentous discovery of the Tel Dan inscription/stele has elicited a lot of discussion as well. I would recommend beginning with an article by Matthew Suriano, "The Apology of Hazael: A Literary and Historical Analysis of the Tel Dan Inscription," *Journal of Near Eastern Studies* 66 (2007): 163–76.

Chapter 4: Tales of Loyalty and Betrayal

1 Harmonizing the passage, many modern translations (e.g., the NJPS) introduce new nuances to the final line (v. 13a). Yet the Hebrew formulation lacks a pronounced sense of urgency. See J. Alberto Soggin, "*wayyithallekû ba'ašer yithallākû*, 1 Sam 23:13a," *Biblica et Orientalia* 14 (1972): 78. If they were fleeing, we would expect the author in v. 13a to use the verbs *bāraḥ* or *nās* that appear elsewhere often. (V. 13a is the transition to a new episode, perhaps 25:2ff.)

Another issue is the fear of David's men in Judah (vv. 3–4, demarcated in brackets and italics in the following). This could refer specifically to Saul and might be an addition. One can remove the lines, and the account would still make perfect sense:

> David was told: "The Philistines are raiding Keilah and plundering the threshing floors." David consulted YHWH, "Shall I go and attack those Philistines?" YHWH said to David, "Go and attack the Philistines and you will rescue Keilah."
>
> [*But David's men said to him, "Look, we're afraid here in Judah, how much more if we go to Keilah against the armies of the Philistines!" David consulted* YHWH *again, and* YHWH *answered him, "March down at once to Keilah, for I am going to deliver the Philistines into your hands."*]
>
> So David and his men went to Keilah and fought against the Philistines; he drove off their cattle and inflicted a severe defeat on them.

The fear of David's men may be understood in the general sense and not refer specifically to Saul. After all, the authors could have easily mentioned Saul here. I am suggesting that the earliest iteration of the account belonged to the HDR. Yet I am not claiming that it must have been included in the first versions of the HDR. It may be represent an early supplement, especially as Keilah is not mentioned again elsewhere. However, the addition of this passage may have caused the name of this town to be deleted from the list in 30:27–31.

2 An observation – one that has been made several times in earlier studies – lends credence to my larger proposal: The account of Keilah's deliverance depicts David consulting the deity through an oracle. We would expect the narrator, when describing this oracular consultation, to refer to the priest Abiathar and the ephod (the instrument of divination or oracular consultation). Yet this is not the case. It is noteworthy that Abiathar only appears in the passages that presuppose the combined Saul–David narrative.

Hence, it makes perfect sense, according to my larger thesis, that Abiathar appears precisely in the part of the Keilah story that relates to Saul – the same part that I've identified, for unrelated reasons, as a supplement to the story. To account for the priest's absence in the older version, the addition explains that Abiathar did not join David, bringing with him the ephod, until after Keilah's liberation. (This is in contradiction to 22:20–23. The Septuagint on 23:6 seeks to resolve the contradiction by adding: "he went down to Keilah with David.")

3 David's second query sticks out in the otherwise tightly formulated passage, with the petition to "YHWH, God of Israel" forming an "inclusion" or frame. (The "God of Israel" assists David against Israel's king, thus confirming that he should replace Saul.) The query also goes unanswered and therefore is repeated a second time (v. 12). What's more, the query does not identify whose "hand" and mentions the name "Saul" only in the following line. The Septuagint provides a much more succinct reading, while many modern translations simply omit the line.

4 The LMLK administrative stamps were impressed into the handles of large pithoi and storage jars that contained valuable foodstuffs (wine or oil). See Oded Lipschits et al., "Royal Judahite Jar Handles: Reconsidering the Chronology of the LMLK Stamp Impressions," *Tel Aviv* 37 (2010): 3–32.

5 The cited letters are, in order, EA 289, EA 290, EA 280. See William L. Moran, *The Amarna Letters* (Baltimore, Maryland: Johns Hopkins University Press, 1992) as well as Nadav Na'aman, "The Political Disposition and Historical Development of the Eretz-Israel According to the Amarna Letters" (PhD Dissertation, Tel Aviv University [Hebrew]), especially 100.

6 I recommend the study by Claudia Sadowski-Smith: *Border Fictions: Globalization, Empire, and Writing at the Boundaries of the United States* (Charlottesville and London: University of Virginia Press, 2008).

7 Likewise, the "hill of Hachilah" is the place where Saul camps and where David discovers him, contrary to the claim of the Ziphites that David was hiding at this hill. Similar points can be made for the first account. The expansion of the first account seems to have taken its cue from the addition of the new introduction in the second account (26:1), although the definite article there may be interpreted as a reference to the group who had already been introduced.

8 See, most recently, John Van Seters, "Two Stories of David Sparing Saul's Life in 1 Samuel 24 and 26: A Question of Priority," *Scandinavian Journal of the Old Testament* 25 (2011): 93–104. It's possible that the many repetitions in the David and Saul accounts correspond to competing versions of the narratives (that is, they constitute rival sources). If so, the authors have selectively included portions of these versions. But why did they include "doublets" (and

"triplets") in some cases, yet not in others? Thus why did the authors include two versions of the account of David sparing Saul's life? This doublet should be appreciated in light of the way David represents Judah and Saul represents Israel, as Judahite kings sought to bring members of Israel back to the fold after 722 BCE. (See discussions in Chapters 1, 2, 3, and 9.) Accordingly, the authors of Samuel wanted impress upon their readers that David went out of his way to show favor to Saul.

9 See Israel Finkelstein, "Rehoboam's Fortified Cities (II Chr 11, 5–12): A Hasmonean Reality?" *Zeitschrift für die Alttestamentliche Wissenschaft* 123 (2011): 92–107.

10 The two Ziphite accounts are separated by the tale about the Calebite Nabal (1 Sam 25), and the following chapters describe David's efforts in the Calebite region.

11 I would be remiss not to mention here how the TV sitcom South Park has parodied the place modern Jewish culture assigns to commemorative activities: In the momentous episode called "Jewbilee" (from the third season), Kenny, who is not Jewish, joins Kyle at "Jewbilee camp." Kenny eventually teams up with a bear to save the campers. In the end, Moses declares that Jews shall meet every year on that day to celebrate Kenny by making macaroni pictures and paper-plate bean-shakers decorated with glue and glitter.

Chapter 5: The Bones of Saul

1 In 1 Sam 31:8–10, only Saul's corpse is pinned to the wall of Beth-shan. Nothing is said about his sons. But in vv. 11–13, the men of Jabesh-gilead recover the bodies of Saul's sons from the wall. The disparity supports my contention that these final lines (vv. 11–13) are an early supplement of the account.

2 Various features accentuate the account's bookends. For example, the city rescues the "body of Saul" (*gewîat šā'ûl* 31:12) just as it had earlier sent messengers to "Gibeah of Saul" (*gib'at šā'ûl* 11:4) when besieged by the Ammonites. Notice too the seven days in 11:3 and 31:13.

3 An Iron Age "crematorium" found at the Amman airport may attest to the burning of bodies in this region. The similarities to Ammonite practices should not be surprising given the close (albeit contentious) interactions between these groups (e.g., Judg 11 and 1 Sam 11). Nelson Glueck identified Jabesh-gilead with Tell Abu Kharaz. An alternative is Tell Maqlub. On the northern edge of Wadi el-Yabis (compare Yābêš Gil'ād), it is strategically located to control traffic close to the point at which the later Roman road crosses the wadi.

4 Compare a similar line: "Some Hebrews crossed the Jordan, to the territory of Gad and Gilead. Saul was still at Gilgal, and the rest of the people rallied to him in alarm" (1 Sam 13:7). See also the Ephraimite insult of the Gileadites as being "nothing but fugitives from Ephraim" (Judg 12:4).

5 The Mesha Stele (an inscription made ca. 840 BCE by the Moabite king Mesha) claims that the king of Israel built the city Ataroth (probably modern Khirbet Ataruz) for the Gadites. That Ataroth is a Gadite city is claimed by Num 32:3, 34, yet there Gad is one of Israel's twelve tribes. For recent discussions of Israel's presence in Transjordan during the Iron Age, see Bruce Routledge, *Moab in the Iron Age* (Philadelphia: University of Pennsylvania Press, 2004).

The Qumran text is known as 4QSam[a]. For Josephus's account, see Antiquities 6.5.1–2. For a discussion of both texts, see Alexander Rofé, "The Acts of Nahash According to 4QSam[a]," *Israel Exploration Journal* 32 (1982), 129–33. For a different option, which differs from mine yet leads the field, see Frank Moore Cross and others, *1-2 Samuel* (Discoveries in the Judean Dessert 17; Oxford: Clarendon, 2005).

6 The account is found in 1 Chronicles 10. Some of the differences from the account in Samuel were noticed long ago by Yairah Amit, "Three Variations on Saul's Death," *Bet Mikra* 30 (1985): 92–102 (in Hebrew).

7 See 1 Chr 12:9–16. In Num 32 and related texts they serve as a vanguard for the Israelites. In 2 Sam 2:7, David alludes to their reputation as valorous soldiers.

8 For a study of the passage, see Simeon Chavel, "Compositry and Creativity in 2 Samuel 21:1–14," *Journal of Biblical Literature* 122 (2003): 23–52.

9 My use of "counterhistory" (*Gegengeschichte*) is drawn from David Biale, *Gershom Scholem: Kabbalah and Counter-History* (Cambridge: Harvard University Press, 1979). See also Amos Funkenstein, *Perceptions of Jewish History* (Berkeley: University of California Press, 1993), 36–49. For the roots of counterhistory in the writings of Wellhausen and Nietzsche, see Daniel Weidner, "'Geschichte gegen den Strich bürsten' – Julius Wellhausen und die jüdische 'Gegengeschichte,'" *Zeitschrift für Religions- und Geistesgeschichte* 54 (2002): 32–61.

Chapter 6: Uriah the Hittite

1 The roster in 2 Sam 23, which likely belongs to (an edition of) the HDR, uses ethnonyms profusely, referring both to nonnatives as well as those from towns within Israel and Judah. In contrast, the

later narratives are much more consistent in their use of ethnonyms for outsiders and patronyms for insiders.

2 See Gen 10:15, 15:20, 23:1–20, as well as Deut 7:1, 20:17, et passim.

3 See Josh 1:4, Judg 1:26, 1 Kings 10:29, 2 Kings 7:7. For another Hittite warrior, see 1 Sam 26:6. For the generic use of Hittite, see Ezek 16:3, 45. A general survey of the Hittites is provided by Meik Gerhards, "Die biblischen 'Hethiter,' *Die Welt des Orients* 39 (2009): 145–79.

4 On the history of attempts to explain Uriah's name, see now Daniel Bodi's study: *The Demise of the Warlord: A New Look at the David Story* (Sheffield: Sheffield Phoenix Press, 2010), 185–186.

5 These lines are 2 Sam 11:1, 17–18, 25, 12:26–31. According to my suggestion, the paragraph in 12:26–31 may be the oldest part of the account that later authors expanded by adding first 11:1, 17–18, 25 (and later the remaining lines).

6 See Jacob L. Wright and Michael Chan, "King and Eunuch: Isaiah 56:1–8 in Light of Honorific Royal Burial Practices," *Journal of Biblical Literature* 131 (2012): 99–119, as well as my piece on "Making a Name for Oneself: Martial Valor, Heroic Death, and Procreation in the Hebrew Bible," *Journal for the Study of the Old Testament* 36 (2011): 131–162.

7 See Wright, "Making a Name for Oneself," as well as Jacob L. Wright, "Human, All Too Human: Royal Name-Making in Wartime," in *War and Peace in Jewish Tradition: From the Ancient World to the Present*, ed. Y. Levin and A. Shapira (London: Routledge, 2011), 62–77.

8 This chapter (2 Sam 10) tells the prehistory of the events at Rabbah. It can be divided into three strata: First, vv. 6b–14 sets the scene for Joab's battle at Rabbah in ch. 11–12 (notice the use of "the gate/city" here and in ch. 11–12). Second, an expansion in vv. 15–19 explains why the Arameans do not come to the help of the Ammonites in chaps. 11–12; it incorporates an older piece about the Arameans (vv. 16–19a) that has nothing to do with the Ammonites or Joab (see 2 Sam 8:3–12). Third, a supplementary episode provides a casus belli (vv. 1–6a) and links the narrative to the Saul narrative (1 Sam 10). Altogether, the chapter exculpates David from reckless ambition by presenting the battle as the climax of a war that the Ammonites initiated.

9 The account likely achieved its transmitted shape after the composition of 2 Sam 13–24* and was meant to serve as the preface to that lengthy narrative.

10 The letters discussed here can be found respectively in A. Goetze (ed.), *Keilschrifturkunden aus Boghazköi, 23. Historische Texte*

(Berlin: Akademie-Verlag, 1928): text – 103 Rs. 14; *Archives royales de Mari*, vol. 26 (Paris: P. Geuthner, 1950), text: 319, lines 27–30; and an unpublished tablet discussed by Karen Radner, *Die Macht des Namens: Altorientalische Strategien zur Selbsterhaltung* (Wiesbaden: Harrassowitz, 2006), 95.

11 Perhaps the most famous case is also from the biblical portrait of David: 2 Sam 5:6–9 tells of the conquest of Jerusalem by David and his men, and concludes with the statement: "David occupied the stronghold and called it the 'City of David.'" For other example of conquerors renaming cities, see Jerusalem / Colonia Aelia Capitolina (the name plays on Hadrian's name and that of the god Jupiter Capitolinus); Sidon / Kār-Aššur-ahhê-iddina ("Harbor of Esarhaddon"); Nappigi / Līt-Aššur ("Victory of Assur," Shalmaneser III). In a study of these and other ANE acts of name-changing, Beate Pongratz-Leisten notes that the toponyms often present the king and his god as the sole agents in the conquest of these cities – an observation that is suggestive for the David texts. See her article "Toponyme als Ausdruck assyrischen Herrschaftsanspruchs," in B. Pongratz-Leisten, H. Kühne, and P. Xella (eds.), *Beiträge zu altorientalischen und mittelmeerischen Kulturen. FS W. Röllig* (Neukirchen-Vluyn: Neukirchener, 1997), 325–344.

12 See Richard F. Hardin, *Civil Idolatry: Desacralizing and Monarchy in Spenser, Shakespeare, and Milton* (Cranbury, New Jersey: Associated University Press, 1992). Given Shakespeare's extensive familiarity with biblical literature, these continuities between his work and the Book of Samuel are likely due, at least in part, to direct influence. See Steven Marx, *Shakespeare and the Bible* (Oxford: Oxford University Press, 2000).

Chapter 7: Ittai the Gittite

1 For recent discussions of the formation of the Absalom account, see Jeremy Hutton, *The Transjordanian Palimpsest: The Overwritten Texts of Personal Exile and Transformation in the Deuteronomistic History* (Berlin: De Gruyter, 2009), and Thilo Rudnig, *Davids Thron. Redaktionskritische Studien zur Geschichte von der Thronnachfolge Davids* (Berlin: De Gruyter, 2006).

2 The paragraph in 15:7–12 must be partly secondary. Note the resumption of theme of "hearts of Israel" (vv. 6 and 13), although portions of vv. 10 and 12 may belong to the older narrative. The reference to a chariots and runners in v. 1 is drawn from the description of Adonijah's attempted putsch in 1 Kings 1:5 and would belong to the addition of vv. 7–12 (and ch. 13–14).

3 Additional support for this conclusion is provided by the narrative strand related to the advice of Hushai and Ahithophel: Every line that refers to David as Absalom's father (15:34*; 16:19, 21–22, 17:8–10) appears to be secondarily stuck into the narrative, which otherwise misses many opportunities to use familial designations. 2 Sam 3:2–5 likely represents a summary based on the final form of the narratives. The author of 2 Sam 13:37–38 does not seem to know that Talmai of Geshur was Absalom's grandfather (2 Sam 3:3).

4 Contrast the different word for "with us" (*'immānû*) in v. 20, where Ittai's name does not appear. For a brief look at Ittai, see Nadav Na'aman's "Ittai the Gittite," *Biblische Notizen* 94 (1998): 22–25.

5 Although I maintain that the figure of Ittai does not represent a Gittite military corps in Judah, war commemoration is used in several texts for other groups of mercenaries: the Cherethites and Pelethites. These include the scene with Ittai leaving with David (2 Sam 15:18); the account of the war against Absalom (2 Sam 20:7); and the account of Solomon's accession (1 Kings 1:38, 44). One of the groups (often translated as "Carites") plays a key role in placing a Davidic king back on the throne in Judah, under the direction of Jehoida the priest. The account bears many similarities to the report of Solomon's accession, with both a priest (Zadok) and a specific unit of soldiers assisting him.

All these texts suggest that their authors were consciously commemorating the loyalty of Cherethites and Pelethites to the Davidic dynasty, claiming that they already faithfully served David and Solomon. Such commemoration would have been acutely needed as a riposte to the resentment many would have felt toward these professional (and originally foreign) mercenaries who were there to do the king's bidding, even against the will of the people.

6 Notice this unexpected word order of "in death and life" (rather than "in life and death"). The relationship between death and statehood was discussed in the preceding chapter.

7 In 2 Sam 18:11, the general Joab says to the soldier who brought him news about Absalom's whereabouts: "You saw it! Why didn't you kill him then and there? I would have owed you ten shekels of silver and a belt." Many Neo-Assyrian images show military officers rewarding warriors for their kills, demonstrated via battle trophies (the heads of enemies).

Both 1 Sam 29 and 21:11–16 [10–15] appear to be unaware of the tradition that David killed Goliath. The Goliath account itself seems to have been interpolated between 1 Sam 18:5–9* (without "and David returned from killing the Philistine" in v. 6) and the account in 14:52 + 16:19–22. If so, the line "Saul has killed his thousand, and David his ten thousands" has nothing to do originally with the killing of Goliath.

8 The same rationale explains the use of eunuchs in palaces. See Jacob L. Wright and Michael Chan: "King and Eunuch: A Study of Self-Preservation (Isa 56:3–5)," *Journal of Biblical Literature* 131 (2012): 99–119.

9 *The JPS Bible Commentary: Ruth* (Philadelphia: Jewish Publication Society, 2011), 18–19. Note also the commonalities between the conclusions to these passages (2 Sam 15:22 and Ruth 1:18–19).

10 *Reading the Women of the Bible: A New Interpretation of Their Stories* (New York: Schocken, 2002), p. 241: "She did not need to invent her lines, for they resonate with Bible's cadences of covenant and contract." Additional parallels to ANE vassal treaties catalogued by Mark S. Smith are very similar to both the context and substance of Ittai's oath to David: "'Your People Shall Be My People': Family and Covenant in Ruth 1:16–17," *Catholic Biblical Quarterly* 69 (2007): 242–258. Ittai's oath on the life of YHWH does not imply worship of this deity any more than Achish's oath on the life of YHWH (1 Sam 29:6).

11 Ittai's pledge, and the quasi-feudal structures undergirded by such vassal oaths, are the concrete articulation of ancient states: 600 men/servants > David > Achish; and 600 Gittites > Ittai > David.

12 An older Saul tradition in 1 Samuel 13–14 begins by reporting that the king chose 3,000 men from Israel for his army while sending the "rest of the people/militia" back home (13:2). Later he has a cohort of 600 men (13:15; 14:2), a conventional number of troops in professional military units. By claiming that "the rest" went in hiding (13:6–7, 15), the narrator identifies these troops as those who remain from the national militia whom Saul had mustered. This editorial maneuver resembles the way the authors of Judges transform Gideon's 300 from the remnant of a huge multitude of "citizen-soldiers" who heed Gideon's call-to-arms and then are gradually reduced in size at the riverbank (see Judges 7).

13 As pointed out earlier, these texts are likely old and originally a part of the HDR, predating 2 Sam 9:1–21:14.

Chapter 8: David in Exile

1 The misplaced reference to Abiathar here may have originated as a marginal gloss. The substratum of the chapter consists of 15:2–6, 13–18, 23, 30, 32a, 37b.

2 Similarly, the authors of the Psalms encourage their readers to view their own experiences, both individual and collective, through the prism of David's life.

3 Notice how the account attributes the bravest acts to the woman. Likewise, the servant girl is loyal, while the boy betrays them. To this we may compare Jael's valor for Israel, in contrast to her husband's alliance with the enemy (Judg 4–5). Elsewhere I treat the issues posed by war commemoration for gender and how biblical authors commemorate the valor of women in wartime.

4 The texts discussed here are, in order, 2 Kings 12:8, 2 Chr 24:6, and 2 Kings 23:5. A recent Emory dissertation situates these moves by Chronicles in relation to the book's larger agenda. See Matthew Lynch, *Monotheism and Institutions in the Book of Chronicles* (Tübingen: Mohr Siebeck, 2013). For other cases in Chronicles and Ezra–Nehemiah, see 1 Chr 15:2, 26–27; 2 Chr 11:13–14, 19:8, 23:2, 29:34, 30:22; Ezra 8:15b–20; Neh 13:10–12, 19–22. For a study that has remained imporant on the Zadokites in relation to David, see Saul Olyan, "Zadok's Origins and the Tribal Politics of David," *Journal of Biblical Literature* 101 (1982): 177–93.

5 The editors also sought to harmonize what were originally separate traditions of David and Solomon. If they were recasting Solomon as David's son, as I have suggested, they had to account for the fact that the older David literary traditions assign the priestly role to Abiathar, while the Solomon traditions assign this role to Zadok. The authors resolved the disparity by claiming that Abiathar had failed to support Solomon's accession and was therefore expelled from office. By reporting that he was exiled to Anathoth, they provide a polemical etiology for the origins of the priestly guild from this town. See 1 Kings 2:26 and Jer 1:1, and compare the polemics against this town in Jer 11.

6 The older statement that David arrived in Mahanaim is found in 2 Sam 17:24. The substratum of the account, which may itself be a supplement, can be isolated to 16:15, 20, 23; 2 Sam 17:1–7, 11–14, 23. Yet notice the resumption of 15:37b in 16:16.

7 Midrashim compare him to Balaam (Num. R. 22), the angels (p. Sanh. 10.2; Yalk. 2 Sam. 142), or even to the Urim and Thummim (p. Sanh. 10.29a).

8 This northern location is curious, since the Arkites were a Benjaminite or southern Ephraimite clan. See Josh 16:1–3. The origins of this tradition may have evolved around the name Yirka (or Yarka), which is said to derive from "Arkite."

9 See 1 Sam 15:31, 15:37, 16:17. "Friend" is also a title for an official position; see 1 Chr 27:33. The narrative strand that relates to

Benjamin is found in 2 Sam 16:1–13 and 19:16–31. The Hebrew verse numbering differs in many English translations by one verse.

10 The charge of David to Solomon (1 Kings 2:1–9) is perhaps an editorial justification for Solomon's actions (2:13–46), which are motivated by spontaneous ad hoc actions (vv. 13–22, 35–43) and only secondarily harmonized with David's charge (30–33, 44). The account is masterfully composed, with the depiction of Shimei going to Achish of Gath – the same ruler David served as mercenary during the time he tore the Kingdom of Judah away from Saul. Notice also the directions in the crossing of the Kidron.

11 Notice the similarities to the valorous warriors of Jabesh-gilead marching all night to rescue the decapitated bodies of Saul and his sons from the wall of Beth-shan (1 Sam 31). In 2 Sam 4, the lines in vv. 2–4 may represent a supplement.

12 Beeroth may be identified with Khirbet el-Burj, where 24 LMLK seal impressions were found.

Chapter 9: Territorial Transitions

1 See column 3, 18–49 of the Sennacherib Prism, translated in Daniel David Luckenbill, *The Annals of Sennacherib*, Oriental Institute Publications 2 (Chicago: University of Chicago, 1924). Likewise, Deut 3:11 claims that among of the prized (war) trophies displayed in the Ammonite capital of Rabbah was a massive iron bed of King Og of Bashan.

2 The texts referred to here are, sequentially, Josh 13:26, 30; 21:38; Gen 32; and 2 Sam 2.

3 See Gen 50:23; Num 26:29, 27:1, 32:39–40, 36:1; et al.

4 The Jordan features so prominently in this narrative because, as a boundary, it symbolizes the otherness of the Gileadites. It is this otherness that elicits the extensive attention to Barzillai.

5 David's offer of a place at the royal table is a mixed blessing. On the one hand, seats at royal tables were great honors limited to most privileged subjects and friends of the king. On the other hand, the table was a place for courts to keep an eye on potential political opponents (see, e.g., 1 Sam 20 or 2 Sam 9). If the text means to suggest that David's offer was more than just a way of rewarding a friend, it would make sense that Barzillai evades David's offer and volunteers his servant in his stead. Ultimately, however, we lack sufficient warrant to conclude that Barzillai is being presented as the king's potential adversary.

6 Notice that the NJPS removes "the Gileadite" from Barzillai's name in the Massoretic text, on the understanding that this reading has

been corrupted by association with the Book of Samuel. The same passage is found in Neh 7:63–65; there, however, the NJPS strangely does not omit "the Gileadite."

7 In the Samuel account, Barzillai has no sons and Chimcham, his servant, accompanies David back to Jerusalem. The Jewish commentator Malbim (Meïr Leibush ben Jehiel Michel Wisser, d. 1879) interpreted these texts conversely, claiming that the disputed priests married a daughter of Barzillai because they needed the good name that Barzillai had achieved in David's time. His interpretation is likely the way the authors of Samuel intended that their readers interpret the passage in Ezra–Nehemiah.

8 Tobiah should be linked to the affluent and powerful clan of the Tobiads who resided in Ammonite territory and who are known from both the Zenon Papyri and Josephus. I discuss this figure throughout my book, *Rebuilding Identity: The Nehemiah Memoir and Its Earliest Readers* (Berlin: De Gruyter, 2004).

9 Compare 15:16b and 16:21–22. These statements would have likely have been originally connected to 19:41 and stood directly before 20:23.

10 All these lines appear to be supplements. They explain why the older substratum of the account presents Judah going out to meet David at the Jordan (19:16, 40–41*) after Israel had fled to their homes (19:9).

11 The two histories were joined via the Book of Judges (and supplements in 1 Sam 1–8). I would argue that portions of the Book of Judges were originally added to the People's History as addenda, and that only later Judges assumed its function as a bridge to the Monarchic History. This terminology (Monarchic History and People's History) is my own. Some would isolate a precursor to the Monarchic History in a Synchronistic History that linked the reigns of the kings of Israel to those of Judah. See discussions in Reinhard Kratz, *The Composition of the Narrative Books of the Old Testament* (London: Bloomsbury, 2005), and Konrad Schmid, *Genesis and the Moses Story* (Winona Lake, Indiana: Eisenbrauns, 2010).

12 Avraham Faust provides a useful overview in *Israel's Ethnogenesis* (London: Equinox, 2008). On marriages, see Gunnar Lehman's study: "Reconstructing the Social Landscape of Early Israel: Rural Marriage Alliances in the Central Hill Country," *Tel Aviv* 31 (2004): 141–192.

13 See Bruce Routledge, *Moab in the Iron Age: Hegemony, Polity, Archaeology* (Philadelphia: University of Pennsylvania Press, 2004), ch. 7. Writings from circles outside the palace may have appealed to a Moabite identity. However, in contrast to royal inscriptions, they

would not have been inscribed on durable monuments and therefore would have eventually vanished. But against such arguments, I would point out that the Moabite identity in Mesha's inscription appears to be in need of assertion. At this early stage, circles outside the court would have had little if any reason to think in this national category. It is more likely that one would have resisted these totalizing claims of the court by affirming older identities that were more local/regional.

14 For example, an Exodus-Conquest narrative, which tells how the people of Israel collectively left Egypt and entered the land under the aegis of the deity YHWH, may have existed already before 722 BCE. However, we cannot be sure to what extent the national character of such a narrative would have resonated with circles beyond the palace. Moreover, the palace would have sought to take ownership of this narrative – if it did not already invent it – by claiming a unique relationship to YHWH.

15 On this subject, see most recently the work of Daniel Fleming, *The Legacy of Israel in Judah's Bible* (New York: Cambridge University Press, 2012).

16 David Goodblatt (*Elements of Ancient Jewish Nationalism* [Cambridge: Cambridge University Press, 2006]) distinguishes between "Judah nationalism" and "Israel nationalism." As he notes in his chapter on "The Role of Scripture," biblical literature "provided materials for the construction of a national identity" and was formative in the later development of Jewish nationalisms.

17 The Samaritans may not have preserved the name if they hadn't emerged in competition with Judah and Jerusalem over the identity over the divinely chosen location for the Temple and the legacy of Israel's literary traditions.

18 *Nations as Zones of Conflict* (London: Sage, 2005).

Chapter 10: Chronicles

1 That David does not go up with "all Israel" in 2 Sam 5:6–10 is due to the likelihood that this passage belongs to the older independent HDR, which presents David as a king who rules solely Judah (not Israel).

2 1 Chr 12:2b. If this is a gloss, it may have been elicited by some of the place names in the list and the reference to the right hand in the preceding line. Compare Judg 3:15, 20:16, and 1 Chr 12:30.

3 The contradiction with 1 Chr 10:11–12 adds weight to the claims that chaps. 11–12 consist to a great extent of later interpolations.

4 See Shemaryahu Talmon, "The Sectarian יחד: A Biblical Noun," *Vetus Testamentum* 3 (1953): 133–40, here p. 136. According to Hugh Williamson, Amasai's words represent an ancient slogan (like 1 Sam 18:7, 21:12, 29:5) transmitted since the days of David as an alternative to the saying of rejection in 2 Chr 10:16 (also 1 Sam 25:6; 2 Sam 20:1, 1 Kings 12:16). Yet given its accent on the leitmotif of these chapters ("help," *'azar*), the suggestion is difficult to accept. See Hugh G.M. Williamson, "'We Are Yours, O David': The Setting and Purpose of 1 Chronicles xii 1–23," *Oudtestamentische Studien* 21 (1981): 164–76.

5 See 1 Chr 12:30. The last line of the verse should be translated: "Up until this point, the majority had kept fidelity to the house of Saul." Benjamin and Judah are often combined in post-exilic literature, pace Sara Japhet, *The Ideology of the Book of Chronicles and Its Place in Biblical Thought* (Winona Lake, Indiana: Eisenbrauns, 2009), pp. 263–264. The references in Chronicles to Benjamin reflect the effort of post-exilic authors to encourage support and solidarity from this region, which competed with Jerusalem and Judah. See Ezra 1:5, 4:1, 10:9; Neh 11:7–8, 31–36; Jer 17:26, 32:44, 33:13, which identify this area as the place whence a population will come to Jerusalem.

6 The text is 1 Chr 12:22a. Baruch Halpern (*David's Secret Demons* [Grand Rapids: Eerdmans, 2001], pp. 78–79), argues that before the insertion of the latter half of 1 Chr 12:20, the account suggests that David in fact did fight against Saul. I do not accept this approach for the following reasons: (1) The redactional history of 1 Sam 29 precludes the existence of such a source. (2) The line in 1 Chr 12:20 is formulated very carefully to refer to the time "when [David] was coming with the Philistines to fight Saul" (not "when he fought Saul with the Philistines").

7 Ralph Klein, *1 Chronicles* (Hermeneia; Minneapolis: Fortress, 2006), 315. See the statement in 12:30b that many of the Benjaminites, Saul's kin, "maintained until then their allegiance to the house of Saul," which might serve to explain the small number.

8 Abigail and Ziba bring many of the same food items to David in times of military peril (1 Sam 25:18 and 2 Sam 16:1).

9 Homer's lengthy register negotiates political membership and status by naming the contingents and their leaders who contributed to the historic war effort. It also includes descriptive epithets of the territories, such as the blessings in Genesis 49 and Deuteronomy 32, as well as in the Song of Deborah. One can easily see how some of the strophes have been expanded with historical-anecdotal material. Most scholars agree that the Catalogue has been supplemented

variously with the names of new contributors and that the names of some participants may have been deleted as a way of criticizing these communities. By stating exactly how many ships each land sent, the Catalogue ranks the level of contribution for each participant. For example:

> Men from Tricca, rocky Ithome, Oechalia,
> city of Eurytus, the Oechalian,
> were commanded by two sons of Asclepius,
> skilled healers, Machaon and Podaleirus.
> They brought thirty hollow ships with them.

Other strophes name the land that sent the best horses (2.761–65) or who represented the best warrior (2.767–68). The Catalogue also notes nonparticipation: "But their minds weren't set / on the grim clash of war. They had no one to lead them" (2.761–62). Later we read that these same troops "stayed behind by their ships" and "amused themselves" in various ways (2.771–79). (From the "Catalogue of Ships" in Iliad 2.494–759. See also the Trojan "Battle Order" in 2.816–877.)

I was delighted to discover that Gary Knoppers also noticed the connections between this passage and the Catalogue; see his *1 Chronicles 10–29* (Anchor Bible; New York: Doubleday, 2004). For more examples of Aegean war commemoration, see the discussion in Chapter 2 or my article: "War Commemoration and the Interpretation of Judges 5:15b–17," *Vetus Testamentum* 61 (2011): 1–16.

10 *1 Chronicles 10–29* (Anchor Bible; New York: Doubleday, 2004), 566. For a seminal study of these chapters, see Kenneth Ristau, "Breaking Down Unity: An Analysis of 1 Chronicles 21.1–221.1," *Journal for the Study of the Old Testament* 30 (2005): 201–211.

11 Previous scholarship has largely failed to take seriously the imbalance between the beginning of the history, with the people of Israel dominating the narrative, and the end, which narrates the destruction of the kingdom in a few short passages and says very little about the people as a whole. Many scholars seem to assume that the narrative corresponds fundamentally to the course of Israel's and Judah's history. Yet others are now responding to this untenable assumption and demonstrating the extent to which the abundant space assigned to the people of Israel in the beginning of these histories (in each of the three configurations mentioned earlier) owes itself to a creative historiographical move to emphasize the peoplehood of Israel. By presenting Israel as nation preexisting the states of Israel and Judah, the authors affirm, on the one hand, a fundamental unity of Israel,

and on the other, the primacy of peoplehood as a survival strategy in anticipation and response to the defeat of the state. See Jacob L. Wright, "A Nation Conceived in Defeat," *Azure* 42 (5771/2010): 83–101.

From a diachronic perspective, the summary statement in 25:21b ("and thus Judah was exiled from its land") may represent the original conclusion to the history. If so, the two paragraphs appended to it would constitute supplements. I maintain that these paragraphs were appended simultaneously. The first paragraph (25:22–26) contradicts the foregoing account by presenting a population of aristocrats and notables in the land. It tells how Nebuchadnezzar appointed Gedaliah as the population's leader, who along with other Judeans and Chaldeans is eventually massacred by a member of the Judean royal family and "captains of the forces." In response, "all the people, high and low, and captains of the forces" take flight to Egypt. The reason for introducing this paragraph seems to have been twofold: first, to show that in the end the land was completely deprived of any Judean community, and second, to direct the reader's attention away from Judah and the (emerging) diasporic center in Egypt.

Not surprisingly, the second paragraph (25:27–30) identifies Babylon as the locus of restoration. It is there that the deported King Jehoiachin, during the first year of the reign of Evil-Merodach (Amēl-Marduk, a.k.a. Nabû-šuma-ukîn), is released from prison. The passage postdates the receipt of rations to the reign of Nebuchadnezzar's successor so as to present a sequence of defeat and restoration: first destruction and deportation, then the assassination of Gedaliah and the flight of the remaining population to Egypt, and finally Jehoiachin's rehabilitation at Babylon. For more on these texts, see Jacob L. Wright, "The Deportation of Jerusalem's Wealth and the Demise of Native Sovereignty in the Book of Kings," in *Interpreting Exile: Interdisciplinary Studies of Displacement and Deportation in Biblical and Modern Contexts*, ed. Brad Kelle, Frank Ames, and Jacob L. Wright (Atlanta: Society of Biblical Literature, 2011), 105–34.

12 Knoppers, *1 Chronicles*, 567.

13 Other post-exilic works present contributions to the building projects as the means by which the members of the nation demonstrate their belonging. A notable example is the Priestly account of the building of the Tabernacle, which appears in tight nexus with (YHWH's!) triumph over the Egyptians.

14 Julius Wellhausen, *Prolegomena to the History of Israel* (Edinburgh: Adam & Charles Black, 1885), 182.

15 This intention also informs the placement of David's coronation as King of Israel before the older account of the occupation of Jerusalem in 2 Sam 5. In this way, the city is to be understood as the central place for all Israel, rather than just a fortress on Judah's northern border.

Chapter 11: Caleb and the Conquest

1 See 2 Kings 8:13 and the extrabiblical material discussed in Dirk Schwiderski, "Wer ist dein Knecht? Ein Hund!" Zu Aufmerksamkeitserregern und Überleitungsformeln in hebräischen Briefen," in *Studien zur hebräischen Grammatik*, ed. Andreas Wagner (Freiburg, Göttingen 1997), 127–141. In Akkadian, the lexeme *kalbu* is often combined with *ardum*, "servant."
2 Compare *Yeraḥme'ēl* and *'Otnî'ēl*, and see 1 Chr 2:9.
3 *Numbers* JPS, 391–92.
4 In Genesis 15, Abraham is dwelling in Mamre, which several texts link explicitly to Hebron, the territory of the Calebites according to other texts. The chapter originally promised Abraham solely the (Kenizzite?) land around Mamre. See the discussion in Chapter 13.
5 This conclusion is supported by the fact that two passages in the Septuagint and Qumran versions of Samuel that depict David showing favor to various clans in Judah have Kenizzites in the place of Kenites (1 Sam 27:11 and 30:29). See the LXX[(B)], which appears to be supported by 4QSam[a].
6 Joshua 15 refers to Caleb as both the son of Jephunneh and as the brother of Othniel, son of Kenaz.
7 On Raba, see *b. Sot.* 11b. For the others, see their commentaries ad loc. Radak also considers the possibility that Jephunneh and Kenaz are different names for the same person.
8 On the difference between "son of Kenaz" and "Kenizzite," see Radak on Josh 15:17.
9 The texts discussed here are 1 Sam 25:3, 27:8–12, 30:14.
10 If we are to read "Kenizzites" instead of "Kenites" (with some versions), it is noteworthy that the Othniel legend tells how Kenizzites came to occupy a southern territory that was originally Calebite (see the use of *negeb* in Josh 15:19 and Judg 1:15).
11 1 Chr 2. (See also Num 26:6, Ruth 4:18.) This Caleb must be the same figure since his daughter is Achsah (v. 49). It is then not surprising that the rabbis sought to harmonize these different genealogies for Caleb.
12 1 Chr 2:50–51. Hur is known from Exodus 17 and 24.

13 P. 509.
14 1 Chr 2:42. See Ran Zadok, "On the Reliability of the Genealogical and Prosopographical Lists of the Israelites in the Old Testament," *Tel Aviv* 25 (1998): 228–54, here 244.
15 The conclusion is derived from Num 14:38 that Joshua and Caleb "lived from those men." Since it is already stated that these two figures survived, the verse is taken to mean that they occupied the lands of the others (b. Bat. 118b).
16 Hur plays a key role in the battle with Amalek (Exod 17). The Sages carry on the biblical war commemoration by claiming that Hur must have died an honorable death because his grandson Bezalel is given the honor of building the Tabernacle. They support this view by appeal to two biblical facts: the sudden disappearance of Hur and the involvement of his grandson in building the Tabernacle. The ceremonious tone of Exod 35:30–35 (see also 31:1–5) suggests that this is when God rewards Bezalel's grandfather, whose mysterious disappearance is explained by the claim that he died for his opposition to the construction of the golden calf (see Exod 24:14).
17 Based on the account in Num 13:30–14:10.
18 Translated by Frederic Gardiner, *From Nicene and Post-Nicene Fathers, First Series*, Vol. 14, ed. Philip Schaff (Buffalo, New York: Christian Literature Publishing Co., 1889).
19 Authorized English Version, translated from the original by Rashad Khalifa (Islamic Productions, 2009).
20 Article in the *Biographisches-Bibliographisches Kirchenlexikon* (Vol. 3, 1992, "Kaleb," 963–64), authored by Siegfried Kreuzer. One can find similar sentiments in Anchor Bible Dictionary and many other standard English lexica and commentaries.
21 Reinhard Achenbach, *Die Vollendung der Tora. Studien zur Redaktionsgeschichte des Numeribuches im Kontext von Hexateuch und Pentateuch* (Wiesbaden 2003), 222–32, 289, 630.
22 Hobab (chap. 10), Moses's Cushite wife (chap. 12), the foreign prophet Balaam (chap. 22–24), scandals with Moabite and Midianite women (chap. 25), et al.
23 If "the Kenizzite" is understood as an ethnonym for a non-Israelite clan, it is worth noting, pace Achenbach, that the authors of the account in Numbers never even employ this designation.
24 The passage belongs to the final redaction of Judges, which introduces an overtly pro-Judahite framework. The authors deduced that Othniel must have been the Judahite who first led Israel since he was the son-in-law of the great Judahite Caleb and had already demonstrated valor in conquering Kiriath-Sepher.

25 An implicit reward that the rabbis identify is that he becomes representative of the tribe of Judah (Num 34:19 and Josh 14:6).
26 For Ezra as the avatar of a new age, see Chapter 6.

Chapter 12: Caleb the Warrior

1 *Religion of Israel to the Fall of the Jewish State*, Vol. 1 (English trans. London: Williams and Norgate, 1874), 138.
2 14:13 may be a supplement that allows Joshua to grant Hebron to Caleb, and bless him in the process. The repetition of "ben Jephunneh" in v. 14 supports this conclusion. If v. 14 were original, we would expect "the Kenizzite" to be stated in it, rather than in v. 15.
3 The relation of Kiriath-Arba to Hebron is not clear; see discussion in Chapter 13.
4 For additional points of conflict, see subsequent discussion. For the relationship of Josh 14:6–15 to Josh 15:13–19, the best discussion remains that of Friedrich Bleek, *Einleitung in das Alte Testament* (Berlin: Georg Reimer, 1865), 321–22. Julius Wellhausen maintained this portion of his revised edition of Bleek's introduction.
5 While the phrase *'el-pî yhwh le-* is characteristic of P texts, this phrase may constitute a late gloss (see 17:5, 19:50, 21:3, 22:9, and following discussion). The rabbis drew attention to this special honor by observing that Joshua and Caleb were the only ones to receive their landholdings *directly* from the deity rather than by means of lot-casting. See *b. B. Bat.* 122a–b.
6 15:15b may be a late supplement.
7 The MT reads *b^e^rākâ* "present, blessing," but could be read *b^e^rēkâ* "pool of water."
8 The pools may be identified with Sēl ed-Dilbe, located 9 km southwest of Hebron. Debir is likely to be identified with Tell Ṭarrāme, situated next to these pools, or in Chirbet er-Rābūḍ, 5 km to the south.
9 In Josh 14 and 17, narratives also interrupt lists, yet they represent the follow-up to promises made in Numbers. What the authors of 1 Chr 1–9 do *genealogically* to unify Israel's population, the authors of Josh 12–22 do *territorially*.
10 The heading to Josh 15 identifies the Calebites as one of many Judahite clans. In telling how all the Judahites were with Caleb when he presented his petition, ch. 14 affirms that the allocation of his territory met with Judahite consent.
11 See Ps. 90:10 and *Pirkei Avot* 5.22. The fact that Joshua's age is not treated to a similar extent (see Josh 23:1 and 24:29) is due to the likelihood that Joshua, whom Exod 33:11 identifies as a boy,

was not originally present with Caleb in the Spy Account (see below). On the chronology of the Conquest and Caleb's age in Josh 15, see Radak's clever calculations (commentary ad loc.).

12 Deut 3:25–28; 34:4; see also Num 14:21–24, 27:12, 32:11. In light of these rhetorical concerns of Deuteronomy, we can understand why this text, in contrast to those in Joshua, is not interested primarily in affirming the right of the Calebites to landholdings in Judah.

13 We can witness a parallel move in Greek literature, with the Homeric aristocratic ideal of martial valor being presented in the poetry of Tyrtaeus as the virtue achievable by a wider body of fighters. Similar developments can be mapped in the medieval West, while modernity has witnessed the emergence of a new masculinity to which all male citizens of the nation-state should aspire. See the discussion in Jacob L. Wright, "Making a Name for Oneself: Martial Valor, Heroic Death, and Procreation in the Hebrew Bible," *Journal for the Study of the Old Testament* 36 (2011): 131–162, esp. n. 23.

14 Deut 1:36 also singles out Caleb. In Josh 14:7–8 Caleb recalls, in the presence of Joshua (!), that Moses commissioned "me" and that "I gave him a forthright report." On Caleb as YHWH's servant, see discussion of the meaning of Caleb's name in Chapter 11.

15 The plague is perhaps an alternative to the punishment of the wilderness wanderings. Josh 14:8–10 noticeably omits mentions of the plague. That both punishments are found in a text strand often assigned to P (see following) reveals the need for an approach that takes seriously the possibility of successive supplementation.

16 Ludwig Schmidt seeks to save the documentary approach to this account (and as a model for the Pentateuch as a whole) by integrating it with the supplementary approach. Ludwig Schmidt, "Die Kundschaftererzählung in Num 13–14 und Dtn 1,19–46. Eine Kritik neuerer Pentateuchkritik," *Zeitschrift für die Alttestamentliche Wissenschaft* 114 (2002): 40–58.

17 See Sidnie White Crawford, *Rewriting Scripture in Second Temple Times* (Grand Rapids, MI: Eerdmans, 2008).

18 Num 14:11–24 and 14:26–35. Martin Noth appealed to the length of the pericope to make a similar point in support of the two-source approach to the pericope.

19 Similarly, the Song of Deborah avoids reference to Judah and the south. While the early exodus traditions likely derive from Israel in the north, it is difficult to imagine a royal court promulgating these traditions. Given their focus on the *people* of Israel and on YHWH as Israel's national deity, these traditions likely took shape at a time after the destruction of Samaria in 722 BCE. For a recent study

of competing exodus traditions, see Stephen C. Russell, *Images of Egypt in Early Biblical Literature: Cisjordan-Israelite, Transjordan-Israelite, and Judahite Portrayals* (Berlin: de Gruyter, 2009).

20 Whether the depiction of the failed southern campaign (Num 14:39–45*) originally belonged to this early version is difficult to determine. That it represents an early supplement is supported by the fact that it refers to the Amalekites and Canaanites (not the Anakites) and to the hill country, which differs from early versions of the account. See following discussion.

21 Thus, in contrast to the narrative in Num 9–10, 13–14, the passage in Exod 13:17–21 does not have the erection of the Tabernacle in view.

22 See 13:17. If this repetition corresponds to two different sources, then Caleb would not be introduced in one of them.

23 The supplementary character of this verse is corroborated by the rough syntax in 14:37, which was likely caused by a later author's attempt to confine the punishment to only those who had brought an unfavorable report about the land.

24 Compare 13:29 with 13:27–28. These lines, usually assigned to P, were perhaps originally connected to 13:31abβ. The mention of "this people" (in the singular) does not cohere well with v. 29, which lists many different peoples. One might include v. 33 here, since it stands out syntactically and is formulated similarly to v. 28b. To be clear, my argument does not require that the Anakites are original to the account but only that they were introduced at an early stage and that v. 39 is later. Notice that Deut 1:28 refers solely to the Anakites.

25 See E.C.B. MacLaurin, "Anak/ 'ANAX," *Vetus Testamentum* 15 (1965): 468–474. MacLaurin's view has been criticized over the years, with many scholars insisting that the word must be West Semitic. "Anak" may originally have been a title for the figure named "Arba." Thus, while the older texts and the legend in Josh 15 refer to the descendants of a legendary ruler called "the Anak," the later texts that use *'anāqîm* (Deut 9:2; Josh 11:21; 14:12, 15) presuppose the widening of the meaning of *'anāq* to signify "giant," which the word denotes in Hebrew up to the present day.

26 (Josh 15:14) In contrast, Judg 1:10 claims that Judah collectively vanquished these three foes. Yet, as I argued in the preceding chapter, this text from Judges represents a pro-Judahite adaption of the Caleb traditions.

27 Num 13:22b states that "Hebron had been built seven years before Zoan (Tanis) in Egypt" (cf. Jubilees 13:13). David is said to have reigned in Hebron for *seven* years before moving to Jerusalem (2 Sam

2:11, 5:4–5). Nadav Na'aman argues that the calculation in Num 13:22b cleverly synchronizes the foundation of Jerusalem and Tanis as capitals of Israel and Egypt. The Torah consciously avoids the name of Jerusalem, so that this late gloss might refers to it under the cypher of Hebron. Nadav Na'aman, "'Hebron was built seven years before Zoan in Egypt' (Numbers XIII 22)," *Vetus Testamentum* 31 (1981): 488–492.

28 The reward is attributed directly to Moses, whom the authors evidently assume to possess great authority for their readers. Moreover, Caleb and Joshua perform here an exegetical deduction: Caleb asks for the hill country where the Anakites dwell in great, fortified cities (14:12). He appeals to Moses's promise of the land on which his foot had trodden (14:9; see Deut 1:35 and cf. Num 14:24). Joshua however gives him only Hebron, in keeping with Num 13:22. Yet in Josh 15, Caleb commands a larger territory. Josh 21:9–12 clarifies that Caleb only received the fields of Hebron and its villages, because Judah and Simeon had given Hebron itself, along with Debir and eleven other cities from their tribal inheritance, to the Levites.

29 One may compare Caleb's words to his daughter's when she appeals for water rights (Josh 14:12 and 15:19): Achsah's demand for water-sources ("give me!") are echoed in Caleb's demand for land ("give me!"). The former may have influenced the latter. The war commemoration on the part of Caleb continues with Hur, who plays a key role in the battle with Amalek (Exod 17). According to the rabbinic sages, Hur must have died an honorable death because his grandson Bezalel is given the honor of building the Tabernacle. They support this view by appeal to two biblical facts: the sudden disappearance of Hur and the involvement of his grandson in building the Tabernacle. The ceremonious tone of Exod 35:30–35 (see also 31:1–5) suggests that this is when God rewards Bezalel's grandfather, whose mysterious disappearance is explained by the claim that he died for his opposition to the construction of the golden calf (see Exod 24:14).

Chapter 13: Caleb the Judahite

1 Moshe Gil, *A History of Palestine, 634–1099* (Cambridge: Cambridge University Press, 1997), 58, citing a medieval Christian source.

2 The reference to Maon in v. 2 is likely a redactional attempt to link the episode to the wider narrative (see 1 Sam 23:24–25). The story repeatedly identifies Carmel as the place of Nabal's residence; see also 1 Sam 30:5; 2 Sam 2:2, 3:3.

3 The framing verses are v. 1a and vv. 43–44. The latter reconcile the fact that David has only two wives (1 Sam 30:5, 2 Sam 2:2) by reporting that Saul had given Michal to another man.

4 Thus the final redactors of the book are likely responsible for the mention of Israel in v. 30b. Yet it is not necessary to ascribe Nabal's reference to "servants who break free from their lords" in v. 10b to a later hand, as it can be understood within the common sociological context of "desperados" who inhabited the fringes of the southern Levant in the first millennium BCE (see, e.g., Judg 11:3 and 1 Sam 22:2). If the verse were a late supplement, we would have expected Nabal to justify his repudiation of David by appealing to his loyalty to the throne of Saul. Although the chapter is likely old, it treats issues of allegiance and belonging in the same manner as the later supplements that presuppose the incorporation of new material related to King Saul.

5 1 Sam 27:11, 1 Sam 30:10, 21–25. Some lines in the account affirm that David protected Nabal from real outside threats: 1 Sam 25:15–16, 21, 28. "Wall-pissers" refer to males of all ages; see 1 Kings 16:11.

6 Both episodes reflect the use of donkeys in the Judahite hill-country. These animals may also be a cultural marker for the Calebites or at least for the inhabitants of the region, in contrast to the camels of the southern Negeb.

7 Compare David's comment when he shares the war booty with the elders of Judah: "Here is a present for you from the spoil of the enemies of YHWH" (1 Sam 30:26).

8 See Jon Levenson, "1 Samuel 25 as Literature and as History," *Catholic Biblical Quarterly* 40 (1978): 11–28, as well as Jon D. Levenson and Baruch Halpern, "The Political Import of David's Marriages," *Journal of Biblical Literature* 99 (1980): 507–18.

9 2 Sam 2:1–4. Even if the explicit identification of Nabal as a Calebite might be editorial, the places where he resides, Maon and Carmel, are squarely within Calebite territory. Moreover, the son of Abigail and David bears a very similar name to Caleb: Chilab (2 Sam 3:3).

10 Levenson and Halpern, "The Political Import of David's Marriages," 510.

11 For Hebron: 78 of Type HIIb, 4 of Type HIIc, totaling ca. 29% of the late group. For Ziph: 74 of Type ZIIb and 6 of Type ZIIc, ca. 28% of the late group. See Oded Lipschits et al., "Royal Judahite Jar Handles" *TA* 37 (2010): 3–32.

12 The Septuagint continues the polemic against Nabal by reading not "Calebite" but *anthrōpos kynikos* ("a doglike, hard, 'cynical'

man"), a play on the Hebrew *keleb* ("dog"). Whereas Radak and especially Ralbag emphasize Nabal's "doglike" character, Rashi, in keeping with several earlier sources, sees Nabal as a direct descendant of Caleb ben Jephunneh.

13 While the HDR refers to a Negeb of Caleb next to a Negeb of the Jerahmeelites, the list in 1 Sam 30:26–31 does not refer to the "towns of the Calebites." It does, however, refer to Hebron, which may mean that the author identified it as Calebite place. "Kiriath-arba" might be the name known among a different population or refer to a larger area embracing "four cities." Alternatively, it may refer to four municipal quarters, a common phenomenon throughout the world. (For the ANE, the examples include Ekbatana, Babylon, Dur-Šarrukin/Khorsabad, and many others). Modern Hebron is located adjacent to the ancient to Tel Rumeida, where the ancient city may situated. No remains were found from the Persian period at Tel Rumeida, which may reflect the flux in names.

14 One may compare the tension between *oikos* and *polis* in Aegean world. For example, Cleisthenes sought to build a stronger state by creating ten new tribes from four older ones that were plagued by rivalries.

15 The Book of Samuel depicts a significant decline from the successes that characterize David's early career. In his old age, he is not fighting like Caleb but fading in strength. In addition to the story of final days with Abishag (1 Kings 1), see the episode in 2 Sam 21:15–17 in which David grows weary in battle. The passage concludes with the oath of David's men: "You shall not go with us into battle any more, lest you extinguish the lamp of Israel." The relationship between these texts is admittedly difficult to determine.

16 See Chapter 10. One can point to other evidence indicating that the earliest sources did not present Jerusalem as David's capital. For example, the author of 2 Sam 5:13–14, in contrast to 3:2–5, has no names to provide for the wives and concubines whom David accumulates in Jerusalem; he likely had the Hebron episode in view and attempted to mimic it.

17 Gen 23:2. We find the same gloss in passages from Joshua; see 15:13, 54; 20:7.

18 35:27 as well as 13:18 and 18:1. Compare the personalization of Mamre along with the places Eshcol and Aner in the late Abrahamic legend of chap. 14 (vv. 13, 24).

19 23:19, see also 23:17, 19; 25:9–10; 49:29–32; 50:13.

20 Gen 50:10–11. Another tradition locates his grave in Shechem, just as Rachel's grave is not at Machpelah (Gen 35:19–20, 1 Sam 10:2, Jer 31:15).

21 See his "Zur Überlieferung der Vätergestalten," *Wissenschaftliche Zeitschrift der Karl-Marx-Universität Leipzig* 3, 1953/4, 265–281.
22 The battle account is found in ch. 14. When removed, it reveals a connection from 13:18 directly to ch. 15. In telling that Abraham refused to take any of the war spoils for himself, the battle account provides a new context in which to understand the deity's declaration: "Fear not, Abram! I am a shield to you. Your reward shall be very great" (15:1).
23 The classic study of the chapter is by Yochanan Muffs, "Abraham the Noble Warrior: Patriarchal Politics and Laws of War in Ancient Israel," *Journal of Jewish Studies* 33, 81–107.
24 See Oded Lipschits, *The Fall and Rise of Jerusalem* (Winona Lake: Eisenbrauns, 2005), 140 et passim.
25 Francesca Stavrakopoulou recently investigated the phenomenon in her book *Land of Our Fathers: The Roles of Ancestor Veneration in Biblical Land Claims* (London: T&T Clark, 2010).
26 See Stavrakopoulou's discussion of Albert de Pury's and Mark Brett's studies (*Land of Our Fathers*, 47–51). For a more recent defense of the ecumenical approach, see Konrad Schmid, "Judean Identity and Ecumenicity: The Political Theology of the Priestly Document," in *Judah and Judeans in the Achaemenid Period: Negotiating Identity in an International Context*, ed. O. Lipschits et al. (Winona Lake: Eisenbrauns, 2011), 3–26.
27 1 Sam 22 and Psalm 52. The polemics against Doeg as Edomite over against the Benjaminites is pronounced in 1 Sam 22. If Doeg had properly informed Saul that David had lied to Ahimelech, Saul would not have had a reason to order the slaughter.
28 I treat these texts in a forthcoming study of war commemoration throughout the Hebrew Bible. In the meantime, see Juan Manuel Tebes, "The Edomite Involvement in the Destruction of the First Temple: A Case of Stab-in-the-Back Tradition?" *Journal for the Study of the Old Testament* 36 (2011): 219–255.
29 1 Macc 5:65. The same book extols the name of Caleb; see my discussion in Chapter 11.
30 Genesis 15 and 36. It is noteworthy that Esau's wife bears the name "Judith" in Gen 26:34; such may reflect early Judahite–Edomite relations. The text avoids these implications by designating her explicitly as Hittite.

Index of Modern Authors

Index of Biblical Passages and Related Texts

Texts

Genesis

Exodus

Numbers

Deuteronomy

Joshua

Judges

1 Samuel

1 Kings

2 Kings

Jeremiah

Index of Historical Figures